# EMERGING DOMESTIC MARKETS

# EMERGING DOMESTIC MARKETS

*How Financial Entrepreneurs
Reach Underserved Communities
in the United States*

Gregory Fairchild

Columbia University Press
New York

Columbia University Press
*Publishers Since 1893*
New York   Chichester, West Sussex
cup.columbia.edu

Copyright © 2021 Columbia University Press

Library of Congress Cataloging-in-Publication Data
Names: Fairchild, Gregory, author.
Title: Emerging domestic markets : how financial entrepreneurs
reach underserved communities in the United States / Gregory Fairchild.
Description: 1 Edition. | New York City : Columbia University Press, 2021. |
Includes bibliographical references and index.
Identifiers: LCCN 2020017277 (print) | LCCN 2020017278 (ebook) |
ISBN 9780231173223 (hardback) | ISBN 9780231553117 (ebook)
Subjects: LCSH: Endogenous growth (Economics)—United States. |
Minority business enterprises—United States. | Business enterprises—
United States—Finance. | Community development—United States—Finance. |
Commercial loans—United States.
Classification: LCC HD75 .F345 2021 (print) | LCC HD75 (ebook) |
DDC 332.1/70869420973—dc23
LC record available at https://lccn.loc.gov/2020017277
LC ebook record available at https://lccn.loc.gov/2020017278

Cover design: Noah Arlow

# Contents

# Acknowledgments

I HAVE the privilege of being named the author of this work. The reality is that the insights shared here are the result of a number of supporters and counselors.

First, my parents. In the chapters of this text, I share relevant examples from my familial narrative. My debts to my parents and grandparents are as much financial as they are educational. These include wealth they were able to accumulate and pass on, knowledge about financial services products and how to manage them, and my father's work in community reinvestment late in his career.

Second, a number of research collaborators have contributed the framing and analyses shared in the chapters that follow. Cory Yemen, Megan Young Kim, and Megan Juelfs helped collect, clean, and analyze data in a number of the studies and analyses found here.

Third, I've been the beneficiary of assistance from a small army of field research assistants. Some of these are former students, some are researchers that were employed in various capacities. Their talents range from interviewing, background research, and development of cases, to detailed statistical analyses. These include Carla Andrews, Vanessa Bean, Angela Briggs, Wilson Brisset, Catharine E. Carrales, Gosia Glinska, Elizabeth Guthrie, Matthew Innamorati, Marc Johnson, Ruth Kidane, Daisy Lovelace, Angela Medaglia, Anthony Mubiru, Claire Murphy, Sindara Oyekola, Natalie Race, Kulwant Rai, Robert Smith, and Ellen Zienta.

Jackie Thomas-Kennedy is an exceptionally talented narrative writer with whom I was able to collaborate on a number of business school case studies and field interviews. I traveled the country with her and learned a great deal on the process of turning interviews into narratives.

Gerry Yemen has been a writing collaborator from my earliest years as a professor. I learned from her how to properly frame a case narrative. She's also become a close personal friend, and has gifted me her family (including her son, Cory, mentioned above).

Ruo Jia came to work with me as a statistician and became a collaborator, co-author, and friend. We worked together for many years, until he left to pursue a PhD at the Stanford Graduate School of Business. Without Ruo, many of the deep quantitative analyses in this book would not have been possible.

Fifth, I've benefitted from careful, thoughtful editing. Many thanks to Elisabeth Jones and Leslie Mullin. Let me state again—thanks to Elisabeth Jones.

Sixth, I must thank the many interviewees that gave weekends and time to explain their businesses to me and my research teams. They also provided documentation and referrals, and some eventually agreed to participate in case studies. I have learned so much from listening to them. There have been many sources. However, I'd like to mention two of them: John Berdes and Jeremy Nowak. Both were founders of iconic CDFIs, both were patient tutors to me, and both have since passed. They are missed by many.

Seventh, Julie Grammer is a talented graphic artist who made my scratchings not only visible but appealing.

Eighth, Michael Stegman was a program officer of the John D. and Catherine T. MacArthur Foundation when he first began speaking with me about Community Development Finance. As those conversations progressed, he supported me with a career-making grant that allowed me to travel the country doing the interviews that have provided so many of the insights that I am able to share. I had no idea then how the relationship with Michael and the MacArthur Foundation would allow me to focus my time on the understudied field of community development finance and alter the trajectory of my career. Likewise, I am deeply appreciative of Debra Schwartz's advice and counsel. Debra was the head of Program Related Investments during the years I studied CDFIs closely. And she was a key informant throughout.

There are many collaborators in community development and economic development institutions. These include colleagues at the Calvert Foundation, MacArthur Foundation, and The Reinvestment

Fund. I am particularly thankful for the long collaborative relationship with Annie Donovan, Greg Bischak, and Oscar Gonzalez of the CDFI Fund. They have been patient tutors and thoughtful partners. Many of these analyses would not have been possible without their frequent support.

Ninth, I must thank a number of faculty colleagues:

- Eric Abrahamson was not only my PhD sponsor, but also encouraged me to follow the voice in my heart to study business in underserved areas.
- Robert L. "Bob" Bruner has been a former teacher, my colleague, and dean. I've shared with Bob that he's whispered in my ear a few times and provided sage advice that led me to pursue topics I likely wouldn't have pursued otherwise. Bob's support and example have been instrumental.
- Ming Jer Chen is a colleague and friend. He also gave me critical advice about where to guide my career as a doctoral student. This book wouldn't exist without a conversation outside his office at a key juncture.
- Robert "Ed" Freeman encouraged me to pursue these questions well before I decided to pursue a PhD. He is a legend in the field, known by most as the father of Stakeholder Theory, of which this work has many echoes. Ed has been a personal friend to me and my family.
- Murray Low was not only a friend; he is someone I admire. Murray first introduced me to the field of inner-city business development. He introduced me to leaders in the burgeoning field, launched a course, and eventually set the table for me to enter the classroom.
- In addition to being great scholars, Andy Wicks and Melissa Thomas-Hunt kindred souls. Love.
- I want to thank my dissertation committee for agreeing to support a topic that was unusual in its effort to bring business school and other disciplines. Thanks for helping me when so many of my ideas and knowledge were unformed: Eric Abrahamson, Peter Bearman, Don Hambrick, Paul Ingram, and Sudhir Venkatesh.

Most importantly, I am thankful to my wife, Tierney Temple Fairchild. In addition to managing my consistent bouts of uncertainty, doubt, and fear, she's been my best thought partner. She's edited draft chapters, answered random questions, and never faltered in encouraging me. This in addition to being the best wife and mother I could've imagined. I love you.

As you read this book, keep in mind that the limitations and oversights are all mine.

# Preface

## *Toward an Inclusive, Resilient Financial Services System*

FOLLOWING THE financial crisis of the 2000s, there was a collective question, "What just happened?" When satisfying answers were in short supply, populist movements from the right and left voiced underlying distrust in our institutions and their ability to serve a broad portion of our society. Protests sprung up around the country. Asset poverty became a topic that people discussed at cocktail parties. Globalization became a negative word. These sentiments grew and stabilized, and were evidenced in Republican and Democratic political rhetoric.

Rather than protest, some chose to exit institutions that had seemingly failed them (or never seriously attempted to support them). Ownership of stocks declined among middle- and lower-income families. Homeownership and marriage rates for millennials declined. The construction of very small homes flourished. A number of workers chose to leave work altogether (there's an acronym, FIRE—Financial Independence Retire Early).

On the other hand, the seeming "winners" in the decline enjoyed uncommon benefits. In the decade of the 2010s, the U.S. economy expanded its share of global output. China was the only other country to achieve this. Affluent families rode the longest bull market in modern history to healthy returns. By 2020, the majority of the world's largest companies by market capitalization were based in the United States.

With lower-income and young families on the sidelines, inequality did not decline, but increased. There were stories that captured the popular sense of this rising disparity. It had long been known that many college students had to leave college early because of a lack of funding. However, in 2019, we learned of a multi-institutional bribery scandal, known as Operation Varsity Blues, in which nearly three dozen wealthy families paid tens of millions of dollars to help their children get into highly selective colleges. The political sphere had devolved into a balkanized, ineffective rhetorical battle with limited results. The "we" of America seemed lost.

## CRISES USHER IN RECKONINGS

As the spring of 2020 arrived, the Covid-19 virus obliterated many of our assumptions about safety and security. Even as the economy stalled, there was a recognition that long-brewing inequality mattered to public health. Data showed us that the ability to protect oneself from contagion and its attendant consequences was influenced by wealth. A relative few could afford to wait out the pandemic in their homes, working online and keeping their families safe. Many could not.

Several weeks into nationwide shelter-in-place orders, protests began in response to the death of George Floyd, who was killed during an arrest for the alleged use of a counterfeit bill. Floyd died in police custody on a street in Minneapolis. Helpless bystanders filmed the final eight minutes and forty-six seconds of Floyd's life, creating the viral videos that led protests to erupt across the country. Floyd was a Black man, and news coverage showed images of multiracial groups calling for fundamental changes to our justice system.

These system-level shocks laid bare what some had long realized: our systems have not been working for many of us. These crises were certainly broad, even global, yet they had differential impact on individual populations (e.g., low-income households, urban centers, racial minorities, small businesses).

Leadership increasingly acknowledged that their collective failure to attend to the least-advantaged had led to loss of life, and that these could threaten our economy. They talked openly about the reality of structural and institutional discrimination. Executives in business and government found themselves stymied because their constituents had so little trust in their ability to solve our problems. It appeared our social contract was broken.

Calls for action spilled over into the corporate sphere—there were demands for attention to the "common good," and for businesses to take on a more active role. Collective economic and physical health

Jamie Dimon, CEO of JP Morgan Chase: "This week's terrible events in Minneapolis, together with too many others occurring around our country, are tragic and heartbreaking. Let us be clear—we are watching, listening and want every single one of you to know we are committed to fighting against racism and discrimination wherever and however it exists."

Mark Mason, CFO of Citigroup: "Racism continues to be at the root of so much pain and ugliness in our society—from the streets of Minneapolis to the disparities inflicted by COVID-19. As long as that's true, America's twin ideals of freedom and equality will remain out of reach."

Larry Fink, CEO of BlackRock: "Importantly, we have to make this a sustained effort. I am writing to you today because recent events have forced us to reflect on the severity of these issues, but these events are symptoms of a deep and longstanding problem in our society and must be addressed on both a personal and systemic level."

Brian Moynihan, CEO of Bank of America: "We can and will build on what our company is already doing. We have already stepped up to do even more during this crisis to serve our clients and support our communities and teammates. This includes our ongoing work to help drive diversity and inclusion, racial equality, economic opportunity and upward mobility, and to deliver on our purpose."

All of these quotes are drawn from a single article: Hugh Son, " 'Appalled'—Here's What Wall Street CEOs Are Saying About the Killing of George Floyd and Protests Rocking U.S. Cities." *CNBC*, 1 June, 2020, https://www.cnbc.com/2020/06/01/wall-street-ceos-speak-out-about-george-floyd-and-protests-rocking-us-cities.html.

mattered, even in the C-suite. CEOs of financial institutions began issuing statements that went beyond trumpeting diversity to discussing racism in American society. Corporations had long talked about diversity and inclusion; now they were talking about inequality and racism.

If we are to take these pronouncements seriously, one important component of future economic growth will be the necessity of broad-scale income supports and asset and wealth development. There are important distinctions between this crisis and the financial crisis of the late 2000s. If we fail to address the trenchant economic and racial inequality in our society, we will sink into distrustful malaise. The strength of our systems requires a breadth of financial capability and a host of institutions that can service a broad set of needs with metrics that include social justice. Rather than viewing them as peripheral to the field of finance, we must recognize that we ignore their centrality at our peril.

It turns out that we have the makings of such a system. It has been in place for some time, but it is less popularly known or understood. There are organizations that work collaboratively to prudently serve the financial needs of low- and moderate-income families and small businesses. For decades, these organizations have focused on a diverse set of demographic groups. This book is an effort to share lessons about these actors and the institutions they serve. We need more like them.

## AN OLD QUESTION

Long before I chose to pursue an academic career, I was curious about financial services—though not because I was interested in pursuing a career in equity trading, financial advising, or investment banking. My questions were about the ability of financial institutions to serve a diverse set of consumer needs. It seemed that somehow, financial service firms veered to the affluent. I had heard that "banks serve people that *have* money." I knew the jargon "redlining," even though I didn't understand its derivation or impact. There was at best a quandary, and at times a skepticism, about the implied justice of the field.

I had a working knowledge of financial services as firms that design, develop, and deploy financial goods (e.g., loans, credit products, retirement savings accounts) to customers (i.e., individuals, households, businesses). I intuitively understood that the institutions and actors in financial services perform a needed transformational function—as intermediaries that collect and ration money—from savings into loans, from stocks into pensions, from government bonds into government spending.

As I will share later, my parents recognized that the on-ramps to the financial services system weren't necessarily equally accessible, and they prepped me to meet a system that might pass me by if I wasn't careful. I understood early that the banking system was something to engage carefully, with a level of vigilance. Yet here was the dilemma: if I took seriously the notion that financial institutions play a critical economic role—transforming and rationing capital to important pursuits at the community and individual level—then there was this nagging lack of evidence that the system was enabling all of those it could. Somehow, with limited evidence to the contrary, I believed that financial services did not need an affluence boundary—that they could be a system for those that were not already wealthy.

This book collects findings from years of quantitative and qualitative research driven by an evolving, linked group of research questions: How can financial institutions develop products for low-income Americans? Can they do so without imprudent levels of associated risks? What skills, routines, and knowledge do organizations that serve these populations have that other, more traditional firms do not? Are there noninstitutional, nonproduct barriers that block access for some? Can we develop a more inclusive, democratic financial services system?

To answer these questions, I've had a stew of influences. From a social science perspective, I borrow from economics and finance, social psychology and intergroup relations, sociology, and behavioral science. Because of this interest in what I think of as representative, resilient financial services, I've pursued quantitative research and case fieldwork with touchpoints in social and economic inequality. During my PhD, I also became a Columbia University Public Policy Fellow, with access to leading scholars such as Theda Skocpol (social policy and civic engagement), Michael Crow (commercialization of technology), Noel Ignatiev (race and ethnicity), Seymour Spillerman (wealth and stratification), and Richard Nelson (economics). Venturing outside of my business school home provided enormously fertile ground for me.

Over the same period, I have continuously "road tested" my academic training, analysis of data sets, and theories through fieldwork. Fieldwork has taken me into truly amazing settings to learn from practitioners across a range of financial institutions and contexts. After spending a few days with a finance professional operating in an environment that at first seemed especially daunting, I have found myself taking notes that lead me to update my perspective once again. Just when I think I understand, I find there's more.

As I've listened to those in the field, I've increasingly been convinced that inclusive models are indeed viable—they are less evidenced and written about, and so less understood in terms of their strategic frameworks and methods. Fieldwork has clarified my view that there are multiple approaches to the provision of economic and asset development services, and that they can even include middle- and low-income families. Unfortunately, a content analysis of the extant literature on financial services would find limited support for the notion that there are financial services models beyond the affluent (I will share more about this later). And, in a form of recursion, my quantitative work has increasingly shown that there are indeed viable models.

## LARGER, WEALTHIER = BETTER?

Given the demography of elite U.S. business schools—at the faculty or student body level—there's a tendency to focus on larger dollar signs and firms. Of course, I am not the first to note that in business schools, we tend to study very large firms with large balance sheets. This has been called the "pro-innovation, pro-size" bias in management research.[1] We spend far less time focusing on the middle and lower ends of the firm distribution, or on products and services that aren't for the affluent.

Candidly, I've wondered if part of the reason for this tendency is a less-discussed belief: those who have less find themselves in that condition because they've made poor decisions, are wasteful or reckless, and thus are higher-risk propositions (and those with more money have made the proper decisions, etc.). An increasing number of us recognize that this logic needs to be questioned. There is increasing evidence that the poor remain poor because of structural inequalities that are durable and consequential. We have often failed to recognize the "cordoned" elements of our social structure and how they influence so many things, including the provision of financial services.

There's a tension that is reminiscent of an infamous literary dialectic between F. Scott Fitzgerald and Ernest Hemingway. In a story published in *Red Book*, "The Rich Boy," Fitzgerald offered the following: "Let me tell you about the very rich. . . . They think, deep in their hearts, that they are better than we are because we had to discover the compensations and refuges of life for ourselves. Even when they enter deep into our world or sink below us, they still think that they are better than we are. They are different."[2]

Hemingway responded to this notion in "Snows of Kilimanjaro." In this short story, published in *Esquire* magazine, one of the characters "remembered poor Scott Fitzgerald and his romantic awe of them and how he had started a story once that began, 'The rich are different from you and me.' And how someone had said to Scott, Yes, they have more money."[3]

I tend toward Hemingway's notion in this debate. Those with more money have unique challenges, and it is easier for us to develop models to serve them. If we spend the time experimenting and learning about how to service middle- and low-income consumers, we will build knowledge and capacity—and we will have fewer wealth disparities.

## UNFAMILIARITY AND FEAR

I was at a recent academic talk with a colleague. There was a fascinating exchange regarding risks, uncertainty, and familiarity in the food industry. In short, the notion was that consumers are fearful of certain foods simply because they are unfamiliar (e.g., insects as protein). The psychological basis for these reactions is a form of uncertainty avoidance. We share a tendency to see those arenas that we know less about as risky, or even dangerous. Our collective biases toward settings and people that are familiar is a natural phenomenon. It's understandable. And we should labor to push past it.

Generally speaking, within business school literature and classrooms, the arenas of social change look mostly to ethnic and gender diversity among white-collar workers, corporate social responsibility, or social entrepreneurship. This has been an important discourse at least since the civil rights movement. However, even as an understanding of the importance of diversity rose, economic inequality increased. Collectively, we've fallen short of acknowledging social dislocations in our society, and the role that business institutions play in facilitating or impeding socioeconomic progress across groups.

In a recent essay in *Time* magazine, Pamela Newkirk directly discusses this dilemma, and the concerning lack of progress.

> The buzzword is emblazoned on blogs and books and boot camps, and Thomson Reuters, a multinational mass-media and information firm, even created a Diversity and Inclusion Index to assess the practices of more than 5,000 publicly traded companies globally. But while business targeting diversity is flourishing, diversity is not. . . .
>
> In other words, the diversity apparatus doesn't have to work—it just has to exist—and it can help shield a company against successful bias lawsuits, which are already difficult to win.[4]

Some will find this description especially cynical. Others will see it as long overdue. My work takes the view that although there may be biases, there can also be factors that contribute to inequality without deliberate bias. The mere path of daily life, particularly for those of us who are affluent, may contribute to inequalities that are not immediately recognizable. Some may argue this means that those of us with advantages aren't "responsible," and perhaps don't need to counter these forces. This may be the case, but I maintain it is important to recognize the way these processes influence economic opportunity and, eventually, social outcomes. Whether or not we chose to intervene is a personal matter.

Those of us with advantages in an increasingly unequal society have the ability to "expand the pie" of opportunity. A collective tendency to ignore current inequality, and a failure to account for how those advantages roll forward over time and across generations, is ethically suspect and institutionally dangerous. This book goes beyond encouraging an opening of our perspective. We need to act.

To that end, I provide examples from the field of ways that practitioners have experimented with new models, innovations, and structures. One useful notion is the concept of "stacking capital"—the way that market-rate, governmental, and philanthropic capital sources can be bundled to provide each contributing entity the return it desires while matching onto relevant risk profiles. These serve as "quasi" market solutions that can have substantial impact if better understood by a broader base of actors.

## THIS IS ALSO PERSONAL

I've drawn as well from personal, familial experiences. My own financial services journey informs these research questions. Throughout these chapters, I share personal reflections—some inclusive, some exclusive—that have become key moments in the development of my scholarly understanding. My own experiences provide insights into the way firms meet potential clients, and don't.

A personally grounded approach like this can be surprising, even misunderstood by some scholars (the phrase is "me-search, not research"). However, a growing number of us recognize that our own experiences are an important way of building depth in our understanding of social phenomena.[5] I find it hard to imagine that any modern writer discussing financial institutions can completely divorce their own experiences with wealth, income, and financial product providers from their research perspectives (whether they acknowledge these influences is an important question). Both scholars and finance professionals tend to come from relatively privileged backgrounds. As a group, we tend to carry biased assumptions about lower-income consumers that are strongly held, and seldom tested (especially since most of the influential stakeholders are also of the same backgrounds).

## WHAT'S AT STAKE?

A financial system that fails to serve large portions of its populace cannot be viewed as successful. If these disparities persist, I am not even sure such a system can continue. Likewise, research frameworks that do not account for structural factors like educational and racial disparities will be unable to respond to the challenges faced by many consumers. I am not confident that "left to our own devices," our inequalities will naturally "work themselves out." There's ample data in what follows about how we haven't, and won't.

A secret wish is that some may read this book and recognize an opportunity for themselves. My fantasy is that the information, techniques, and models presented will encourage some who are skeptical of the financial services system to see an alternative future that includes a larger set of consumers. I hope these skeptics will recognize that the system needs their personal interest, support, and efforts. My bet is that they may see in the narratives the promise of the finance industry's capacity to assist others—within their own communities and beyond—in achieving a higher standard of living and an improved quality of life. And perhaps they may choose to leverage that potential by pursuing a career in helping finance live up to its promise of rationing wealth and investment to the betterment of all society.

EMERGING DOMESTIC MARKETS

# CHAPTER ONE

# The Best Investment
# I Never Had to Make

Less than a year into my first job at Banker's Trust, I surprised
no one more than myself by becoming suddenly, uncharacteristically,
and inextricably bored with analyzing American companies for the
bank's credit department. For some reason, the dynamism of the
world seemed to lie elsewhere.[1]

IN 1984, Antoine W. van Agtmael of the International Finance Corporation of the World Bank coined the term "emerging market" to
describe nations with low but rising per capita gross domestic product (GDP) that were instituting reform programs which would allow
them to "emerge" into the arena of global economic competitiveness.
His ideas were counterintuitive for some, at least initially. Agtmael
shares an anecdote about once being told by a superior that "there are
no markets outside of the United States!"[2]

Key underlying themes of Agtmael's thesis were the notions of rapid
economic transition and burgeoning investment opportunity. Agtmael
began his investment ventures abroad at Banker's Trust, including
helping to finance airplanes for Iran Air (with Ethiopian crews) and
developing cocoa exports in Ghana. He relates fascinating stories like
having a gun pulled on him by a military policeman in Seoul, South
Korea, during an investment research trip. Appetite sparked, Agtmael
joined the International Finance Corporation (IFC), the World Bank's
private investment arm, and as their experience and investment returns
grew, he and his colleagues leveraged the IFC platform to help spread
their knowledge and foster interest among investors.

These early entrants practiced humility, recognizing that their background came with bias and represented "baggage" for some in former European colonies. They understood that they would be learning as they invested, and would inevitably make mistakes. They acknowledged that they were seeking business opportunities in unusual places, often led by unfamiliar entrepreneurs. However, they believed that the costs of early entry would eventually be offset by competitive advantages: in-country knowledge, trusted in-country networks and relationships, and relatively little competition from other investors. Over time, investment in emerging markets became not only legitimate but also viewed as an important way to diversify a portfolio.

## A BIT CLOSER TO HOME

Agtmael's experiences caused me to question the field. Perhaps there were also domestically based developing markets in which a cadre of early, knowledgeable investors could gain an advantage through learning, and by doing so, recoup considerable returns? Recently, a small cadre of researchers began using the term Emerging Domestic Markets.[3] I authored *In Your Own Backyard*, which laid out a thesis that there were economic opportunities closer to home that might prove promising and that were being overlooked.[4] As with Agtmael's early efforts, I encountered some skepticism.

What had been observed in international development investment intrigued and encouraged me. I recognized common features relating to macroeconomic changes that signaled potential for growth (e.g., rising per capita incomes, increasing manufacturing capacity, launch of local stock markets). Likewise, three macro societal trends became the principal foundations of the Emerging Domestic Markets (EDM) framework: demographic shifts, rising educational attainment, and housing preference trends toward increasing urbanization. Let me share a bit of data about each of these.

### Demographic Shifts

Since 1970, the percentage of racial and ethnic minorities in the overall population in America has increased from 16.5 percent to 36.3 percent (a 120 percent proportional growth rate), and the nation is estimated to become a plurality in just over 20 years, meaning that no racial or

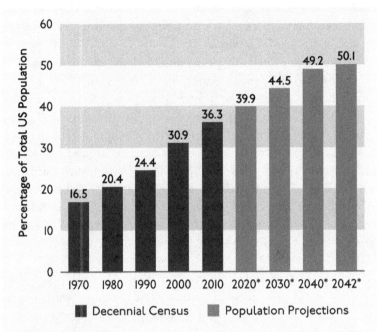

*Projected population as of July 1

Note: "Minority" refers to people who reported their ethnicity and race as something other than non-Hispanic White alone in the decennial census

Data source: US Census Bureau, decennial census of population, 1970 (5% sample), 1980 to 2010, 2008 Population Projections, 2020–2042.

*Figure 1.1* Minority population percentage and projections, 1970–2042. *Note*: "Minority" refers to people who reported their ethnicity and race as something other than non-Hispanic White in the decennial census. *Source*: U.S. Census Bureau, Decennial Census of Population, 1970 (5-percent sample), 1980 to 2010, 2008 Population Projections, 2020–2042, accessed from the presentation "A Look at the 1940 Census," https://www.census.gov/newsroom/cspan/1940census/CSPAN_1940slides.pdf.

ethnic group will represent more than 50 percent of the population.[5] Since 2012, more than 50 percent of the children born in the United States have been nonwhite.[6] Figure 1.1 shows the nonwhite composition of the U.S. population since 1970.[7]

## Increasing Educational Attainment

Matching a movement away from a manufacturing-based economy, postsecondary educational attainment has exploded. Between 1976 and 2008, high school graduation rates grew from 52.1 percent to 87.1 percent (up 67.2 percent), and degree-granting college enrollment rates increased 73.5 percent.

These trends are certainly promising, but the composition of this enrollment is linked to prior demographic trends. In 1976, 17.8 percent of college students were nonwhite and 48 percent were female. By 2008, 36.7 percent of enrollment was nonwhite and 56.9 percent was female (proportional increases of 106 percent and 18.5 percent).[8] The 2008 college enrollment rates for both Asian and Black adults exceeded rates for all races in 1980 (and Hispanic rates are nearly equal to those of whites at the time).[9] From 1999 to 2008, the total number of Black and Hispanic students taking an Advanced Placement (AP) exam more than tripled.[10] Achievement gaps between groups remain, however, and will be discussed with greater focus later.

The rising educational attainment of these demographic groups, particularly in the postsecondary arena (college and beyond) suggests pent-up workforce productivity. The aggregate and per capita spending power of formerly underserved groups is growing, along with their exposure to managerial career paths within the private sector. These shifts form a basis for burgeoning underserved consumer and labor markets. The third factor involves the geography of growth.

## Density and Urbanization

America's growth over recent decades reflects trends toward urbanization. A larger proportion of Americans are living in cities and within this larger trend is movement toward central city neighborhoods.

First, between 1982 and 1997, the U.S. population grew by 17 percent, while the population living in urbanized areas rose by 47 percent.[11] Second, an analysis of residential permitting between 1990 and 2007, shows a trend toward central city as opposed to outlying areas.[12] Third, the number of cities with over 500,000 residents grew explosively between 1940 and 2010 (see figures 1.2 and 1.3).

In their annual Gross Metropolitan Product report in 2019, the U.S. Conference of Mayors reported:

Combined, the nation's 10 highest-producing metro economies generated $7.2 trillion in economic value in 2018, surpassing the

| | | |
|---|---|---|
| ❶ New York | ❻ Cleveland | ⑪ Washington DC |
| ❷ Chicago | ❼ Baltimore | ⑫ San Francisco |
| ❸ Philadelphia | ❽ St Louis | ⑬ Milwaukee |
| ❹ Detroit | ❾ Boston | ⑭ Buffalo |
| ❺ Los Angeles | ⑩ Pittsburgh | |

*Figure 1.2* U.S. cities with populations above 500,000, 1940. Data from U.S. Census Bureau, "A Look at the 1940 Census," https://www.census.gov/newsroom/cspan /1940census/CSPAN_1940slides.pdf.

output of the sum of 38 U.S. states. Their combined output exceeds all the nations of the world save China, and is 45 percent greater than that of Japan, the 3rd largest economy of the world.[13]

Cities are becoming more attractive destinations for a number of reasons, including their walkability, technological infrastructure, access to mass transit, convenient retail stores and restaurants, and increasing proximity to our workplaces (especially in the skilled service industries). From a demographic standpoint, it is clear that in many U.S. economic centers the labor force tends toward racial plurality and tends to have higher educational attainment. Each year, metropolitan

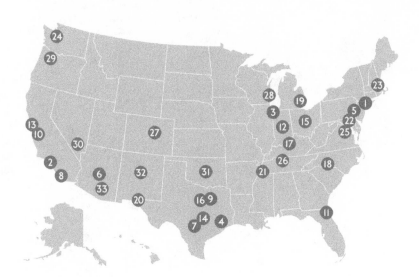

## US Cities with a Population of 500,000 or More in 2010

- 1. New York
- 2. Los Angeles
- 3. Chicago
- 4. Houston
- 5. Philadelphia
- 6. Phoenix
- 7. San Antonio
- 8. San Diego
- 9. Dallas
- 10. San Jose
- 11. Jacksonville
- 12. Indianapolis
- 13. San Francisco
- 14. Austin
- 15. Columbus
- 16. Fort Worth
- 17. Louisville
- 18. Charlotte
- 19. Detroit
- 20. El Paso
- 21. Memphis
- 22. Baltimore
- 23. Boston
- 24. Seattle
- 25. Washington DC
- 26. Nashville
- 27. Denver
- 28. Milwaukee
- 29. Portland
- 30. Las Vegas
- 31. Oklahoma City
- 32. Albuquerque
- 33. Tucson

Source: U.S. Census Bureau, 2010 Census

*Figure 1.3* Cities with populations above 500,000, 2010. Data from U.S. Census Bureau, "A Look at the 1940 Census," https://www.census.gov/newsroom/cspan/1940census/CSPAN_1940slides.pdf.

workers and consumers become more diverse as the younger generation enters the workforce.

Taken together, these trends are transforming *who* will produce economic growth as well as *how* and *where* that growth will occur. As with emerging markets in Asia or Latin America a generation ago, awareness of incipient opportunities is increasing, yet how to benefit from these changing structural factors is not broadly understood. Some are skeptical, confusing these with philanthropic or "social" efforts. Some fear what these changes portend.

This is not to suggest a lack of any positive reception. These notions have diffused to investment institutions like the California State Teacher's Retirement System (CalSTRS) and the nonprofits Community Wealth and the Aspen Institute. And there are echoes of these realizations in a number of other pension and venture funds.

These trends are not fleeting, passing fads. They are spurring growth in consumer and labor markets characterized by increasing educational attainment, disposable income, and sophistication in demand for quality products and career satisfaction. Accompanying this growth is a new cadre of entrepreneurs positioned to create innovations to serve these growing markets. Furthermore, these markets are growing faster than relatively older, less diverse, and less urban market spaces.

To provide a bit of perspective, the aggregate revenues of minority-owned firms in 2016 were $1.26 trillion. One way of understanding this level of economic output is to compare these revenues with GDP in purchasing power parity (PPP) of nations (aggregate size of the economy normalized for local price differences). Taken together, the revenues of minority-owned firms would be one of the 20 largest economies in the world (table 1.1).

Following Agtmael, emerging market investors had to approach their tasks with humility and a scholastic ethos. They displayed willingness to navigate cultural differences and legal structures, manage political and currency fluctuations, and recognize their own postcolonial biases that could scuttle deals. The EDM opportunity shares many of the same challenges, requiring accounting for the social and policy realities of our nation.

## SOCIAL, PHILANTHROPIC? YES. INVESTMENT? YES.

Early in my doctoral studies, I was given an early draft of "The Competitive Advantage of the Inner City," an article that would be published in the *Harvard Business Review*.[14] I became excited when I saw

TABLE I.I

Emerging Domestic Markets: GDP Purchasing Power Parity by Country

| | |
|---|---|
| China | 23,160,000,000,000 |
| European Union | 20,850,000,000,000 |
| United States | 19,390,000,000,000 |
| India | 9,459,000,000,000 |
| Japan | 5,429,000,000,000 |
| Germany | 4,171,000,000,000 |
| Russia | 4,008,000,000,000 |
| Indonesia | 3,243,000,000,000 |
| Brazil | 3,240,000,000,000 |
| United Kingdom | 2,914,000,000,000 |
| France | 2,836,000,000,000 |
| Women- & Minority-Owned Firms (combined)[a] | 2,717,764,645,000 |
| Mexico | 2,458,000,000,000 |
| Italy | 2,311,000,000,000 |
| Turkey | 2,173,000,000,000 |
| Korea, South | 2,029,000,000,000 |
| Spain | 1,774,000,000,000 |
| Saudi Arabia | 1,774,000,000,000 |
| Canada | 1,769,000,000,000 |
| Iran | 1,645,000,000,000 |
| Women-Owned Firms $ | 1,451,115,521,000 |
| Minority-Owned Firms $ | 1,266,649,124,000 |
| Australia | 1,246,000,000,000 |
| Thailand | 1,234,000,000,000 |
| Egypt | 1,201,000,000,000 |
| Taiwan | 1,185,000,000,000 |
| Poland | 1,121,000,000,000 |
| Nigeria | 1,119,000,000,000 |
| Pakistan | 1,057,000,000,000 |
| Malaysia | 930,800,000,000 |
| Argentina | 920,200,000,000 |
| Netherlands | 916,100,000,000 |
| Philippines | 875,600,000,000 |

GDP (purchasing power parity) compares the gross domestic product (GDP) or value of all final goods and services produced within a nation in a given year. A nation's GDP at purchasing power parity (PPP) exchange rates is the sum value of all goods and services produced in the country valued at prices prevailing in the United States. Source: CIA World FactBook, 2019, https://www.cia.gov/library/publications/the-world-factbook/fields/208rank.html.

[a] US Census business receipts data from 2016. Source: US Census Bureau, American Factfinder, Statistics for U.S. Employer Firms by Sector, Gender, Ethnicity, Race, Veteran Status, and Employment Size of Firm for the U.S., States, and Top 50 MSAs: 2016, 2016 Annual Survey of Entrepreneurs, https://factfinder.census.gov/faces/tableservices/jsf/pages/productview.xhtml?src=bkmk#.

the name of the author, a legendary scholar, Michael Porter. I needed no introduction to his work. Porter's name would have been recognizable to anyone who had studied for an MBA, as I had. His presence looms large across a broad range of topics.

Porter opened his article by saying,

> Past efforts have been guided by a social model built around meeting the needs of individuals. Aid to inner cities, then, has largely taken the form of relief programs, such as income assistance, housing subsidies, and food stamps, all of which address highly visible—and real—social needs.

He went on to argue that past efforts to address economic deficiencies were based on faulty models, and thus had limited results. The article was well received and influential, although there was a bit of controversy over his sweeping, dismissive comments about past aid efforts in inner cities.[15]

Porter founded a nonprofit, the Initiative for a Competitive Inner City (ICIC), to directly apply his ideas in the field. I soon became involved with Porter's ICIC, specifically with an initiative to encourage business school faculty to develop courses and foster research on inner city development. At an ICIC-sponsored conference, I was surprised to run into Robert "Bob" Bruner, who had taught my first MBA finance class. He led a session on the investment opportunities in America's inner city areas.

As we talked, I learned that Bruner's notion was not unlike my own: there were economic opportunities in America's developing areas. Years later, I would join Bruner in an entrepreneurial finance research program examining the performance of equity capital firms run by women and minorities in the nation's underserved yet developing areas. In the next section, I draw from my personal story to share a few factors—some historic, some contemporary—that must be included in our models.

## VALUABLE GIFTS I DID NOT REQUEST

In the summer of my sixteenth year, I landed my first real job as a busboy and dishwasher at the Hickory Palace. The job was "real" because I received a check I could convert into cash that did not originate from my parents' largesse. Once I had my first paycheck in hand, I had tangible proof that I was becoming an adult. It is a stark, empowering memory that stands in sharp relief to other transitional events of the period.

After six months at the Hickory Palace, I saw an ad in the newspaper for a job as a waiter. I applied and was hired the same day. Once I became a waiter, I was essentially receiving my compensation every evening, with a small residual check every two weeks. This created a novel dilemma: I was carrying more cash than I had ever before personally held or needed to manage.

After each shift, my mother required me to report my tips to her and turn 10 percent over as a fee for drop-off and pickup service. While this was the ostensible reason, the funds were actually placed into a savings account that she managed on my behalf, only revealed to me years later.

I imagine that my being flush with cash every evening caused my parents concern. First, there was a safety concern. A tipped job meant that I would be carrying wads of cash after leaving a public venue in the dark of night. A second worry was more behavioral. My father had a conversation with me about cash "burning a hole in my pocket." He understood that with ready cash came an increased propensity to spend and, in turn, diminished savings.

Around this time, my father presented me with my first plastic card. As with many things in my family, the card came with a lengthy lecture. My father explained the card was not a credit card, but something he called a "check" card. Dad explained that although I could use the card in all the places credit cards were accepted, this type of card had a ceiling equal to the available dollars in my checking account. Using accounting terms, he explained that this was an "asset" card, and that it would "debit" my purchases from my account as I made them. Debit cards had only been introduced a few years earlier, around 1977, and by that point had only diffused to a few banks and their customers.[16]

The card came with further requirements. On the first night he picked me up after I'd received the card, we stopped by the local bank branch. It was past midnight, long after operating hours. Dad passed me a piece of paper with a four-digit number and told me to commit the sequence to memory. He then required me to deposit all but a bit of my cash into the first ATM I had ever used.

This was a behavioral transition. Up until that time, money had been tangible: I received an allowance from my parents in cash, managed daily transactions through my wallet, and tracked my savings through a passbook savings account. The debit card created a set of practices in which currency was transformed—cash into account, debit spending, and electronic record-keeping.

My use of a debit card as a teenager was, at first glance, a transitional moment into adulthood. In reality, it was a carefully managed learning opportunity. Through daily repetition, monitoring, and training, I was being "pushed." My parents were providing me with something beyond plastic finance or the accounts to which my card linked. Later, my mother gave me a small bound notebook and had me write down the date and amount of the deposits I made.

Financial self-efficacy, defined, is the condition of having the knowledge, comfort, and confidence to manage day-to-day banking and commercial matters in a fashion that helps build financial well-being over time.[17] In practice, my parents were deliberately socializing me with the expectation that I would (1) engage with a broad range of financial products (cash, checks, electronic transactions); (2) know when best to use each product; and (3) internalize a set of values in their use (no overdrafts, regular savings of 10 percent of gross earnings).[18] Research indicates that financial socialization in the home pays dividends over time, raising one's likelihood and amount of saving[19] and reducing destructive financial behaviors (e.g., overdrafts) up through adulthood.[20]

If, in reading my account of my parents' training, you experienced head-nodding recognition, you may not realize that this is not a given practice. In fact, it may be relatively uncommon. The extant research on familial financial socialization shows that, first, many parents have limited experience of their own with bank accounts. Second, some are reticent to engage their children in using relatively new products because of informational asymmetry—that is, gaps in their own understanding of how best to use financial products. Other reasons include embarrassment at revealing poor familial "money management" practices and outdated or inaccurate knowledge. In some families, there are religious or cultural moratoria on discussing money with children. What follows is an obvious question: how can one advise on a matter in which one has limited or no experience?

Cultural capital theorists assert that it is the transmission—through parents, relatives, and friends to children—not only of technical knowledge but of attitudes, values, behaviors, and even relationships that aid the entry into and management of consumer products.[21] Bourdieu and DiMaggio, among others, have recognized that "cultural capital" can provide value in the navigation of various class-related interactions.[22] A base accumulated knowledge of, say, how to manage the financial system can confer very real economic value over time.

Cumulatively, I was provided with a set of layered and reinforcing advantages intergenerationally—a rare form of financial cultural capital. When I arrived at college, I soon learned just how valuable that was. Some of my peers had never opened a bank account, and many applied for their first credit cards as students (which, without knowledge of how to use them, was likely a poor idea). The methods of proffering credit cards to college students did not seem to address gaps in knowledge at this critical starting line in professional life.

I am now embarrassed to confess that I judged these peers as profligate. Many years later, I recognized that although I would never have described my upbringing as wealthy, there was real economic value in the knowledge I was given. These discomforts raised prescriptive questions. Do our financial services systems address knowledge disparities across sets of consumers? If not, how could the system respond to varied asset holdings?

My early experiences provide one of this book's primary insights: financial self-sufficiency is not accidental. My personal journey obscured the importance of financial cultural capital. Some of us receive technical knowledge, behavioral support, even mentoring; some do not. The good news is that there is a set of institutions that recognize these differences at the starting line and build systems to address them. The other news is that some firms seem to be operating under another logic: *caveat emptor.* In the next section, I discuss another influential set of factors that I had taken for granted: where I had lived and the schools that provided my education.

## TWO IMPORTANT GIFTS, FROM FEDERAL POLICY

My father was still in high school in 1948 when President Harry Truman issued Executive Order 9981, abolishing workplace segregation in the armed services. Following this lead, President Eisenhower continued the desegregation of daily military life that Truman had begun by integrating military schools, bases, exchanges, and medical facilities. In 1954, the year my father graduated college, the last of the all-Black units closed. That same year, my father took his commission as a second lieutenant and was among the first Black officers to serve within, or command, an integrated U.S. military unit. Unlike his early years, his post-college life was an integrated one.

In July 1963, Robert McNamara issued Department of Defense Directive 5120.36, which required base commanders to use the financial resources of the U.S. military to ensure integration off base, including housing and services. Coincidentally, that same year, I was born in El Paso, Texas, while my family was stationed at Fort Bliss. My father's military career is likely the reason I grew up never living in segregated housing or attending segregated schools. Once again, I took for granted what I later learned was exceptional.

Even with the growth in diversity of our population discussed earlier, a large body of research shows that we are still segregated— in our neighborhoods, in our daily working lives, and in the schools we attend.

In the early 1990s, Doug Massey and Nancy Denton's *American Apartheid: Segregation and the Making of the Underclass* was a wake-up call.[23] Massey and Denton showed through a series of analyses that residential segregation by race was a durable feature of American life, and that the levels observed in major cities were evidence of "hypersegregation." They noted that American levels of segregation were comparable to only one other nation in modern history: South Africa under apartheid. Because of the relative integration on the base settings where I grew up, I was shocked to learn the novelty of my experience.

In 1999, leading economists David Cutler, Edward Glaeser, and Jacob Vigdor published a paper, "The Rise and Decline of the American Ghetto," in which they analyzed the degree of segregation in the U.S. over the course of a century (1890–1990).[24] They offered a striking conclusion:

Across all these time periods there is a strong positive relation between urban population or density and segregation. . . . By 1990, the legal barriers enforcing segregation had been replaced by decentralized racism, where whites pay more than blacks to live in predominantly white areas.

Gary Orfield and Chungmei Lee reviewed progress in school segre-gation fifty years after the Supreme Court's *Brown v. Board of Education* (1954) decision, in an article titled "*Brown* at 50: King's Dream or *Plessy's* Nightmare?"[25]

> Our new work . . . shows that U.S. schools are becoming more seg-regated in all regions for both African American and Latino students. We are celebrating a victory over segregation at a time when schools across the nation are becoming increasingly segregated.

As for patterns in the workplace, the *American Sociological Review* published a paper that concluded: "Most strikingly, black-white workplace desegregation essentially stops after 1980 . . . there is also some disturbing evidence of resegregation after 1995 in old economy sectors."[26]

Segregation reflects differences in the composition of people over geographic space. These differences are not an issue in themselves. However, physical separation of demographic groups creates closed markets that depress the opportunity for segregated minorities to accumulate knowledge, jobs, and wealth. In time, I did my own research analyzing the costs of segregation. Growing up in residen-tially segregated neighborhoods, schools, and workplaces is associated with depressed labor market attainments as an adult, largely due to racially circumscribed social networks.[27]

There is an unsettling realization about persistently high levels of segregation. If they are left unchecked, we should anticipate rising inequality across groups *without* the requirement of what we often think of as racial or ethnic prejudice. For so many years, we have built our research frames and social prescriptions under the assumption that the reduction of individual prejudice would lead to equality of oppor-tunity. Perhaps the physical and social space between us was missing from our consideration set?

Geographic and social space is consequential. Given this reality, it now seems difficult to construct theories of market action or business strategies in which hypersegregated lives—by race and class—would not result in education, income, and wealth disparities. As with my naive assumptions about my college classmates when they accepted credit cards they likely should not have, it also seems a mistake to assume that those cordoned off from the larger market and educational systems would easily transition into positive relationships with financial service providers. Some financial institutions have recognized the deleterious effects of segregation and have taken steps to mitigate them; some are featured in this book. Having recognized the influence of financial socialization in the home and social segregation, I discuss the role of governmental policy in the next section.

## ANOTHER BENEFIT: GOVERNMENT INNOVATION

My father grew up in a racially segregated enclave of Tulsa, Oklahoma. My grandparents were college graduates, who both served during World War II—my grandfather as an educator and marksmanship trainer for troops in Georgia, my grandmother working for the Tennessee Valley Authority (TVA).

After the war, they purchased a new home.[28] Their loan was secured through a financial innovation created by the Servicemen's Readjustment Act of 1944, or "GI Bill," which provided a range of benefits for the millions of veterans returning from World War II. Without this intervention, it is doubtful they would have secured a loan. In the America of that period, precious few banks made loans to families like mine; there were exclusionary home ownership covenants in segregated white neighborhoods, and perceived high risks in Black ones.

There was a coincidental difference in where my grandparents chose to settle after their service. Studies show that in the Deep South—Georgia, Alabama, Mississippi—Black veterans were blocked from using many of their promised veterans' services, including home mortgages and educational funding.[29] My grandparents' decision to settle in Oklahoma created a positive inequality that provided me benefits years later. This brings me to another uncomfortable fact: policy intervenes in ways that provide benefits to some and not others, and these can influence the acquisition of financial wealth.

I share these three contributing factors—cultural capital, segregation, and their linkages to policy—to introduce elements I worry are sometimes missing from our discussions about disparities across demographic groups. There is a sizable and powerful breadth of academic literature on the topic of workforce diversity with a basis in the field of psychology. Typically, these frameworks provide diagnoses and prescriptions to recognize and reduce bias. The psychologically based, "prejudice is the cause" approach to relations between groups has practical roots in the notion that someone is explicitly or implicitly carrying bias toward one group or another.

As helpful as these are, I worry that they obscure other considerations. The contribution of physical and social structure must be reckoned with in our prescriptions. If demographic groups are not at the same point at the educational and socioeconomic starting line, or if policies provide benefits to some and not others, there can be an exacerbation or compounding of existing gaps—without anyone having bias or practicing stereotypes. If groups are fundamentally separated, we first should expect ignorance between them (with or without any animus or bias). If groups start out with differences in education, income, and wealth, the rising tide may not equally float all boats. Some financial providers recognize that the scales are not always balanced and develop product innovations that address these disparities.

Becoming antiracist is a process. At the personal level, it involves often uncomfortable reflection. At the institutional level, it involves recognizing entrenched structures, and building systems that help us overcome them. It may be counterintuitive to some, but we must recognize the key role of financial capital in these efforts.

## AN ARGUMENT FOR INCLUSIVE MODELS

By now, readers should understand that I sample a diverse set of disciplines—economics and finance, social psychology and workforce diversity, sociology, and behavioral economics. There are references in this text to a broad portfolio of research topics that might initially seem loosely connected to the financial services industry. Residential segregation, socialization and relationship networks, educational achievement gaps, intergenerational wealth, and immigration policy are quite integral elements of customer engagement in the business and financial services marketplace and, in turn, of outcomes like wealth accumulation and disparity.

In recognition of the place of business within the larger society, I also reference relevant government policies. This extends from local initiatives to pivotal Supreme Court decisions. This integrative approach, predicated on the fact that businesses operate "in society" and do not somehow exist in a separate sphere, is central to the work of business ethicists like my colleagues Ed Freeman and Andy Wicks.[30]

The combination of approaches is meant to add grounding, not unlike the demographic, cultural, and policy analyses that an investor venturing abroad would undertake.

The relative exclusion of these factors in some research likely reflects a preference for parsimony. The process in most peer-reviewed journals is to attract scholars with deep knowledge of specific streams of discourse. Work that bridges boundaries is encouraged, but harder to deal with and review. This is why the expressed appetite among academics for "cross-disciplinary" work is greater than the supply.

The intent of the review process is, of course, benign—to focus scholars onto avenues of inquiry that deeply develop paradigms and provide rigorous research to answer relatively focused questions. A consequential yet unintentional effect is that work that spreads beyond the traditional boundaries tends to meet a challenged reception. Journals also have a finite number of issues each year and pages in each volume, and, like universities, their value is assessed in part on their degree of rejection.[31] Incentives shape behavior. Attending to messages of "fit" is an important consideration for research authors.

Perhaps a second reason some scholars have been less likely to include some of these topics in their work is the fear of having their research or conclusions potentially face accusations of bias. I can imagine that for some, it may simply seem easier to leave these topics unaddressed. There is a cost to all of us in this circumstance. Like a family that colludes to avoid uncomfortable topics, our collective failure to include factors like these lowers the likelihood of our finding appropriate prescriptions. The lack of discussion, coupled with fear of variance from the status quo, may discourage market action in what are actually viable markets. Collectively, we fail to learn what works and why.

Book-length projects like this one afford scholars the breadth and length to cover their interests broadly, and provide the opportunity for integration across fields and concepts. What is reflected here is the culmination of years of quantitative and qualitative research driven by an evolving, linked group of research questions, which I referenced in the preface: How can financial institutions develop products for low-income and underserved Americans? Can they do so without imprudent levels of associated risks? What skills, routines, and knowledge do organizations that serve these populations have that other, more traditional firms do not? How can we develop a more inclusive, democratic financial services system?

## THE IMPORTANCE OF HISTORY

During my doctoral studies, I had the opportunity to meet the famous economist Richard Nelson, who shared a paper on "history-friendly" models of economic development.[32] Nelson's sense was that researchers in industrial economics, business organization, and strategy had been limited by a reliance on theorization that was not informed by qualitative facts. Nelson held that researchers should strive to be grounded in their work—that "formal economic models ought to proceed well informed by the empirical literature on the subject matter they purport to address."[33]

Nelson's notions were encouraging to my evolving thinking: policies have influenced financial accumulation in unequal fashions across demographic groups. Inequality can be inherited and passed on, without demonstrable intent. Our research frames should consider these impacts.

## COUNTERING THE "FINANCE STEREOTYPE"

If you asked the average American their opinion about bankers and finance, they might share a set of adjectives that reveal a sense of disconnection. The salaries and bonuses bankers receive, the homes and neighborhoods they live in, and the ways they choose to enjoy themselves can seem extreme, overplayed, and otherworldly. In 2009, during the financial meltdown, President Obama described the magnitude of that year's bonuses as "shameful." As job losses and unemployment mounted, everyday Americans learned that John Thain, formerly of Merrill Lynch, had spent $1.2 million to remodel his office suite, including the installation of a $35,000 toilet. Whether or not there had been a crisis or a bailout, few readers could generate reasons why this was not extreme behavior.[34]

Gold-plated commodes aside, the very real ties between Wall Street and Main Street were made plain in the recent financial crisis. Most felt then, and still feel, that blame somehow rested on Wall Street; however, they would be hard-pressed to explain the chain of linked organizations that contributed to their own financial difficulties. The dominoes that fell eventually reached the front doors of common folks living far away from Wall Street, physically and economically. The prevailing view was that events unfolded because of greed.

For many, something seemed amoral, imbalanced. There seemed to be little or no relationship between salary and the performance of Wall Street firms. For some, this was evidence that the system was somehow "fixed" in ways that benefited those at the top, and that financial institutions were central players in a modern-day version of the "good old boys" network.[35]

For others, the controversy was an example of ignorance and class warfare. In framing the issue, one explanation drew on long-standing theories popular in business and economic circles: Markets are efficient, and the compensation of executives represents both the value of their work in economic terms and the level of compensation necessary to attract that level of talent.[36] As Marc Hodak of New York University's Stern School of Business wrote in *Forbes*:

> I know it's hard for someone making $50,000 a year to imagine that anyone can be worth 10 or a hundred times that. But, they well might be. How do I know? Because if I don't pay them, someone else will. When an executive across the table tells me, "The guys down the street are offering $2 million a year," he's not bluffing. The experienced buyer of managerial talent can see the difference between a $500,000 executive and $2 million executive as surely as a home buyer can tell the difference between a half-million-dollar home and a $2 million home.[37]

As I read Hodak's explanation, I suspected that few average Americans could tell the difference between a half-million-dollar and two-million-dollar home. For perspective, in 2009, the time of Hodak's article, the median price of a new home in the United States was $216,700.[38]

## IS THE FINANCE STEREOTYPE REALLY A PROBLEM?

If stereotypes about financial professionals as "disconnected" spread and reify, a social and structural gulf between the spheres of finance professionals and average consumers will follow. Some may avoid the field altogether. Who wants to work in an industry labeled "unethical" and "greedy"?

The representation of the finance industry and its managers as greedy, villainous, and different from you and me may be widespread and may have institutionalized in the popular imagination. However, what if the popular negative perception of finance is just what scholars of rhetoric would term a *trope* or a *shibboleth*?

Perception is not always fact, and some strongly held beliefs about groups turn out to be stereotypes. Despite what we see on evening television dramas, the reality is that the average police officer is highly unlikely to have ever used their weapon in the line of duty. Likewise, the majority of managers working in financial services firms have not been indicted for fraud or other unreputable acts.

Beyond the hype and headlines, at its core, finance is a set of practices—even an art—that can be applied across a broad range of social and demographic contexts and levels of affluence, which can be used for purposes beyond personal asset growth. It is our responsibility to highlight research and narratives that provide a counter to the "finance problem" rhetoric.

## GETTING BEYOND DISCOURSE
## TO POTENTIAL IMPACT

In business school, we tend to study very large firms with enormous balance sheets and market capitalizations. This has been called the "pro-innovation, pro-size" bias in management research.[39] Collectively, we spend far less time focusing on the middle and lower ends of the distribution.

I have wondered if part of the reason is a less-discussed belief: that those who have less are that way because they have made poor decisions, are profligate, and are therefore high-risk. The impoverished remain so because of structural inequalities that are durable and consequential. This reminds me of my mistake when I observed my classmates taking credit cards, or my erroneous assumption that everyone had grown up in integrated settings.

I am one of a group of scholars choosing to wade into thorny, some would say controversial, topics that find their way into the public interest: immigration and nativity, racial and gender disparities, residential segregation. These are all fraught topics, with complicated histories. They also require careful, multifaceted solutions that will take patience and time—and collective support.

We include in our frames the role public and financial institutions have historically had, and still have, in effecting or exacerbating inequalities between groups. We observe the rigidity of these differences between us and find that market-efficient equilibrium models of change are insufficient.

Research that includes these considerations may reveal *inclusive* models that provide prescriptions for financial institutions to operate efficiently, without high levels of risks, and with uncommon returns. There is a potential "trickle-down" benefit of an inclusive approach. A financial system that continually fails to serve large portions of the populace cannot be taken as successful. Likewise, research theory or models that are silent on societal matters like the various "isms" that are clearly evident—for example, in durable wealth disparities—fail to respond to the very realities of daily life for so many.

I am encouraged that this work has influenced policy. My colleague Ruo Jia and I developed a risk model that was adopted as a key input to the financial model for the Community Development Financial Institutions (CDFI) Bond Fund. This funding innovation provides capital to community development financial institutions, recently more than $1.5 billion.[40] Likewise, my fieldwork with CDFIs eventually culminated in a request to participate as a researcher in the review of the CDFI Fund at its twenty-year anniversary.[41] I have also had the benefit of sitting on the boards of a number of development organizations and financial institutions.

I have additional motivations as an academic. Certainly, I am serious about our roles to produce scholarship. I also take seriously our roles in social progress, with the mission to serve more than the affluent. I believe this about all educators, and especially my colleagues in public institutions.

## ORGANIZATION OF THIS BOOK

The approach I have adopted is reflected in the organization of this book. The next few chapters provide perspective based on research I have completed on financial institutions pursuing EDM strategies.

A number of these are large-scale econometric models. The first two chapters deal with questions of the riskiness and efficiency of financial institutions operating in developing communities. The third examines social movements in the field of what has been alternatively called "social" or "development" finance.

There is strength in narrative. Some ideas are difficult to comprehend when presented solely as quantitative and statistical analyses. Thus, the remaining chapters provide accounts from extensive fieldwork with depository banks and credit unions, venture capital firms, development loan funds, and financial services providers.

The work featured in this book covers three areas of community development: work focused on people, on places, or on areas of impact. For example, the chapters on the achievements of the Citizen Potawatomi Community Development Corporation and the push by American Express to build a business among lower-income consumers represent work focused on specific consumer groups ("people" projects). The chapters on Shorebank's efforts on Chicago's South Side or the Reinvestment Fund's efforts in North Philadelphia are focused on geographic areas ("place" projects). The chapter detailing efforts by Pacific Community Ventures to provide equity to a set of entrepreneurs that met their impact goals represents yet another approach. Each of these has varied benefits and challenges, as we will see.

I have spent years visiting, interviewing, and writing about the individuals who run financial institutions operating in developing areas. Exemplars from the field bring nuance from behind quantification. Field research is not an endorsement; my effort is not to lionize these entrepreneurial managers. There are both successful and cautionary tales. It is clear to all of us that these are complicated challenges. Experimentation is necessary, and comes with error. We should accept this reality.

I consider these "facts on the ground" to be entrepreneurial experiments in action. Others have called them "policy through demonstration." Either way, there is a recognition that there may be more happening in the field that we have not collected, analyzed, and digested in our understanding of how business does and does not happen in our communities.

I had two secret wishes in writing this book. One is that we recognize a shared purpose in our markets, neighborhoods, and working lives. There are easy symbols of our disconnection these days. This book recognizes that there are indeed entrepreneurs building connections, and that we need more of them. The second wish is that some may read this book and recognize a path for themselves. I am hoping that the information, techniques, and models presented will encourage some who are skeptical of the financial services system to see an alternative future that includes their personal interest, support, and efforts—that they might see in the narratives the promise of the finance industry's capacity to assist others, within their own communities and beyond, in achieving a higher standard of living and an improved quality of life. Perhaps they may choose to leverage that potential by pursuing a career in finance.

A long-standing, implied promise of America has been that anyone can achieve to the extent of their abilities and efforts. Now there is an increasing recognition that perhaps this notion may not fit the facts: inequality is higher than in other Western nations and rising, health outcomes lag, educational gaps persist, and trust in American institutions is falling. Equilibrium is not "taking care of it."

The protests of 2020 were a stark reminder that we sorely need to address structural and institutional barriers. A looming question is how we achieve this. There is real potential that financial innovators like those featured in this book can assist in fulfilling America's promise of opportunity for all. This type of labor can overcome some of the structural barriers we have yet to surmount. This will require careful study, experimentation, and diffusion of innovations that prove efficacious. The hope of this book is that readers will recognize the unique contribution that these efforts can make, and that more will engage in helping us find solutions.

# CHAPTER TWO

# A Fool's Errand?

## *The Riskiness of Financial Services in Low-Income Areas*

TWO HUNDRED & FIVE DOLLARS REWARD—At the great
baseball match on Tuesday, while I was engaged in hurrahing, a
small boy walked off with an English-made brown silk UMBRELLA
belonging to me, & forgot to bring it back. I will pay $5 for the return
of that umbrella in good condition to my house on Farmington Avenue.
I do not want the boy (in an active state) but will pay two hundred
dollars for his remains.[1]

SAMUEL CLEMENS, *HARTFORD COURANT*, MAY 20, 1875

"YOU'LL BE denied."

That was my father's verdict when I'd called him for advice on a
condominium my wife and I were interested in purchasing at auction
in Hartford, Connecticut. As a former commercial loan officer, he
seemed a wise resource. I was dumbstruck at his response. After all,
this would not be a large loan: The real estate agent assisting us estimated the winning bid at monthly payments of less than $200, even
with a shorter, fifteen-year term.

Our agent pointed out that the bank had chosen to put the property up for auction with a reserve that would allow them to recoup
only the remaining unpaid balance on the loan—a clear indication of
an intended quick sale. When I mentioned this detail, Dad indicated
that the low potential acquisition price was actually a disadvantage.
"From the bank's perspective, the effort to complete a small loan like

yours makes it overly expensive in terms of the amount of paperwork and the salaries of the employees who will work on it."

In graduate school, I'd been introduced to the economic reasoning behind transaction costs and marginal returns—I just hadn't imagined this logic would apply to my own aspirations to increase familial wealth.

Dad went on to explain. "Even if the loan officer could get past the relative expense of assisting you, her next concern would be the past owner's default. Few banks want to take another loan on a property that has previously gone into default."

I countered that there was an understandable reason for the owner's default, and it had nothing to do with the property's value. Tragically, the reclusive owner had passed painfully and slowly from HIV/AIDS. Dad reminded me that accounting statements don't note extenuating circumstances.

Further, the property was located in a historic area with personal resonance for us: The homes of Harriet Beecher Stowe and Mark Twain were only a few blocks away. In the late 1800s, the area had attracted a community of politicians, artists, and writers with progressive ideals, including feminism and the abolition of slavery. After I'd laid out these details, Dad countered that they were "incidental, at best, even if the small loan size and past default issues could be explained to a loan review committee."

Apart from Dad's counsel, there was something else: the neighborhood. Although West End was once a destination for wealthy luminaries, it was now starkly different. The 2000 Census data told the story: Of the roughly eleven thousand units of housing in the zip code, 13 percent were vacant, and the vast majority (86 percent) were renter occupied;[2] the median family income was less than $30,000; 30 percent of the population lived below the poverty level; and 16 percent of its working-age adults were unemployed. Demographically, the zip code was racially and ethnically pluralistic (i.e., no racial or ethnic group represented a majority). For us, this was attractive.[3]

Though I was well aware of the historical practice of redlining, I also understood that it was illegal for banks to avoid lending solely based on a neighborhood's racial composition. I had read enough to know that lending institutions would not focus on race *per se*, but on the correlates of race: the age of housing stock, median family incomes, and the percentage of homeowners versus renters. The fact that the residents of an individual complex had high education and income status might not overcome other concerns. Dad reminded me that lenders would be paying attention to features on spreadsheets.

The pivotal question that remained was: "How do families like ours finance a home purchase in neighborhoods like these?" Dad explained that the options were pretty limited. Most buyers self-fund the purchase and essentially pay in cash. Some have other collateral assets, such as large deposits with the lender bank, but most just give up and move elsewhere.

As the financial realities and our limited options began to sink in, I realized that, although I had studied the benefits of increasing income and racial diversity in terms of social outcomes in lower-income neighborhoods, there was another factor in socioeconomic change: funding—that reality-based intersection of personal wealth decisions, espoused progressive ideals, and the rigors of the financial services system. I also realized that the lack of financial services and products had another unintended consequence. Even if a family desired to move to neighborhoods like this one, a relatively small number of buyers would have cash on hand to purchase properties. Gentrification and racial displacement would be difficult to avoid. As if to prove this point, the residents of the condominium complex tended to be white (including a very helpful and encouraging African American Studies professor).

Recognizing we would need to go without the financial support of a bank, my wife and I placed a closed bid on the property with our available savings. The amount was less than the price of a *used* luxury car. Two days later, the real estate agent informed us that we'd won our first home, and we were ecstatic. We were preparing to move into our unit—or so we thought.

A few weeks prior to moving day, there was a fire. It had started in a local warehouse and quickly spread to a number of nearby buildings, including ours. According to the fire department's report, embers from the warehouse fire ignited the wooden decks at the rear of the complex and, within minutes, the entire building went up in flames.

Insurance covered the property's repair and restoration, but the building's reconstruction took more than thirteen months. The one good piece of news is that when we sold the unit, we took a profit that assisted us in securing our next home. I recently looked up that Hartford property on Zillow. It sold in 2015 for four-and-a-half times what we paid through our winning bid. The value of the property had grown just under 11 percent per year—an attractive rate. I've wondered how often other buyers like us fail to find lenders to assist them in purchasing similarly "difficult" properties that actually have economic potential.

## A DECIDEDLY DIFFERENT TYPE OF FINANCIAL INSTITUTION

We'd had a challenging experience that ultimately ended on a positive note. Nevertheless, I mused on how barriers in the lending process could be overcome in similar neighborhoods. When I began studying the business models of financial institutions that operate in lower-income communities, I soon came across a set of banks, credit unions, and nonprofit lenders that *choose* to serve areas like the Hartford neighborhood. These encompass minority-serving depository institutions (MDIs), for which race or ethnicity is an intentional area of impact,[4] and community development financial institutions (CDFIs), which serve low-income communities. At the time Dad and I were talking about financing the condo purchase, I didn't know about these types of financial institutions, or that some may have been willing to provide a mortgage loan to a couple like us.

## "AREN'T THEY RISKIER?"

Community Development Banking Institutions (CDBIs) are depository banks that serve low-income, underserved markets. CDBIs are defined as "depository institutions with a stated mission to primarily benefit the underserved communities in which they are chartered to conduct business."[5] They are one category of Community Development Financial Institution (CDFI)—the U.S. Treasury designation for mission-driven financial institutions, which include credit unions, loan funds, and equity funds.

CDBIs provide depository, credit, and counseling services to low- and moderate-income (LMI) individuals or communities. CDFIs were created under the Riegle Community Development and Regulatory Improvement Act of 1994 (P.L. 103–325), which established the Community Development Financial Institutions Fund as a "wholly owned government corporation to promote economic revitalization and community development."[6] The fund was initially proposed by President Clinton who advocated its mission-driven aspects: "By ensuring greater access to capital and credit, we will tap the entrepreneurial energy of America's poorest communities and enable individuals and communities to become self-sufficient."[7]

Similarly, MDIs are a federally recognized set of banks and credit unions with missions to provide financial services to minority populations reach back to the Freedmen's Savings and Trust Company, a federal initiative that created depository banks to serve the needs of recently emancipated slaves in the wake of the Civil War.[8]

It is possible for a single depository to be an MDI, a CDFI, neither, or both. As regulated financial institutions, CDBIs and MDIs must meet the same safety and soundness requirements as any other depository.

There are *prima facie* reasons to suspect that CDFIs and MDIs face greater risks of institutional failure than otherwise similar depositories. Most of the prevailing concerns center on their stated commitment to provide financial services to LMI and minority clients. There is a general recognition that consumers from these households tend to have fewer assets, greater risk of unemployment, and lower average incomes. The logical progression is that consumers with these characteristics expose financial institutions to heightened risks of credit default and, in turn, eventual institutional failure.

There is some evidence to support these associations. Studies indicate that CDBIs tend to establish branches in LMI neighborhoods and place more of their loans in these communities. A recent report by the National Community Investment Forum (NCIF) found that, in 2016, the median CDBI had 55.2 percent of their branches in LMI communities and made 75.3 percent of their loans in these areas as well.[9] Comparable banks that are not CDBIs have considerably fewer branches and services in these markets.[10] Likewise, other researchers report that MDIs are more likely to serve minority consumers than comparable non-MDIs.[11]

Some demographic trends offer a measure of support for the conjecture that service to these consumer segments exposes institutions to undue risks. Disturbingly high levels of residential segregation by race, income, and education cluster poverty and concomitant social dislocations in geographic space (and likewise in depository operational areas). For example, a recent analysis by Intrator, Tannen, and

Massey concluded, "Given their higher overall levels of segregation and income's limited effect on residential attainment, African Americans experience less integration and more neighborhood poverty at all levels of income compared to other minority groups. The degree of black spatial disadvantage is especially acute in the nation's 21 hypersegregated metropolitan areas."[12]

By 2014, there were more than 174 Federal Deposit Insurance Corporation (FDIC)–insured MDIs with assets in excess of $181 billion. With a history dating to post–Civil War Reconstruction, it is not surprising that, over time, the demography of the communities served by MDIs has evolved. By 2014, 44 percent were categorized as serving Asians, 18 percent served Hispanics, 11 percent served Native Americans, and only a minority focused on serving Blacks (14 percent).[13] As I continued my research, I learned that many MDIs (about 40 percent) were also CDBIs.

The MDI designation was created in 1989 as a component of the Financial Institutions Reform, Recovery, and Enforcement Act (FIRREA) with the objective of sustaining and increasing the number and capacity of depositories operating in minority markets.

## THE QUESTION

Something else nagged at me about the Hartford condo: Wouldn't a lender providing mortgages in a neighborhood like ours be taking on undue risk? Wasn't it just "chancier" or more costly to lend to lower-income consumers? Even if the individual lendee wasn't of low income, weren't there multiplicative "spillover" risks associated with the neighborhood in which a mortgage was granted?

Recognizing that these questions are relevant, what I term the "good but risky" question became a central theme in a project I engaged in a few years later. CDFIs target their services to poor and low-income communities—providing a societal benefit, or "good." However, these are also perceived *a priori* to be riskier markets for financial institutions. The "good but risky" question seemed critical to any credible discussion of CDFIs' performance over time.[14]

In 2014, my research team was invited to assist the U.S. Treasury in its evaluation of the CDFI program on its twentieth anniversary.[15] One reason we were invited was that, a few years earlier, we had performed an initial exploratory analysis that created a predictive model on whether a CDFI was likely to fail within two years of its creation.[16] This work was a component of a research project on the business models of CDFIs supported by a grant from the John D. and Catherine T. MacArthur Foundation.[17]

## DOING OUR HOMEWORK: A REVIEW OF RESEARCH ON CDFIs

As we set out to develop a model that would provide a comparative measure of whether MDIs and CDBIs were at greater risk than their "traditional" counterparts, our first task was to perform background research. I knew that business academic literature, even finance journals, contained precious little about these types of banks. First, there was a study I performed with Ruo Jia that used a modified CAMEL (Capital Adequacy, Asset Quality, Management, Earnings and Liquidity) model to predict the comparative likelihood of failure among CDFI banks and credit unions, which found that CDFIs were not statistically different in their failure risks.[18] Second, Kashian and Drago used CAMEL models to examine the risks of MDI failures from 2009 to 2014, and found that failure rates were high among Black and Asian serving MDIs. Beyond these, there was little peer-reviewed research carefully examining CDFI or MDI institutional failure risks.

The quantity of academic research did not match the degree of "common wisdom" on the topic. I have felt for some time that this lack of interest is an opportunity.

## DIFFERENCES BETWEEN MDIs AND CDFIs

In most ways, there are marginal differences between CDBIs and MDIs and their counterparts. At their heart, like all financial service firms, they are financial intermediary organizations involved in the transformation of capital from one form to another. A CDFI or MDI could be the bank or credit union just around the corner.

During our background research, collaborators at the CDFI Fund of the U.S. Treasury, Greg Bischak and Oscar Gonzalez, shared a particularly helpful study that categorized census tracts in which financial institutions provided loans according to median family income (that is, low, moderate, middle, and higher incomes) and then compared these data to the area's overall income.

Bischak and Gonzalez's analyses showed that CDFI awardees consistently focused their activities in low-income areas and, not surprisingly, outperformed mainstream lenders on a number of socially relevant measures—e.g., where they placed their loans and where they deployed award capital. To illustrate, CDFIs placed 91 percent of their loans in LMI areas, while non-CDFIs placed 59 percent in these areas.[19] From these data and other indicators, we concluded that MDIs and CDFIs indeed lend in low-income, underserved markets to a greater degree than their comparable counterparts. We wondered whether these efforts included programs to aid in creating financial security for low-income populations, increasing affordable home ownership, and providing capital to minority entrepreneurs.

## MISSION AND PROFITABILITY ENABLED BY THE BALANCE SHEET

At least one reason for these differences in orientation might be the coupling of mission and balance sheet. The missions of MDIs and CDBIs address a constellation of social concerns, ranging from refugees and victims of domestic violence to energy efficiency; though, the majority explicitly target their assistance to low-income clients and communities.

However, these missions may create an inherent tension: How do CDFIs balance their social mission with profitability? Conceptually, there should be scant reason to find a conflict in navigating shareholder and stakeholder returns. However, in practice, there are dilemmas—decisions about which loans to make, how to price them, where to adjust decisions about creditworthiness, among others. In some decision-making regimes, these questions might "push" some products into a market, or retract others.

There is one additional challenge. The effects of certain CDFI social efforts—for example, funding charter schools or early childhood educational centers—may not be realized for some time. The problem of how to accurately measure social impact further complicates the question of whether CDFIs are meeting their objectives and, if so, how effectively. There is a careful interplay among financial expediency, fiduciary responsibility, and production and dissemination of financial products that presents a unique challenge.

One way CDFIs manage these tensions is through the leverage provided in their balance sheets. For example, CDFIs are eligible to receive grants for projects that align with their missions. Many times, these grants don't have to be repaid or vary in their need to be serviced compared to the debt and loans from private sources that may appear on their balance sheets. Grants can come from federal, state, and local governments, from private philanthropies such as foundations, or from private donors.

Grants may be received for certain types of lending (home energy retrofit, affordable housing, fresh-food small businesses); targeted areas (post-Katrina New Orleans, Willapa Bay Watershed, the Bronx); or designated groups of people (Sudanese refugees, Native Americans, victims of domestic violence).

During austere times, when many families are in distress, there is a greater need for the types of services CDFIs can provide. A number of CDFIs' sourced funds became available through the American Recovery and Reinvestment Act (ARRA, P.L. 111–5, February 2009), a countercyclical government stimulus program. So in periods like the Great Recession, when federal programs expand social safety nets temporarily, CDFIs may receive additional funding, through initiatives like the Troubled Asset Relief Program and New Markets Tax Credit funds.[20] Further, philanthropic funders may request that CDFIs "double down" and extend an even greater portion of their lending capital in low-income areas. During the recent Covid-19 crisis, CDFIs received $10B in additional funds as a part of the Paycheck Protection Program (PPP).

In sum, our background research confirmed suspicions that the missions and emphasis of CDFIs and MDIs either encourage or explicitly require them to enter low-income, underserved markets and to use their fundraising efforts to create "space" or "leverage" on their balance sheets for this type of work.

## THE ANALYSIS: ANSWERING THE QUESTION

During the 2008–2010 mortgage market collapse, market interconnections led to a cascading set of banking and credit union failures. To analyze this impact, we became interested in whether CDFIs and

MDIs were more vulnerable because of their exposure to challenged loans in lower-income mortgage markets.

We wanted to ensure we were comparing across categories in a way that would eliminate any misleading correlations due to other effects, such as the size of a firm's assets, its location in a rural area, the level of poverty in the community, or other factors that do not directly tie to the risks of the firm itself. We found that the best tools to perform this type of evaluation are based on a statistical modeling process called logistic regression.

To perform this study, we needed access to comparable, regular performance data that extended over a period of time longer than three years. Ideally, these data would be available on a quarterly basis so that we could add sensitivity to our analyses that included differences in performance within a single year.

As it turned out, other researchers had also looked into the failure risks of CDFIs. However, they did not approach the issue with either the same econometric techniques or the same breadth of firms for comparison.

We had confidence in our approach, at least in part because of the positive response to our past analyses that had used similar techniques. As mentioned earlier, in our initial work, we were able to accurately predict a CDFI's likelihood of failure within two years of operation based on its quarterly financial statements.

To illustrate, if a given bank were to fail in the fall of 2009, our model could predict that failure using financial reports from the fall of 2007. The model captured the evolution of underperformance in periods leading up to a bank's failure. This approach also had prescriptive value and could be used as a tool to diagnose financial institutions in the early stages of distress.

The phrase "systemic risks" in mortgage lending generally refers to the likelihood that either a cascade of failures will affect a significant portion of the financial system across lenders, or a series of failures will be created by the interconnections among lenders with shared experiences in their mortgage markets. By way of comparison, a similar situation can occur with contagious diseases. For example, an individual's likelihood of catching the flu is directly related to the number of contagious people she may come in contact with during flu season.

As we moved forward in our effort, we recognized the potential benefit of answering additional questions: Are CDFIs at greater risk for failure when markets are especially challenging and failures abound? Is the likelihood of a loan default directly related to the health of other homeowners within the same service area? One way to answer these questions was to evaluate banks and credit unions through their "connectedness" within the local mortgage markets where they lend in the same low-income neighborhoods.

The importance of accounting for systemic risks became clear during the 2008–2010 global financial crisis, when there were a record number of banking failures. One of the primary factors of the crisis was the significant decline in the value of mortgage portfolios of individual financial institutions, and a record number of mortgage delinquencies leading to foreclosures.

In theory, in shared markets, banks that make poorly qualified loans negatively impact peer lenders that have been considerably more careful in their specific lending practices. Firms that have underwritten qualified loans could be thrust into failure because their loans are collocated in areas beset by "contagious" firms that have underwritten their loans poorly. In light of that, we included a systemic risk mortgage market analysis to simulate the impact of such a market collapse in the mortgage industry, and to estimate whether CDFIs would be more vulnerable.

The primary statistical methods we applied to the question of failure risks have a long history, but had not been used to study MDIs and/or CDFIs. These methods and associated statistical models have roots in the work of Edward Altman and are generally referred to as "Altman's Z-score."[21]

As a tool for analysis, the logistic regression Z-score model is especially useful in predicting values that are discrete, rather than continuous—that is, predicting the likelihood or probability of an event happening or not happening, such as a bank failure within two years. Since first proposed by Daniel Martin in 1977, these models have been used to monitor banks and have remained a staple of the credit risk and banking industry ever since.[22] Over the years, many regulatory and rating agencies have developed their own proprietary methods for evaluating the risk of institutional failure, and many private consulting firms do the same for their clients in related areas.

To examine systemic risks through mortgage markets, we focused on the potential that individual firms hold similar assets that are correlated with one another. Because specific holdings of financial institutions are rarely available for analysis, research generally looks at the way the performance of different financial institutions—with similar distributions of assets—trend with one another with respect to return and volatility. In this case, the subject was mortgage loans.[23]

We wanted to ensure that our model adjusted for geographic and other focal factors when attempting to estimate systemic risks of failure. To achieve this, we defined shared markets in the way an epidemiologist studying the spread of viruses might examine shared spaces, like workplaces or schools.

We based our measure on the overlap two financial firms have with respect to a region in which they both do mortgage origination. This made sense because bank failures at the individual loan level—or the level of the entire firm—affect other financial institutions by undermining the stability of asset holdings they all share and the valuations of the mortgage loans they hold in their portfolios. In this way, the transmission of "illness" is through lowered valuations of the properties that the mortgages support, which are brought on by foreclosures. The quality of the properties or the creditworthiness of families paying their loans has not changed, but the behavior of the foreclosed lendee next door has. When a set of local homeowners are foreclosed upon, it affects the value of properties within proximal distance. Firms that overlap in their mortgage lending can mutually affect one another in this way, and the going-in hypothesis to our research was that the greater presence of mortgage loans in low-income neighborhoods would make CDFIs and MDIs especially vulnerable.

## MEASURING SYSTEMIC RISKS THROUGH CONCEPTS FROM SOCIAL NETWORK THEORY

In examining systemic risks through mortgage market interconnections, we needed a quantifiable way of measuring the degree or extent of overlap across firms. The optimal place to look was social network analysis. Social network methods provide quantitative and symbolic representations of the relationships between different entities, including people. The most common visualization of these relationships is through sociograms that illustrate the connections of individuals to others inside a graphic set of relationships.

Again, we were interested in determining how interconnected various financial institutions were to one another through their presence in shared mortgage markets. The simplest quantitative measurement would be simply to count the number of connections any particular firm has with others. Using this approach, one mortgage lender may be more connected than another because it holds a larger aggregate number of shared mortgage markets.

However, this measure is somewhat limiting because another firm could actually be better connected, even though both lenders have the same aggregate number of connections in shared mortgage markets. The difference lies in "network distance," or the number of steps needed to reach any other lender's markets. Two lenders could have the same number of shared mortgage markets, but the number of steps (or network distance) to reach other units in the network could be, on average, shorter for one than the other.

Figure 2.1 provides a graphical representation of two networks that have the same number of connections but different levels of centrality and dominance. (The concept of dominance is also known as *power* in network structure research.)

In the illustration on the left, the circle at the very center of Network A is what network theorists would term *central*, though not very *powerful*. In the illustration on the right, Network B, the center

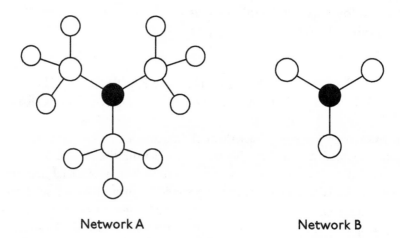

Network A                                  Network B

*Figure 2.1* Networks illustrating centrality and dominance. Source: Zachary Neal, "Differentiating Centrality and Power in the World City Network," *Urban Studies* 48, no. 13 (2011): 2733–2748, fig. 1.

circle has the same number of connections, but is more dominant. In either situation, the bank offers mortgages in the same markets, but the exposures are substantially different. We can imagine these simple diagrams represent the on-the-ground composition of mortgage markets and mortgage loan providers.

We recognized that epidemiological viral researchers had developed a set of measures that could capture the degree of centrality of an institution's connections within a network—eigenvector centrality and Bonacich centrality.[24] These ways of measuring networks have been commonly used yet, to our knowledge, had not previously been applied to the measurement of connectedness across mortgage markets. We used both measures because together they can provide a nuanced understanding of how central, dominated, or dominating a financial institution may be at a given point in time. This approach measures two attributes: how "in the thick of things" firms may be, and how dominated they are by others around them.

Using eigenvector and Bonacich centrality would allow us to capture both types of systemic mortgage risks. It would be appropriate to term this form of systemic risk "interbank lending risk."[25] Armed with a way of measuring failure risks and systemic risks, we next set out to build the data set we would use for our work ahead.

## BUILDING OUR DATA SET AND TESTING THE MODEL

In our initial study, we built a substantial data set by securing the quarterly call reports for every bank and credit union chartered in the United States with assets below $8 billion. This was necessary because even the largest CDFIs are capped at $4 billion. We were also interested in quarterly data so each observation in our data set would represent a firm-quarter. To give a sense of our sample's magnitude, the eventual data set included more than 147,000 bank observations and 170,000 credit union observations—that is, financial measures per quarter, per institution, for the period 2001 to 2012.

The use of CAMEL models to predict institutional failure risks for U.S. banking institutions dates back to the 1970s. They rely on a combination of financial ratios and direct observation, and are generally structured as logistic regression models. Presently, CAMEL models are the prevailing method used by regulators to determine the safety and soundness of banks. Essentially, one or more of the variables we applied in our model reflect all CAMEL measures (with the exception of the M, or management measure).[26]

Equipped with our large data set, we applied logistic regression models to all the depositories, whether CD bank, CD credit union, or comparable mainstream institution.[27] To reiterate, our outcome variable of interest, or dependent variable, for each firm was whether it would be predicted to fail within two years or less.

We developed testing models for banks and credit unions separately, because there were many organizational and structural differences between them that merited differentiation. There was one additional environmental factor we wanted to learn more about. We included a measure of the degree of density surrounding the location of a firm's headquarters as a proxy for whether it served a rural or an urban area (known as rural-urban commuting area [RUCA] codes).[28]

## GETTING DOWN TO THE ANALYSIS: WHAT WE FOUND

Given the size of our data sets and the complexity of the models we applied, it took the computer many hours to run these analyses. And, as any researcher doing this type of work will tell you, one run was insufficient. Since our analysis period included the pre–financial crisis period, it was important to critically interrogate our analyses to determine if we were capturing sustained differences or if our data were skewed by an epiphenomenon (individual firms, periods, or variables that might be outliers). For weeks, we tweaked the model and reran it, changing an individual variable here or there, or running the analysis minus a bank or credit union that seemed different from the norm.

When we were satisfied that our model was representative, we found some things that were expected. Nonperforming assets or loan delinquencies, for example, were like kryptonite for banks and credit unions. Given the environmental challenges brought to the field by the mortgage loan crisis, this measure alone was sufficiently powerful to constitute the largest factor contributing to failure.

A number of other financial ratios fell along anticipated lines. For example, we found that a credit union's larger size, in terms of assets, provided relative protection from failure. Location in a rural area was less associated with failure than location in an urban area.

Regarding the study's primary question of failure risk, some findings differed for credit unions and banks. We found that a certified CDFI bank was less associated with failure than one not holding that designation; however, status as a certified CDFI credit union was statistically insignificant. Taken together, our results showed that CDFI banks were less likely to fail than their counterparts of similar size and scope, and that there was not a greater likelihood of failure among CDFI credit unions relative to peers.

When we examined the impact of systemic risks, we also found differences between banks and credit unions. For banks, we found that, of the network measures, only the eigenvector centrality measure was statistically significant. This meant that there was a heightened risk of failure if a bank had a greater level of network centrality in the mortgage-loan overlaps among banking institutions (that is, if the bank's loans were in neighborhoods with a high degree of overlap with those of other banks). It is important to note that this risk of eigenvector centrality was important for any bank, whether a CDFI or not. However, when we examined the influence of these centrality measures on CD banks and credit unions, we found that both measures mattered and were statistically significant, although they exerted influence in reversed directions.

Put differently, for CDFIs, risks were due not so much to the intensity of mortgage lending in the markets in which a CDFI operated, but more to the extended, outside-of-the-area loans made by other lenders operating in the same neighborhoods. CDFI banks and credit unions were "infected" by other areas of mortgage lending. The cautionary advice here is that CDFI banks should pay attention to the lending decisions of their peers.

There was one notable element we did not include: a measure of the quality of the institution's management (the M in the CAMEL acronym). In practice, reviewers do this. We did not have the bandwidth to visit and score literally hundreds of institutions.

We wondered whether the M was indeed the relevant, unmeasured variable for a number of reasons. First, after becoming a certified CDFI, it may be that a bank's leadership has access to management training, development, and advice that are unavailable to non-CDFIs of similar size and scope. We know, too, there are important best-practice sharing opportunities for institutions serving low-income communities that may not be open to others. Another conjecture is the mere decision to enter a challenging market. Perhaps the process of becoming a CDFI compels the management team to carefully consider their strategic priorities and the realities of having a large number of low-income households as members. A fourth notion is that the presence of increased philanthropic capital during difficult times, such as the recent Covid-19 pandemic and related economic crisis serves as a protective factor for CDFI credit unions. Alas, we were not able to test these ideas.

Although the project had a number of features, the "good but risky" analysis received attention to such an extent that we were asked to present our findings to the Federal Reserve Board. In the end, our model was adopted in what became a major piece of governmental policy: the CDFI Bond Guarantee Program of 2013. The ensuing legislation created a set of federally guaranteed bonds to support community development and included a total potential appropriation of $500 million.[29] Most recently, we replicated this analysis on MDIs for a research paper commissioned by the Federal Reserve Board of Governors.[30] Once again, we found that MDIs face no greater risk of failure and, in certain circumstances, are less risky than their comparable counterparts.

## UNDERSTANDING AND ASSESSING THE DIFFERENCES

If asked to catalogue consequential differences between traditional and what I often call "mission-driven" financial institutions, I have found complexities that make easy distinctions difficult. There are easily observable differences in the wealth assets of the customers served by these firms and in their relative behavioral and knowledge advantages. There are also market-relevant sources of risks (e.g., the degree of competition for consumers, lending market interlinkages). I have also noted internal differences, including the extent and currency of technological resources, compensation levels, and quality of training systems. In addition, there are financial sources of difference, such as the cost of capital and the availability of grant funds. Finally, there seem to be some differences that accrue from the approach to values within organizations, including orientations toward which risks to engage with

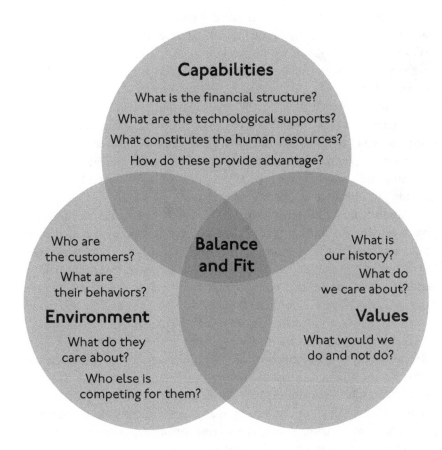

*Figure 2.2* Cataloging relevant risks and advantages.

and how much to expose the organization through credit activity. The intersections of these make easy answers and careful analysis difficult.

I have developed an approach based on a set of frameworks I use in my consulting engagements: values, environment, and capabilities. As illustrated in the Venn diagram in figure 2.2, each of these areas is distinct, yet they are interconnected within a firm's operation. These elements create the unique assemblage that constitutes a firm's strategy (and for this discussion, provide an insight into sources of differential risks).

**Values**. Every organization has a set of values, whether they state these explicitly or consider themselves a "mission-based" firm. An organization's values are not necessarily found in slogans developed by a corporate communications office. I tend to categorize a firm's values by interrogating the "glue" that holds the organization together: What is the organization's purpose, and how has it developed over time? Which interest groups are valued? Which are overlooked? What makes a firm significant to important constituents?

**Environment.** In this framework, environment indicates where a firm operates and who it serves, and accounts for consequential trends and movements. Who are the firm's key clients? Partners? What are their desires, behaviors, and expectations of service providers (advantageous and disadvantageous)? What key regulatory or technological trends can influence the firm's operations?

**Capabilities.** The term "core capabilities" is popular in strategic management. In this context, I tend to focus on three areas that help evaluate how the firm serves its markets: Who are the *people* in the firm, and what are their relevant skills? What are the *processes* the firm uses that are unique and complement the markets they serve (or are misapplied)? What economic and noneconomic *resources* are leveraged to serve clients, and do they provide an advantage?

When we apply this framework to firms such as CDFIs and MDIs, we can begin to distinguish meaningful differences that influence the presence or absence of risks. For example, these firms elect to serve markets in which consumers have lower average wealth and income. If these weren't sufficient challenges, many of these consumers are unfamiliar with or distrustful of financial institutions (these risks would be located in the environmental sector).

In terms of these firms' capabilities, the relative quality of the lending and underwriting operations, the type and extent of training for the team, and the amount of equity or grant capital on the balance sheet can provide advantage or create sources of relative risk. Finally, the underlying ethos of actors within a firm can drive the perception of markets and service areas that are clearly avoided by others.

I suspect they will find calling out the risks relatively easy. The more arduous task is noting the balance created between what may appear to be risks and a risk-taking culture, on the one hand, and the corresponding organizational practices and balance sheet that can offset those risks Herein lies the reason for the otherwise surprising findings about the risks of CDFIs and MDIs, and the related finding in the next chapter on these firms' relative efficiencies.

## AN IMPORTANT ANSWER TO
## A LINGERING QUESTION

The question of whether MDIs or CDFIs have systematically greater risks of failure has been a topic of some conjecture for a long time. There is logic to the notion of greater risks, given these observations.

Yet sometimes the common wisdom isn't, or at least hasn't been, tested. My colleagues and I have set out a number of times to analyze the relative institutional default risks of both CDFIs and MDIs when compared to similar financial institutions without their unique missions. Each time, we have examined the risks using a set of robust data and a modified version of a logistic regression modeling technique with broad applicability, CAMEL. And each time, we have continued to find similar insights and a surprising counternotion. These institutions are less likely to fail than their traditional counterparts.

The questions asked in this chapter have important policy implications. First, decades-long government support has provided these types of financial institutions both subsidy and technical assistance. Our analysis suggests that this level of support may have been appropriate.

Second, given their missions, the viability and expansion of CDFIs and MDIs can have important societal impacts that go beyond prudent efforts for financial safety and soundness. Increased investment in their operations could well result in broadened participation in financial services and decreases in the considerable wealth gaps across racial and income groups.

Taken together, if there were greater numbers of institutions like CDFIs and MDIs, and increasing numbers of consumers who were familiar with their inclusive approaches to lending, then families seeking to purchase homes in neighborhoods like the one in the western end of Hartford would have the interest and support of capital providers.

# CHAPTER THREE

# Efficient?

## *Are Development Financial Institutions Expensive to Operate?*

IN THE spring semester of my final year of college, with only a few months until graduation, I was still without a clear vision of what I would be doing afterwards. If you had asked me, I would have told you my primary interest was journalism. For me, the opportunity to wield language as a change agent—as a member of the fourth estate—was an energizing career I could get passionate about.

Passion is wonderful, but so is income. So, I began to look beyond journalism and found my way to retailing. One Friday, I drove an hour to a job fair with copies of my one-page resume in hand. Later that summer, I began working at Saks Fifth Avenue, a venerable, high-end department store. I had been hired into the executive training program, and by the fall was working as an assistant manager in what Saks would call a "moderately priced" evening dress department.

After a year as an assistant manager, I was promoted to manager, and it was quite the placement—the company's couture dress department in the flagship Fifth Avenue store. This department offered the soft goods of major designers I had never heard of only two years earlier—Jil Sander, Victor Costa, Christian LaCroix, and

St. John. The customers were not only affluent but also recogniz-able. It was common to serve well-known entertainers, and even some of the celebrity journalists who worked across the street at Rockefeller Center.

As rarified as the context may have been, when I finished my first fall selling season as manager, I learned something that surprised me: My high-flying, service-to-the-stars department was not especially profitable. In fact, the gross margins were fractional to some of the other, more pedestrian departments, including the moderately priced one I had first managed. Was there an illusion of affluence? Weren't high price tags and profitability correlated?

Looking beyond the price tags, it became clear. A couture dress department was central to Saks's brand and image but costly to run: Full page ads of featured dresses appeared in the *New York Times*. The combined sales staff salaries of eight women reached into seven figures. When a single blouse can run to $2,000, the margin for error in inventory management tightens. The risks of obsolescence are espe-cially high in high fashion. The ability to predict demand is notoriously difficult in a market with so few customers, especially when so many variables that can influence sales are out of your control. A dress worn by the first lady or a celebrity can lead to high demand and even stock-outs (which are nice to have, but not necessarily good for margins).

I wondered how my leadership determined the value of a depart-ment. Were gross margin or dollars-per-square foot sufficient? I recog-nized that the couture dress department was built on the notion that it would draw customers. They would sightsee the merchandise on my floor and then purchase elsewhere.

Further, how would Saks's leadership compare two otherwise iden-tical departments in different cities? How would my department stack up against couture departments in Beverly Hills, Boca Raton, Dallas, or Chicago? I knew it was indeed the largest of the couture depart-ments across the chain. However, that somehow seemed an incom-plete analysis. All of Saks's locales featured high-end addresses and customers, though my department was actually located on Fifth Ave-nue, arguably the epicenter of luxury shopping. Still, how could the firm account for differences in cities, weather, tourists, and the idio-syncrasies of elite families in each of these places? Without accounting for these factors, it would be difficult to compare performance *ceteris paribus* (all things being held constant).

## MEASURING RETAIL PRODUCTIVITY

Decades later, I would read the research of Hean Tat Keh and Singfat Chu on retail efficiency.[1] In their work, they listed a number of ways that efficiency could be considered in retailing, beyond the generally accepted, noneconomic measures. Their primary factors were:

1. *Accessibility.* How easy is it for consumers to patronize the store?
2. *Assortment.* What are the breadth and depth (varieties within a product line) of product lines?
3. *Delivery.* Are the products available at the desired time and in the desired form?
4. *Information.* What are the prices, availability, and other characteristics of goods and services that are available?
5. *Ambience.* Are customers attracted to the store atmosphere and design?

Looking back to my time at Saks Fifth Avenue under these categories of efficiency inputs, I recognized that my store and department were likely more efficient than I had thought. My sense was that although my department had lower gross margins than others in my store, it would tend to fare quite well on these nonfinancial efficiency measures. Heah and Chu collected and applied a statistical model that incorporated all of these and noted the customer-centric nature of efficiency.

Thomas, Barr, Cron, and Slocum, a group of marketing researchers, have taken a slightly different approach to the measurement of efficiency, focusing on differences across a chain.[2] Thomas and coauthors developed four general categories of inputs (labor, experience, location, and internal processes) that would reveal differences across a chain of stores. I knew there were forty other couture departments like mine across the country. Their methods could help determine which ones were actually more productive, and could even assist in learning which departments were best suited for additional or decreased investments. My department was indeed on Fifth Avenue, and was larger than others, but would the supports I received be better placed elsewhere?

## PERSPECTIVES: FASHION INTO FINANCE

When I began studying financial institutions that operate in low-income communities, I developed a related set of questions. When compared to financial institutions of similar size and scope, are these banks and credit unions less operationally efficient? That is, when we examine the investments in funds, materials, and labor that flow into community development financial institutions (CDFI), do they tend to process, or transform, these funds in a fashion that is less efficient than comparable financial institutions?

In my sense of things, these differences in efficiency could stem from a number of factors that had little to do with the affluence, or lack thereof, of clients. These included the use of technology to process transactions or applications or to analyze the performance of portfolios.

For example, one of the primary operational sources of potential efficiency differences between smaller, community development institutions (CDI) and what we might term "mainstream" institutions is the relatively higher application of "relationship finance" among smaller, community development institutions. Relationship finance is the notion of close, personal relationships between financial services providers and their depositors and borrowers.[3] One view is that personal relationships provide insights and information that relatively impersonal, arms-length commercial relationships cannot. In a Federal Reserve speech in 2004, Chairman Ben Bernanke explained its benefits:

> By relationship finance I mean financial services whose value-added depends importantly on the ongoing personal interactions of bankers with their customers, interactions that improve the flow of information and allow for more customized services. Relationship finance strengthens the economy by allowing credit and other financial services to be provided more *efficiently* [emphasis added].[4]

## THE CHALLENGE OF SERVING TWO MASTERS

The crux of this chapter can be illustrated by a dialogue from the iconic American film *It's A Wonderful Life* (1946). In this scene, Mr. Potter, the film's traditional business villain, is explaining to George Bailey why his father, Peter Bailey, was not a competent founder and president of Bailey Building and Loan, the local community-based lender. The exchange captures the essence of a long-standing tension in American popular culture and opinion, which holds that smaller, local, community-based institutions are managed and staffed by honest brokers who work for the greater community good, while larger, national, more quantitatively based organizations are soulless and lack concern for the rank and file.

The Potter-Bailey exchange supports another common hypothesis, that larger organizations are more efficient because smaller organizations let their hearts get in the way of sound business decisions. I also wondered about the influence of mission on efficiency. Is it possible that mission-driven firms are less likely to be explicitly efficient? Would they be more likely to seek social impact and value personal relationships, instead of profits?

The clash between the traditional view, "smaller is beneficent," and the more recent "larger is efficient" was the impetus for an analysis comparing the efficiency of community development banks with comparable mainstream institutions to determine whether the former were indeed less efficient in their operations.

As in the risk analysis chapter of this book, our research team chose to use depository minority-serving institutions and CDFIs because of their strong proxy for local, community financial institutions that operate in lower-income settings. There are three primary reasons why they are optimal for this comparison. First, they tend to be smaller in asset size, and the vast majority are chartered to operate intrastate. Second, community development institutions are certified as serving low- and moderate-income communities, and third, they are known to use relationship finance to a greater degree.

To perform our analysis, we applied a method long used to examine efficiency in industrial analysis: data envelopment analysis (DEA). DEA methods have been employed for decades to examine similar questions in a broad range of industries, including depository banks; they were also used in the Hean and Chu retailing analysis described earlier.[5] We share our methods and results below.

## GOOD MONEY AFTER BAD?

Beyond the primary interest in understanding productivity, we also wanted to answer another question: Were the subsidies provided to development institutions worth it? Or were they perhaps finding their way into relatively inefficient financial intermediaries?

When a financial services provider obtains a CDFI certification from the U.S. Treasury, it is able to tap into resources unavailable to other institutions. For example, a CDFI certification allows a bank or credit union to access technical advice and assistance as well as training to improve its operational fitness. Certification also allows firms to tap into financial assistance awards, such as the Bank Enterprise Award (BEA), the New Markets Tax Credit (NMTC) Program, the CDFI Bond Guarantee Program (CDFI Bond), and Troubled Asset Relief Program (TARP) funds.[6] Philanthropic supports are also available from local and national nonprofits, foundations, and even other depositories. This research would answer the question of whether these supports were landing in institutions with inefficient operations.

We were also interested in the performance of minority depository institutions (MDIs), the federally recognized set of banks and credit unions that tend to serve minority populations in their provision of financial services. In chapter 2, I shared the mission, requirements, and supports of MDIs.

A recent analysis by researchers from the Milken Institute suggests that the number of MDIs has decreased at a faster rate than the number of non-MDIs, and that smaller asset sizes are associated with institutional failure risks.

> Compared to commercial banking institutions on average, they are very small; the largest institution has only $38 billion in total assets. . . . Accordingly, and for Black MDIs in particular, the smaller scale may translate to difficulty navigating and operating in a highly regulated, quickly transforming industry, which limits their ability to serve the communities that need their help.[7]

## A REVIEW OF THE RELEVANT LITERATURE

We began our research by reviewing the literature. While there was a sizable base of research on the efficient performance of banking institutions, there was very little examining the relative performance of MDIs or CDFIs. There were, however, some early studies that had long-term influence, at least on perceptions of these institutions.

As early as 1930, Earl L. Brown published his Boston University doctoral dissertation, *Negro Banks in the United States.* Brown's work came just decades after the failure of the Freedmen's Banks. Created in 1865, as a component of a suite of post-Civil War Federal policies that became known as Reconstruction, the program collapsed in 1874 (although a few of the original banks persisted). For Brown and many observers, the causes of its failure were the extreme poverty of emancipated slaves, who were the bank's primary customers; questionable management practices; a lack of revenue from commercial customers of its product lines; and the collective resistance to Reconstruction policies in the South.[8]

In May 1971, *Journal of Finance* ran two articles on Black-owned banks. The authors, despite their contrasting analyses, were in agreement that Black-owned banks tended to be less capitalized than comparable institutions, tended to have higher costs, and tended to service predominantly Black customers. They differed on prescriptions, however.

In "The Black Banks: An Assessment of Performance and Prospects," Andrew Brimmer, the first Black governor of the Federal Reserve Board, found that Black banks trying to do business in "urban ghettos" appeared to operate at a substantial disadvantage and experienced higher operating costs and lower margins."[9] (The term "urban ghettos" appears in the text and was the author's vernacular of the period.) Brimmer cited a few causal factors.

This experience, of course, is intimately related to the inherent risk of doing business in the urban ghetto: the high unemployment rates, low family incomes, the high failure rates among small businesses (compounded by high crime rates) make the ghetto an extremely risky place for small banks to lend money.[10]

He also cited a lack of depth in management talent.

In fact, the severe shortage of management talent is probably the most critical problem facing the black banks. . . . The reason for this severe shortage of management talent is widely known: because of racial discrimination and segregation. Negroes historically were kept out of the economic mainstream and thus lacked the incentives to acquire a mastery of skills in economics, finance, accounting, and business administration, which form the foundations of bank management.[11]

Given his position in the Federal Reserve, Brimmer's observations were influential. On the question of governmental support for black-owned banks, he observed:

At this point, I must take note of the possibility that some observers (especially in the black community) even in the face of the substantial evidence presented here may still wish to encourage the establishment of new black-owned banks. For them, such banks may be a source of racial pride, and this is a positive consideration for a rapidly growing segment of the community—particularly young people. Moreover, these banks may also render some marginal—although high-cost—financial services.[12]

Edward Irons, chairman of the Business School at Howard University, performed a companion analysis using different methods, which also showed the relative performance decrements in the Black-owned banks of the period. While Irons's analysis revealed convergent findings, his prescriptions were starkly different.

The prospects of black banks in the United States can be summed in two words. They are a "societal contingency." Today's black banks are a mirror of contemporary American society, in the same manner as Black doctors, Black lawyers, Black businessmen or Black economists. They reflect all the past constraints imposed by society. Potentially, they can be as sound as any group in the United States. Black banks are no different.[13]

Implicit in this assessment was continued government support of these institutions with a goal of eventual comparable performance. Over the years, the general assumptions about these institutions' inherent risks and operational efficiencies have persisted, and to some degree, each of the general policy approaches has continued.

It is my sense that, comparatively, Brimmer's perspective looms largest, likely because of his prominent position at the Federal Reserve, whereas Irons's came from a minority-serving educational institution. I also find it important to note that the most recent paper we could find on the efficiency of minority-serving financial institutions was published in 1977.[14] Given the considerable change in the communities and families these institutions serve, it seemed remarkable that there had not been any updated research on the question.

Both Brimmer's assertions about talent and costs, and Irons's notions that these institutions would evolve are nearly half a century old. Are they still relevant? Take talent, for instance. Certainly, the educational and professional attainment of minorities has increased considerably since the 1970s. However, the competition in recruiting financial talent may create a human resources market in which relatively undercapitalized MDIs are outbid for top minority talent. Examining the relative efficiency of MDIs would be an important update for research and policy reasons.

## APPROACHING THE EFFICIENCY QUESTION

This approach would have prescriptive benefits as well. Research by Berger and Mester (1997) found that relatively inefficient, high-cost banks were more prone to failure.[15] By using a model like DEA, interested researchers would be able to evaluate the relative efficiency of a group of banks such as CDFIs and be better prepared to respond with policies that could help prevent systemic failure. Additionally, a researcher or regulator might be able to ferret out potentially vulnerable individual firms in a diagnostic fashion, even before a crisis. This method could be used to (1) identify poorly performing institutions, (2) provide insight into areas that might improve their operations, and (3) target support to bring performance in line with industry efficiency levels (and avoid unnecessary failures).

In this specific analysis, we were interested in evaluating what some term "the efficient frontier" for MDIs and community development banks (CDBIs), as well as for a comparable group of peer institutions. The efficient frontier is a concept used in modern financial theory in the following way: a combination, or portfolio, of inputs into a firm is referred to as "efficient" if it has the best possible expected level of return for its recognized level of risk.

In addition to examining the level of output commensurate with the level of risk, DEA allows for statistical comparison within and across a group of similar firms. For a manufacturing firm, inputs could be natural resources, labor, utilities, technology, and, of course, the level of financial investment. The resulting outputs might be furniture, lumber, or iron ore.

If we wanted to compare like institutions—say, Norwegian sawmills or fisheries—we could agree to the typical inputs and outputs, compare entire industry groups to determine where the most and least efficient firms fell, and even identify the factors that drove their relative efficiencies. These approaches are not hypothetical. An analysis of Norwegian sawmills using stochastic, DEA methods was published in the journal *Forest Science* in 2003, and another by Ian Vazquez-Rowe and Peter Tyedmers on fisheries management was published in *Marine Policy* in 2013.[16]

As one would expect, in a DEA analysis of financial institutions, the inputs and outputs are overwhelmingly financial in nature; however, there are some nonfinancial inputs, such as labor (management and staffing). Given the unique nature of the development firm's mission to serve lower-income consumers, their relatively uncertain markets, and the additional emphasis on relationship finance, we assumed that CDFIs would likely be less efficient in terms of their ability to convert a portfolio of financial inputs into outputs.

On the other hand, we recognized *a priori* that CDFIs often receive a considerable amount of their income from restricted and unrestricted federal, state, local, and private foundation grants. Grant funding may be used to subsidize loan activities. CDFIs are able to enjoy a lower cost of funds through grants, which may offset the additional expenses and risks of the markets in which they operate. They are also able to access technical assistance that comparably sized mainstream institutions would have difficulty finding. This factor produced a counterhypothesis that the subsidy contribution might lead CDFIs to be equally as efficient as, or even more efficient than, their peers.

## WHAT IS DATA ENVELOPMENT ANALYSIS (DEA)?

Data envelopment analysis assumes that firms within an industry take inputs and transform them into outputs. DEA makes no assumptions about how the inputs are used or altered once firms manage to generate the outputs. From an agreed set of inputs and outputs, DEA estimates a production frontier and assigns efficiency scores to a firm relative to that frontier.

Figure 3.1 provides a simple graphical illustration of the efficient frontier. In this example, the most efficient firm is the one whose position draws the steepest line between its location and the origin. Here, the square dot representing firm A is the most efficient of all the points given. To score the efficiency of all the points, the simplest way is to take the ratio of their slopes relative to the steepest one.

To further illustrate the degree of complexity in DEA modeling, figure 3.2 is based on the slightly more complex case of two inputs and two outputs. When organizations have more than one output or many inputs, comparing the relative efficiencies of different firms is more difficult. To illustrate, figure 3.2 plots the output/input ratios of two inputs and two outputs.

The points representing firms A, C, and D effectively constitute a production frontier, which "envelops" (hence the E in DEA) all the other points. Consequently, a natural measure of firm efficiency is how near or far it is from the production frontier. In both examples, an analyst may quantitatively determine how an efficient firm operates more efficiently, by either lowering certain inputs or increasing specific outputs. These two examples illustrate the magnitude of the task involved in a DEA model containing only two inputs and two

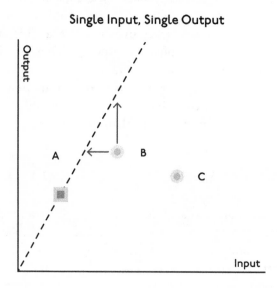

*Figure 3.1* Single input, single output.

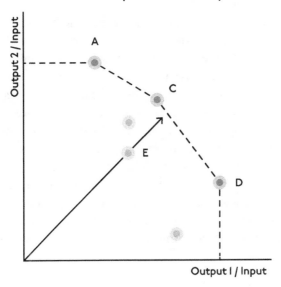

*Figure 3.2* Double input, double output.

outputs. In most industries, there will be multiple inputs and outputs and a three-dimensional chart would be required to illustrate the comparison points and the complexity of combining those points into parsimonious efficiency scores.

Scholars know DEA as a nonparametric frontier analysis. It is called "nonparametric" because it makes no assumptions about how the inputs are used or altered to generate the resulting outputs. Instead, this method projects where a firm's inputs *ought* to rank it in terms of the overall output productivity described by the data, and then scores it by how far the firm's actual output is from that optimal point.

Before we offer more information about our analysis, let us return to the example of fishery operations. In one of the DEA analyses, the task was to analyze a group of forty-one vessels operating in the Atlantic and Pacific Oceans, each having a diverse set of inputs, to include the performance of the individual skippers managing the vessels.[17] One easy way to think about measuring efficiency would be to determine which vessels and skippers tended to bring in more fish during the season. The reason this approach is blunt at best is that so many elements differ—vessels, ports, oceans, fuel usage, engine and ship size, and so on.

To accurately capture efficiency requires a method to measure each of the important input variables and equalize them, and to identify the impact of each variable, distinctly and separately, on total productivity. If this could be done using regular, agreed-upon, systematic data sources, we might begin to answer the efficiency questions about each vessel and, from a managerial standpoint, the performance of the individual skipper at the helm. Another obvious element might be the economic returns generated by each vessel.

The researchers were able to collect a large data set, with multiple inputs and outputs accumulated over time, and then chart an average annual efficiency score based on the entire set of data. They were even able to identify individual skippers who might have had higher rates of efficiency once all other elements were accounted for in the statistical model.

## APPLYING DEA MODELS TO FINANCIAL FIRMS

Going into our project, we recognized that the range of variables necessary to perform a DEA efficiency evaluation of the type we envisioned meant that we would have to create a unique and comprehensive data set. Unfortunately, this was not available from a single source.

We also attended to different ways of thinking about outputs. One approach involves models that evaluate a financial institution's ability to attract loan applicants; we call this a production approach to efficiency. The alternative approach is concerned with the economic value generated by a financial lending firm while also managing profitability and risk; we call this the intermediation approach to efficiency. We examined the firms using both approaches, and made sure we collected data that would allow us a diversity of perspectives.

## CONSTRUCTING THE DATA SET FOR ANALYSIS

Because our evaluation required a substantial data set with systematic reporting, our eventual data set included more than a decade of quarterly call report data from a large and diverse set of financial depositories. It is important to recognize that the performance of credit union and banking institutions may differ considerably based on local conditions in their chartered service area. To add controls for local conditions, we gathered socioeconomic indicators (levels of poverty and unemployment) for a bank's chartered and headquartered areas from the Bureau of Economic Analysis and the Bureau of Labor Statistics.

Our final data set included a large set of variables available for analysis. Similar to the Vazquez-Row and Tyedmers's fisheries study, we based our variable list on our knowledge of the field. It consisted of ten variables, including cost of funds, equity over assets, and return on average assets, among others. We collected these data for every bank and credit union in the United States between 2002 and 2011, then limited the analysis to firms with asset sizes below $10 billion because CDFIs tend to be smaller.

## RESULTS: WHAT DID WE FIND?

Our primary research question focused on whether CDFIs, as proxies for financial firms that service lower-income consumers, typically had lower efficiency ratios than mainstream institutions. Drawing from past research indicating that inefficient, high-cost banks were more prone to failure, if we found that CDFIs were less efficient, then it would raise questions about the purported value of the governmental and charitable subsidies CDFIs receive. Furthermore, it would provide fuel for the argument that regulatory policy or charitable giving designed to encourage smaller, local depositories focused on lower-income consumers was "good money chasing after bad."

Since we were examining a decade worth of performance data and three different DEA models, we had a large base of year/model combinations in which we might find differences between MDIs, CDFIs, and comparable institutions. From a statistical standpoint, we were seeking statistically significant differences in mean efficiencies between groups.

In our first analysis, we did find some statistically significant differences in efficiency between MDIs, CDFIs, and other institutions.[18] Of the potential year-and-model combinations, there were only seven combinations that resulted in a statistically significant mean difference between institutional types (a difference in 23.3 percent of cases). Taken together, the summary results indicate that in the majority of tested model/year combinations (23/30, 76.6 percent), CDFIs and mainstream institutions had mean efficiency ratios that were not statistically different.

A deeper examination of the directionality of these differences provides even more provocative findings. In 2004, the mean efficiency of mainstream institutions was considerably higher than for CDFIs. However, in 2005, the relative efficiency of the two groups reversed: the mean efficiency of the community development institutions was greater. The differences across all models were more interesting in 2007, primarily because these findings occur at the start of the recession of 2007–2009.

If community development institutions tended to underperform in efficiency during the crisis, this would suggest that their risks of failure were greater and that efforts to provide capital, as through TARP funds, would be an imprudent strategy. However, when we examined the directionality of these 2007 differences, CDFIs showed higher mean efficiencies, and this difference was robust across models. In summary, this study indicated that in four of the seven periods in which there was a difference, CDFIs showed higher mean efficiencies.

We also performed an analysis that specifically focused on MDIs. This review returned a complementary finding: we found that MDIs were not systematically less efficient than their non-MDI counterparts. These findings are surprising, given the observed relatively lower inputs of MDIs. They suggest that programs designed to support MDIs— their viability and expansion—have had a critical impact in the field. Further, the ability of MDIs to provide financial services products to the communities they serve has likely been attenuated by a relative lack of investment capital. Our findings suggest that although MDIs may have lagging *average* levels of productive efficiency, their inputs or starting points are likewise lagging. Nevertheless, they outperform in apples-to-apples comparisons.[19]


## WHAT THESE FINDINGS TELL US

Our primary interest was in comparing the performance of a set of CDFIs with a set of similar-size mainstream peers, with an eye toward determining whether there were differences in efficiency performance. Using a well-established operational efficiency analysis method (DEA), our analyses revealed two principal findings.

First, over the decade-long period we analyzed, the efficient frontier was declining for all depository firms. Second, we found that the efficiency of CDFIs was virtually indistinguishable from that of mainstream institutions; in fact, in some years, CDFIs were more efficient than peer institutions.

Two questions not addressed in this analysis are nonfinancial inputs and outputs, a limitation because we only examined depository institutions. Our model was based on financial performance measures and did not directly measure inputs not found in financial statements or government data sets. So, for example, this analysis does not capture measures of branch locations, drive-by-traffic flow, or consumer sentiment about a bank or credit union. One particularly important area of interest might be the input of various technological enhancements that have come into the retail banking field in recent years. This analysis is silent on the impact of those innovations, although they could have a material influence on a financial institution's performance.

Technological innovations in retail finance go to the heart of core questions about CDFIs versus mainstream institutions—that is, CDFIs' greater reliance on relationship retail banking practices. These "high touch" practices can be alternatively seen as disadvantaged by human error and biases or as enhancing the effective targeting and servicing of clients. It is important to note that the growth of electronic and mobile banking services is also happening during a period when traditional brick-and-mortar branch banking is declining.

There are a number of theories about this decline. Some see these trends as evidence of the relatively higher cost of managing a retail branch, coupled with a rising application of technological platforms that lower the overhead and transaction costs in retail banking—notably, online banking, mobile banking platforms, telephone banking, automatic teller machines (ATMs), computerized credit-scoring models, and loan approval systems. Others see the decline of branches as evidence of the dollars available to acquisitive banks, and that merger and acquisitions activity is driving out the locally based, closely held players.

What is certain is that there is not an even distribution of technological investments across the industry, especially among smaller banks that serve lower-income consumers. This logic suggests that CDFIs will have to rely on a greater degree of subsidies to perform relatively costly banking services.

A second area of potential investigation is the influence of the rise and fall of external, charitable funding on individual CDFIs, or groups of similar firms. On reflection, it is remarkable that CDFIs continued to perform at competitive efficiencies while one of their prominent sources of funds was variable and declining. It begs the question, "What would have happened had these supports evaporated altogether?"

I hope research like this will encourage banking practitioners to use similar approaches in a prescriptive way, to learn "what has worked." One of the advantages of approaches like DEA is that these models can be used to assist in locating underperforming institutions and to provide advice on how they might increase their efficiency. I have wondered whether there are firms that have especially noteworthy efficiencies, at both the high and low ends of the efficiency scale. Using these methods, an analyst or organizational leader could reveal actionable, strategic data at the firm level. Broad-scale use of data and methods like these could help raise the efficiency of financial institutions overall, identify best-performing firms, and assist those that may be lagging. Since few of these firms compete directly, this prescriptive knowledge can improve the field overall.

Our large-scale, quantitative studies did not directly examine the role of technological innovation. My hopes look toward future research to directly examine the effect of technological platforms and investments on overall efficiency levels within the community development finance industry and determine if there are important differences between community development and comparable institutions. Is it possible that improvements in the scope, specificity, magnitude, and processing capabilities of larger financial institutions allow them to build algorithms and machine learning that erode the advantages of close, confiding relations in relationship banking? Will technological capabilities mediate or replace altogether the benefits of personal relations?

A 1991 research paper by Chicago Federal Reserve economists Evanoff and Israilevich presents this theory of technological change and mergers into larger firms as destroying the traditional advantages in banking:

Because of changes taking place in the banking industry, the importance of efficiency has increased substantially. As geographic and product deregulation occurs, the resulting increase in competition should place banks in a situation where their success will depend on their ability to adapt and operate efficiently in the new environment. Banks unable to do so will have difficulty surviving.[20]

Andrew Brimmer provided a dubious assessment of minority-serving institutions and their prospective ability to provide financial services to their communities. Edward Irons offered a relatively optimistic assessment. While recognizing the real and substantial challenges these organizations faced in the marketplace, Irons argued that they could become as sound as any comparable depository. Both the literature and commonly held wisdom suggest that Brimmer's assessment has proven more influential. Our analyses suggest that, given the proper resource inputs, Irons's assessment may have been the more prescient one.

# CHAPTER FOUR

# Changing the World Through the South Side of Chicago

Twenty-five years ago, [my father] spent a small personal fortune, his considerable talents, and many years of his life fighting, in association with NAACP attorneys, Chicago's "restrictive covenants" in one of this nation's ugliest ghettos. That fight also required our family to occupy disputed property in a hellishly hostile "white neighborhood" in which literally howling mobs surrounded our house.

LORRAINE HANSBERRY[1]

LORRAINE HANSBERRY was born in Chicago, one of Carl and Nannie Hansberry's four children. Just a few days after her seventh birthday, Lorraine's father bought a home near the University of Chicago, in the all-white neighborhood of Woodlawn. The property the Hansberrys purchased had been vacated some time earlier by its previous owners, the Burkes.

Properties in the neighborhood were under racially restrictive covenants. In 1928, about five hundred property owners had signed an agreement to ensure that properties in the neighborhood would not be "sold, leased to, or permitted to be occupied by any person of the colored race." These agreements conveyed with the properties and applied to any future owners, whether they agreed with them or not.

Fully aware of the governing covenants, yet anxious to sell a property that had been empty for some time, Mr. Burke arranged a dummy transaction in which the property was sold to a third party, and then on to the Hansberrys.

Once the Hansberrys moved into their new home, Woodlawn's residents requested they vacate the property, subsequently suing them for violation of the covenants. Since the property had been financed by First National Bank of Englewood, the Woodlawn homeowners sued the bank, along with James Joseph and Olive Ida Burke and the Hansberrys, for knowingly violating the covenants—a warning to others who might consider violating them. In 1934, the Cook County Circuit Court ruled that, indeed, the covenants were valid.

With the support of the NAACP and its attorneys, the Hansberrys appealed the case to the U.S. Supreme Court. After a few years, the Court ruled for the Hansberrys, and they were able to legally keep the Woodlawn home they had purchased.

For the Hansberry family, winning may have been a Pyrrhic victory. They now had to live among hostile neighbors in a neighborhood where they were not welcome. Reflecting later, Lorraine would say that the experiences had left her father not only emotionally but physically damaged. In 1946, Carl Hansberry experienced a cerebral hemorrhage and died at the age of fifty.[2]

These experiences left an indelible mark on young Lorraine—only seven to ten years of age at the time—and they would become the basis for one of her iconic works. At the age of twenty-nine, she would become the youngest playwright and the first Black person to receive the New York Drama Critics Circle Award for her play *A Raisin in the Sun*. It is telling that today the Woodlawn community is nearly 80 percent Black, one of its streets has been renamed Martin Luther King Jr. Drive, and the neighborhood will be the future home of the Obama Presidential Library.[3]

## VISITING A HISTORIC BANKING INSTITUTION

The concept of residential segregation was first coined by two University of Chicago sociological researchers, Otis and Beverly Duncan, based on their observations of neighborhood changes in the school's surrounding areas.[4] Over decades, Chicago had experienced noticeably high levels of residential clustering of white ethnic groups (Germans, Poles, Italians, Irish, Greeks, Jews), with a corresponding pattern in which a relatively acculturated immigrant group was replaced by a set of more recent immigrants.

At the time of the Duncans' work, the ethnic group of recent entry into Chicago's neighborhoods was Blacks, with the outmigration coming from ethnic whites, mostly Italians and Jews. Rather than representing the "melting pot" metaphor common in the popular imagination, Chicago was more akin to a revolving lazy Susan—each racial or ethnic element in rotation, yet completely separated. Chicago's neighborhoods had been undergoing ethnic change for decades, and the city's residential history had long been marked by cyclical patterns of segregation, mass exodus, and neighborhood transformation.

In late winter of 2008, I went to Chicago for a field visit with the leadership of one of the nation's historic financial institutions, ShoreBank. Its headquarters was in South Shore, a neighborhood very near Woodlawn. The tagline on the bank's logo read "Let's Change the World."

ShoreBank Corporation, a bank holding company, began as an idea conceived by the president of Chicago's Hyde Park Bank, Ron Grzywinski. Along with other investors, Grzywinski had acquired the bank in 1967, and shortly after, the newly purchased bank moved to actively lend to minorities living in the highly segregated metropolis.

Grzywinski came to believe that his ultimate social goals—profitable banking and community development—would be best served by a new model of financial institution. He joined Milton Davis, head of the Chicago chapter of Congress for Racial Equality (CORE); Mary Houghton, an executive with the Johnson Foundation; and James Fletcher, a former official in the Nixon administration's Office of Economic Opportunity (OEO), in discussing the creation of a bank, a credit union, or a housing loan fund that would help stem Chicago's mounting segregation. This strategy was, in itself, an audacious theory of social change—first, that integration would contribute to a better society, and second, that the interjection of capital would enable minority homebuyers to purchase homes in formerly segregated neighborhoods.

Much like their banking initiative, their leadership composition was also novel for the era: Davis and Fletcher were Black; Grzywinski and Houghton were white. Their efforts came at a time when Chicago, like many major U.S. cities, was convulsed by riots following Martin Luther King Jr.'s death on April 4, 1968.

"We were products of our times, inspired by the Civil Rights Movement and the kind of idealism that John F. Kennedy espoused," Grzywinski would later write. "We were also frustrated. We saw that community organizations had identified the right issues but lacked the capital and technical competency to make a difference."[5]

The four cofounders eventually decided to structure their financial institution as a bank holding company. There was a reason: the Bank Holding Company Act (1970) allowed bank holding companies—a collection of financial institutions under a singular structure—to invest in community development corporations if the primary investment target was a low-income area. This was an important element in their strategy to create a suite of social finance levers because a bank holding company could have subsidiaries, such as a commercial bank and a nonprofit community development organization.

Grzywinski led the capital raise and helped secure a $2.4 million loan, in part by using his own personal property as collateral. This enabled a new organization, the Illinois Neighborhood Development Corporation (INDC), to purchase the South Shore National Bank.

The South Side was experiencing tumultuous Black settlement and white flight in a time of widespread neighborhood transitions. This is illustrated through the concept of racial "tipping points" in housing. The term was originally coined by two researchers, Martin Meyerson and Edward Banfield, based on their observations working for the Chicago Housing Authority.[6] They used the phrase to conceptually describe the behavior of white public housing complex residents when the level of racial diversity surpassed one-third Black residents. They noticed that when this threshold was reached, white residents would rapidly move out of a project until it soon became all Black. Because of the popular author Malcolm Gladwell, the phrase is now associated with a less negative practice.[7]

With its purchase, the bank became known as South Shore Bank—a newly formed financial institution committed to servicing low-income and minority communities. Among ShoreBank's founding principles was to employ "a comprehensive approach to community development, one that could be self-sustaining," according to Grzywinski.

At the time the founders were establishing their bank, South Shore's local institutions had begun to "manage for deterioration," in Grzywinski words. The value of single-family homes had begun to fall precipitously. Given that a home's value was the key collateral element in mortgage lending, financial services firms were reluctant to make loans to African Americans. Likewise, the tenuous status of Black migrants' employment prospects raised reasonable questions among lenders, as did the knowledge that recent-migrant Blacks tended to have fewer assets and be at a higher risk for job loss.

There is a logical sequence in assuming that, all things being equal, loans in transitioning white-to-Black neighborhoods would represent elevated credit risks. As the South Side housing market continued to contract, some homeowners abandoned their properties, contributing to lenders' collective sense of an increasing and durable social dislocation.

While seemingly rational, this progression in thinking requires pattern recognition, and even what we must call stereotyping. Although these observations may be true for many, arguably even the majority of Blacks migrating to Chicago, it would not be correct to conduct lending practices under the assumption that they were true for all Black borrowers.

Even if one were unsure about the assumption's accuracy, there would be cost considerations in collecting and analyzing data to "disconfirm" this belief. Known as "statistical discrimination," lenders may make what seem to be rational assumptions based on the statistical likelihood of an occurrence. Ethically speaking, observers tend to find statistical discrimination less objectionable because there is a normalized logical pattern supporting a recognized discriminatory practice. (Note: A normalized pattern of logic need not be accurate.)

ShoreBank's founders challenged this set of practices by showing that a financial institution could prudently lend to Black borrowers in ethnic minority neighborhoods without taking on undue institutional risks.

The team's approach was, in fact, aligned with one of the core tenets of economic theory: discrimination is expensive, and eventually firms will innovate to exploit the blind spots of others. Leading economists, including William Darity and Nobel laureates Gary Becker and Joseph Stiglitz, have written extensively on the economic underpinnings of discrimination and its essential costliness as a business practice.[8]

This process can roughly be collapsed into a six-stage set of assumptions. First, regularly avoiding consumers who can be served is economically irrational and ultimately costly. Second, when firms discriminate, other innovative firms will pursue the opportunity to service the avoided group. Third, firms will develop the means to effectively deliver products and services to the group, and fourth, their resulting innovations in service delivery will bring these firms uncommon profits. In the fifth stage of this theory, the resulting profits will lead other firms to follow their example, and in the sixth stage, through the pursuit of profits realized by innovators, discrimination against the focal group will be ameliorated over time or completely eliminated.

Whether explicitly recognized or not, ShoreBank's founders were field-testing the theory. On the first evening of our visit, Houghton spoke forcefully about the synthesis of their personal beliefs with their business model. When I asked about the bank's biracial management team, Houghton asserted that this was one of the reasons the bank survived in its early stages.

"Milton and Jim [who are Black] were unusual because they were working in a white-owned, socially-oriented business that was going to do something about social problems," she stated. From the start, the founding team sought the embrace of both white and Black communities:

> Two or three nights a week, Milton Davis—then president—and I went to neighborhood meetings, to PTAs and block clubs, church basements and potluck suppers, committing the bank to the community. We told people who we were and what we intended to do, and we invited them to tell us what they considered to be the community's greatest needs.[9]

## EXPANDING AN ECONOMIC EXPERIMENT INTO A BANKING INSTITUTION

At the outset, it was not easy to transition the newly acquired South Shore National into a community development bank. Because of the exodus of white ethnics who had traditionally lived in South Shore, the bank was losing deposits, and the likelihood of becoming profitable was unclear.

The bank's first institutional investment came from the board of Homeland Ministries of the United Church of Christ, followed by capital from the Legal Foundation in Chicago. At this point, the bank was still undercapitalized and had nothing in its reserve account for loan losses. During this time, the prime lending rate rose to 21 percent, and the bank had to service debt in the form of monthly interest payments on a loan from American National Bank.

Through a mission-based approach to fundraising, the bank was able to secure grants from the Ford Foundation and the Mott Foundation, which allowed it to continue its work, at least for the short term. Over the following two decades, the bank continued to sustain itself and grow. In 1973, the bank was renamed ShoreBank, reflecting the expansion of its geographic footprint.

Given its mission, ShoreBank's founders saw their bank as both a model and an advocate for prudent, effective ways to provide credit in segregated markets and influence the economic fortunes of residents. The culmination of their efforts came when Ron Grzywinski was invited to speak before Congress in discussions leading to passage of the Community Reinvestment Act (CRA) of 1977. It was the bank's opportunity to influence federal policy and practice through its experience and demonstrated success. It is notable that Grzywinski was the only banker to testify in favor of the act's approval.

In 1995, the bank acquired Indecorp, Inc., a minority-owned bank holding company with two banks (Independence and Drexel). The acquisition doubled ShoreBank's assets, from $200 million to $400 million, but it was also a subject of social controversy.

Indecorp was criticized for its transition from a purely minority-owned institution, which held symbolic meaning beyond products and services for some in the South Side community. The sale of Indecorp to a white-owned company created a feeling of loss, if not disloyalty, as reported in *Chicago Business*:

> To many, the prospect of selling black-owned Indecorp to a white-controlled company is unthinkable. . . . If the deal does go through, . . . black ministers will pull church deposits out of Indecorp and urge their congregations to do the same. Other community leaders say they would direct business to other black institutions. . . . In failing to forge alliances before the merger was struck, Shorebank may have underestimated the power of neighborhood leaders to derail its plans. [10]

It is telling that the bank, with its integrated founding team and South Side customer service location, was still perceived as a nonblack institution. The legacy of Chicago's history of racial disconnection, verging on mistrust, was playing an unanticipated role.

After the Indecorp merger, the bank's ability to attract capital increased significantly, and with a larger retail banking operation, ShoreBank was able to connect with many Black homeowners, borrowers, and depositors across a greater swath of Chicago. The acquisition brought the potential of scale to ShoreBank.

Soon after, Continental Bank made an equity investment of several million dollars and encouraged other downtown Chicago banks to follow its lead. Financial institutions took note, and ShoreBank started to receive "traditional" sources of investment capital. Continuing this trend, in 1998, ShoreBank bought Omni Bank's assets, including approximately $18 million of uninsured public deposits. ShoreBank restructured Omni Bank to become ShoreBank Detroit, which eventually merged with the Chicago bank.

## EXPANDING THE FOOTPRINT, INNOVATING IN THE PORTFOLIO

Throughout its various expansions and acquisitions, ShoreBank's primary market was concentrated in South Shore's low-income neighborhoods, where multifamily housing emerged as a hub of innovation to become one of the bank's core products.

Multifamily housing lending allowed the bank to demonstrate its mission in an economically impactful and socially symbolic fashion. White flight from Chicago's south side had decimated housing values. Many recently migrated Blacks to the area sought homeownership. However, they faced two obstacles: their financing options were limited, and properties were overpriced by less-than-scrupulous, even predatory, sellers. (See Beryl Satter's *Family Properties* for a historical account of pent-up African American demand and rampant real estate speculation.)[11]

By providing capital for housing, ShoreBank could help accomplish three objectives: (1) build asset wealth for those recently migrated families; (2) curtail ongoing predatory pricing practices; and (3) offer itself as a model for community development practitioners across the nation.

ShoreBank was by now a highly visible and influential community bank, and as such, it was well connected to funding sources and political networks. Its leaders believed that to drive its social mission, Shore-Bank must be a vehicle for policy change. The bank had scope, and it had relationships that were essential to securing funds for continued innovation, research, and acquisition.

ShoreBank expanded beyond its core mission to address the needs of the underbanked when, in 2006, two bank executives, Ellen Seidman and Jennifer Tescher, created the Center for Financial Services Innovation (CFSI). During our interviews, Grzywinski referred to this forward-leaning organization as "the most innovative part of Shore-Bank." In a departure from offering credit and deposit services to the underbanked, CFSI taught other financial institutions how to most effectively serve this underserved market.

On the retail side, ShoreBank hoped to reach the mission-driven market online. Its expanded target of investors comprised those who were attracted to ShoreBank's mission yet might have limited, if any, ties to either Chicago or the South Side. It was a market that generally consisted of college-educated depositors who lived beyond the bank's geographic footprint. The prevailing notion was that accessing bank products online, instead of by filling out a paper form, would likely increase this segment of the bank's depositors.

## INFLUENCING CHANGE THROUGH NETWORKS

In addition to the founders' deeply shared vision of reduced segregation, social and political networks played a significant role in Shore-Bank's growth in assets and reputation. Whether recognized or not, the ShoreBank team was illustrating the practice of policy through demonstration.

As their social experiments on the South Side of Chicago gained notice, ShoreBank officials were frequently requested subject-matter experts at an increasingly broad range of community development convenings. Its leadership team, in particular, leveraged social networks and relationships ranging from local community organizers to influential state and federal officials to high-profile international figures. ShoreBank leveraged noneconomic assets to diffuse best practices.

These relationships frequently became conduits to increasingly powerful thought leaders and policy makers; for example, Jan Piercy, who joined ShoreBank in the 1980s, was the former college roommate of Hillary Rodham Clinton. This is conjecture, but Piercy's relationships were at least a partial factor in eventually drawing then-Governor Bill Clinton to visit the bank. His association with ShoreBank was likely an influence on Clinton's subsequent legislative agenda and the creation of the Community Development Financial Institutions (CDFI) Fund once he became president.

As ShoreBank grew over time, and given the state of racial relations nationally, the founders became lionized public figures.

During our visit with Grzywinski and Houghton, they discussed the rise in lending activity within their core neighborhoods. They were experiencing more competition than they'd seen in the past, and much of the new lending activity was coming from nontraditional lending organizations. I would not understand until some time later how that uptick in lending activity would contribute to the eventual fall of ShoreBank. Arguably, the rise of subprime lending represented a realization by many financial providers that segregated neighborhoods constituted an attractive cluster of commercial opportunities.

It can be argued that political support, endorsements, and celebrity associations were integral components of ShoreBank's early ability to launch, scale, and grow. However, as the institution expanded, a human resources challenge arose in finding the right, experienced banking talent to helm a financial institution of significant size.

Over its first three decades, the bank had recruited increasing numbers of bankers. More recently, it appeared that a large portion of ShoreBank's executive staff was drawn from policy-related fields rather than from the ranks of financial services professionals. It was unclear whether this was due to challenges in meeting the salaries demanded by experienced banking professionals, a reticence to hire talent from fields already connected to social justice movements and community development, or a combination of both.

I wasn't the only one to notice this unconventional human resources approach. Richard Taub, after extensive fieldwork with ShoreBank, wrote:

> Most [Shorebank] personnel are not orthodox bankers. They are smart people found in other worlds, trained by management, and then encouraged to be creative. There is the sense that because they come to the task with few preconceptions, they are able to forge new instruments and devise new tactics.[12]

A prominent example could be found in the bank's cornerstone revenue-generator, its multifamily housing lending unit. It was initiated and developed by Jim Bringley, who expanded the portfolio with little formal financial services or lending background. In his own unique approach, Bringley literally walked through South Shore neighborhoods looking for properties viable for rehabilitation.

Once he had identified a suitable building, Bringley would speak to the property's owner about financing for improvements or buying nearby housing stock. "We . . . were able to prove the hypothesis that if you could find someone who would invest in a product, you would see demand," Bringley stated.

By financing multifamily rehab, ShoreBank essentially created a local industry that contributed to its growth. Bringley called this "build[ing] a homegrown entrepreneurial base." By 2009, his department had $800 million in loans under management, and Bringley eventually became ShoreBank's executive vice president and senior lending officer.

## GETTING TO KNOW A CREDIT:
## THE HALLS OF CHATHAM

When I inquired about an exemplar ShoreBank loan or financing project, I was referred to Clarence and Lisa Hall, real estate entrepreneurs with whom the bank had built a long relationship. The couple owned multiple multifamily properties throughout Chicago's South Side and were an example of ShoreBank's efforts to help create an economic ecosystem.

While in Chicago, we stayed in a hotel just across from Grant Park, firmly in the city's central business district. In that neighborhood, you are likely to encounter the city's breadth of racial and ethnic diversity. As we taxied to the Chatham neighborhood where the Halls' offices were located, we passed block after block of inhospitable city landscape, and the visual evidence of decades of segregation was clear. Given the social-change goals of Gryzwinski, Houghton, and the other founders, I began to wonder to what degree their vision had actually been achieved.

By way of background, Clarence Hall had spent time in the corporate world before deciding to transition into entrepreneurship. His wife, Lisa, was born and raised on the South Side; she wanted to help make a difference and saw high-quality, affordable housing as a means to that end.

"Well, we knew it wouldn't be easy," she said, "but we had to do something."

Not long after becoming real estate developers, the Halls learned about ShoreBank's efforts to build a cadre of affordable multifamily home developers. According to the Halls, ShoreBank played a signifi-cant role in helping the couple transition and access the knowledge they needed to succeed at their entrepreneurial efforts.

Under Jim Bringley, ShoreBank financed housing redevelopment projects of small, "rookie" buildings of two to six units and partnered the properties with potential developers, usually owner-occupants. The bank then pitched the benefits of redevelopment to the own-ers, making them aware of the bank's long-term commitment to the neighborhood.

Bringley indicated that ShoreBank preferred to work with blue-collar developers because it found that these entrepreneurs had a real-istic sense of the arduous work involved in renovation. They were familiar with the often volatile nature of tenant-landlord relationships and could cut down on overhead using their practical knowledge of maintaining buildings on the cheap. Once a team of developers had proven their abilities, ShoreBank offered to put them on larger mul-tiunit projects.

ShoreBank's relationship with the Halls didn't fit the established profile. First, they had corporate, professional backgrounds; second, they were not owner-occupants; and third, they proposed an initial project that involved renovating a twenty-four-unit residential build-ing. Nevertheless, ShoreBank took a chance on the couple and their project. There were multiple challenges and a long list of lessons learned. However, the Halls renovated the building, found lessors, and turned the building around. Other projects followed.

At the time of our visit, the Halls owned a portfolio of multiunit properties. As we toured a few completed projects and several under-way, the Halls shared with us that they were considering taking on a new challenge: commercial real estate.[13] The couple had recently pro-posed buying and renovating an abandoned, derelict office building on a main thoroughfare of the South Side. While the ShoreBank team had deep confidence in the Halls' capabilities in redeveloping multi-family housing, office buildings required a different skill set. Given their long relationship with the bank, as well as their collateral in mul-tiple properties, ShoreBank agreed to finance the $825,000 project and reduced its down-payment requirement by half, from 20 percent to 10 percent of the purchase price.

Beyond financing, the project brought many new challenges: work-ing through the intricacies of purchasing property from the city of

Chicago; gaining endorsements from the alderman blessing the project; and adhering to legal requirements to separate the development and contracting functions—rules that meant the Halls would be unable to use their seasoned rehab and construction team.

These were barriers and bumps that the real estate entrepreneurs had not previously faced. The city required explicit hiring and labor commitments, Lisa explained. "Fifty percent of the local labor had to be drawn from within the city limits, with 24 percent of it from minority-owned businesses and 4 percent from businesses owned by women. And the latter two had to be certified by the city in advance. That challenged the budget."

The fact that a minority-owned business was attempting to develop an abandoned building in a low-income, segregated neighborhood did not seem to alter these requirements.

There was another goal in the Halls' project: a green building. They had decided to seek LEED certification at the Silver level.[14] The Halls were not prepared for the amount of documentation required, the time it added to the development process, and its substantial additional cost.

"I was surprised at the total budget costs going up by 22 percent," Clarence admitted.

The couple told of their plans for the building, a 12,000-square-foot, two-level, mixed-use structure. Retail stores would be on the first floor, offices on the second, and even a "green" roof up top. Sitting in the offices of their small but impressive real estate empire, the Halls talked passionately about their desire to bring an energy-efficient structure to the South Side.

"There are buildings downtown, on the North Side and in the suburbs that are green," Lisa said. "We decided to try to be the pioneers on the South Side. Our building will rival any office building in those [other] areas. The bottom line is we want it to be a gem in Chatham." Despite a project with considerable hurdles and risks, they seemed appreciative of the support ShoreBank had provided over many years, and certainly on this adventurous initiative.

## THE MORE THINGS CHANGE

My research team and I spent a bit of time with Census data to get a sense of the demographics in the area directly abutting the bank's headquarters. In the latest data, the ShoreBank zip code reported a population of 54,823, 98.9 percent of which was Black. The median household income was reported to be $27,699, significantly lower than the national average of $41,994.

Poverty indicators were no better. One-fourth of families were found to be living below the poverty level (23.3 percent, compared to the national average of 9.2 percent), and 26.3 percent of individuals lived below the poverty level, more than twice the national average of 12.4 percent.[15]

Forty years after the launch of ShoreBank, its efforts at innovative finance hadn't diminished segregation. Residential segregation, at least as experienced by Blacks in Chicago, had proven more resilient than had been anticipated. Even with the bank's expansive growth and its product innovations, there was less success than expected in altering housing patterns. There was still a strong tendency of homeowners to pay higher rates for the right to live next to people who looked like themselves (a reality confirmed by other research).

## SEGREGATION, SOCIAL NETWORKS, AND STRATEGIC CHALLENGES

At the time of our field visit, ShoreBank was the nation's largest community development financial institution, with assets exceeding $2.4 billion. In addition to a sizable and diverse geographic footprint, the ShoreBank Holding Company had also become a relatively complex entity through multiple associated nonprofit organizations. Over time, the bank's growth strategy appeared to be an effort to add complementary services and product lines that would meet an expanding, broader set of community development needs than those typically managed by a financial intermediary organization, including health care, charter schools, and consumer research.

I marveled at the breadth of their work and the innovations underway to improve the communities in which they operated, although I wondered about the influence of the bank's heft on their attendant risks—financial, strategic, and operational. For example, we spent considerable time with ShoreBank's lending group because it had been a trailblazing demonstration of how multifamily lending could be offered within geographic areas that were often overlooked. We had a number of questions, however. One, in particular, was how the bank developed structures and staffing for risk management, as it did not appear that these functions were evolving at the same pace as the bank's market expansions.

Another question concerned loan delinquencies. These were managed under the purview of the chief lending officer, and in some cases, it appeared that individual loan officers were responsible for managing their own delinquent credits. This type of close-confiding relationship between a lender and lendee is common enough in character-based lending, but understandably makes poorly performing loans difficult to manage. If, over time, a loan officer had trained and groomed a lendee, he or she might be reticent to call the loan as a loss because of the resulting questions about their own professional judgment.

ShoreBank's training and development operations raised additional questions. As in many CDFIs, training and development followed an apprenticeship—an on-the-ground, "learn-as-you-go" model. In interviews with staff of the core multifamily lending unit, it surfaced that, prior to joining the bank, few managers had experience in commercial lending or in organizations with formal risk management departments. Clearly, finding and compensating finance executives with those credentials would be expensive and challenging, and most CDFIs would find it expensive from an overhead perspective to staff internal training and development functions. As the complexity of the bank's operations increased, it appeared that a corresponding expansion in training was not funded. In retrospect, my sense is that the apprenticeship method of training had been sufficient in prior market conditions but that an emerging new market merited novel approaches to risk management.

As it happened, we began our fieldwork with ShoreBank just as the rapid rise in subprime lending on the South Side of Chicago was beginning to be understood. Lenders like Jim Bringley spoke with us about a new and increased level of competition, with lenders entering from outside of the city. This was not viewed as a welcome prospect. He talked about their activity as creating "perverse incentives on behavior," with house prices being negotiated higher than their underlying value. He noted the rise in "flipping properties," which encouraged borrowers to resell and leave their assets in search of a quicker equity payout. This was before the slew of foreclosures began.

## RISING CLOUDS

About six months after our visit, ShoreBank began to face a number of regulatory challenges related to vulnerabilities on its balance sheet, including loan delinquencies and interest rate risks. These eventually led the FDIC to issue a cease-and-desist order on July 14, 2009. It stated that the bank had engaged in a number of "unsafe or unsound banking practices," including "operating with policies and practices that are detrimental to the Bank and jeopardize the safety of its deposits"; "operating with an excessive level of adversely classified loans"; "operating with inadequate liquidity and excessive dependence on noncore funding"; and "operating with a less than satisfactory sensitivity to market risk position."[16]

In response, the bank announced a plan to raise $30 million of capital.[17] By November 2009, 15 percent of the bank's $1.5 billion loan portfolio was at least ninety days overdue.[18] The bank had tried to protect its multifamily portfolio by being selective—financing only fifty projects totaling $75 million—and choosing not to lend to new investors who lacked experience in managing property. Despite these precautions, some of ShoreBank's borrowers were using their lines of credit to excess, buying and flipping properties without completing due diligence. ShoreBank's multifamily lending group saw delinquencies rise from its usual range of 1 to 3 percent, to as high as 5 percent.

Two executive resignations took place in autumn 2009: Jim Bringley, after more than thirty years at the bank, and Joseph Hasten, the sitting CEO, after three years in the role. George Surgeon, who had worked at the bank since 1976, left his position as CFO of the bank holding company to become the bank's CEO.[19]

Between 2008 and 2010, ShoreBank's challenges in the field were reflected in accounting performance. The bank's percentage of nonperforming loans (NPLs) spiked to over 20 percent, and with it came damage to its equity and assets. The bank's asset size dropped from a high of $3 billion in 2009 to $2.5 billion in one quarter. Its loss of equity was so acute that its debt leverage descended into the negative (which is only possible if debt exceeds the value of assets).

In addition to these concrete problems, the bank had to confront an overarching question concerning both its mission and its operations.

Deep local knowledge of the community it served was essential to the bank's initial success and growth. However, by 2009, ShoreBank was a large institution with assets of $2.5 billion, geographically far-flung operations, and a diverse assortment of product lines. Although getting to scale and maintaining local connections were not mutually exclusive, they required different resources and skills. Furthermore, local knowledge was not a static set of relationships and a fixed understanding of the operational ecosystem.

In May 2009, ShoreBank appeared to be close to its goal of raising up to $140 million from megabanks Goldman Sachs, Citigroup, JP Morgan Chase, Morgan Stanley, and Bank of America. In addition to these commitments, ShoreBank was reportedly seeking another $75 million from the U.S. government in order to complete its recapitalization. Given the public disdain for further bank bailouts and the bank's obvious political ties to Washington, regulators wisely turned down ShoreBank's request for funds under the Troubled Asset Relief Program (TARP). Considering its poor financial condition, regulators concluded that even with the additional TARP bailout, ShoreBank still would have been undercapitalized and unsafe to remain open. Regulators were left with no options.

On August 20, 2010, ShoreBank closed. The bank's assets were purchased from the FDIC by a newly chartered banking institution, the Urban Partnership Bank of Chicago. There was a subsequent turn of events, however. It was clear that providing direct cash from the TARP to ShoreBank would have been highly visible and controversial. Instead, ShoreBank was recapitalized through loss-share guarantees from the FDIC, and a $367.7 million loss was taken by the FDIC Insurance Fund. Although the government did not directly bail out ShoreBank, it appeared to some in conservative political circles that a "stealth bailout" for the owners of ShoreBank had been conducted. The following excerpt captures the ensuing controversy:

> The bailout of ShoreBank is certain to be controversial for the following reasons: In an almost unprecedented action, the FDIC allowed the current management team to remain in place and maintain ownership of ShoreBank by allowing them to purchase ShoreBank through the newly chartered Urban Partnership Bank. Although ShoreBank's president, William Farrow, was brought on after regulators ordered ShoreBank to raise additional capital, it is

highly unusual for the FDIC to resell a bank to the managers who ran the failed bank.[20]

ShoreBank's iconic status and celebrity meant that it also received outsized attention. In part because of President Clinton's role in the industry, the firm's relationships with prominent Democrats had created unforeseen scrutiny and likely contributed to the bank's inability to receive funds it might have otherwise.

In August 2013, the FDIC sued five ShoreBank lending executives, including Bringley. The suit alleged that they "repeatedly fail[ed] to undertake the analysis necessary to evaluate loans and approved loans without sufficiently informing themselves of information needed to evaluate them fully."[21] The suit was settled in November for $17.3 million, the largest settlement of its kind at that time.[22]

Throughout its history, ShoreBank epitomized the strategy of linking policy, practice, and networks, and its venerable status and subsequent closure had substantial impact on other CDFIs. The demise of the field's symbolic flagship (the bank that would "change the world") could leave the impression that mission-driven banking was a flawed business model. Further, ShoreBank's elite, sophisticated group of investors and supporters left many wondering, "Who knew and when?"

Using the CAMEL model described earlier, our own analysis suggested that ShoreBank's eventual failure was predictable, at least based on the model we developed. However, even as this analysis indicated substantial financial warning signs, we did not examine the M in the model, which assesses the management capacity of an organization. I can imagine that among most observers, ShoreBank's leadership team may have received high ratings, and their celebrity may have buoyed an otherwise troubled balance sheet. Because ShoreBank was, in so many ways, the model firm for community banking, for CDFIs, and for community reinvestment, its failure reverberated across the field. In some quarters, this scrutiny extended to other community banks and CDFIs with less challenged balance sheets, that felt the sting of a certain form of discrimination based on association.

Despite the bank's eventual closure, ShoreBank's founders influenced the art of finance in Chicago and beyond. Their work certainly inspired me, and many others. I am also sure that families like the Hansberrys were able to secure homes and build assets as a result of the bank's efforts and achievements. I also cannot help but feel that ShoreBank was in some ways a victim of its own success. The founders had built a firm designed to demonstrate that one could lend in segregated neighborhoods. Eventually, other firms figured that out, but unfortunately, they were not prudent about their approach. They may have been attracted by the sizable underserved markets in neighborhoods like the South Side of Chicago, yet were not careful about constructing the proper loans that suited these consumers. In short, it appears they were more focused on transactions than on creating long-term wealth for their clients. The practices of these new entrants to the field contributed to a contagion that ultimately compromised or ruined asset accumulation among many individuals and families. More than that, their untoward actions cast a blight on a pioneering bank that, through its long, distinguished history, had helped and advocated for those who, for too long, had been overlooked and underserved by the finance industry.

# CHAPTER FIVE

# Corn Tostadas and a Changing Compton

I'VE SHARED elsewhere that the particular experiences my family navigated in interracial and international relationships were the product of my parents' choices to take up careers in the U.S. military. To borrow a term I became familiar with, my parents were at the "tip of the spear" in our nation's civil rights experiment. They and their peers had to literally "learn on the job" the necessary sensitivities of managing cross-race interactions.

My parents talked passionately about the value they saw in the opportunity to penetrate the envelope of segregation. They believed that their entry into integrated work settings and residences was personally beneficial and societally meaningful, and shared with their children their roles as agents of social change.

I can recall assisting my mother as she prepared for lunches and tea services with her fellow officers' wives. In the military, hosting these gatherings was expected, yet the adult me recognizes that they were likely a challenge. Outside of our bases, there were racial and political upheavals. I can appreciate how uncomfortable these seemingly pleasant afternoon chats might have been for her and her guests. They were all in uncharted territory.

There was a secondary, nonprofessional benefit. I can recall the many friendships my parents collected and nurtured that lasted across years and global geographic postings. The integration of work obliterated former boundaries, leading to intimate, personal relationships.

As I grew older, I came to understand that the factors that brought me into interracial or even international contact—attending racially integrated schools, living in integrated housing, regularly interacting socially with non-Americans—were atypical advantages. In the next section, I share some of the research that informed me about just how unusual those early experiences were for Americans of my generation and, perhaps, even for the ones that follow mine.

## SOCIAL DISTANCE, RACE, AND CLOSE CONFIDANTS

One of the longer-running interests of sociological scholars is the study of closeness and intimacy in personal relationships. In the 1920s, while a graduate student at the University of Chicago, Emory Bogardus began writing about a concept he termed "social distance."[1]

Interest in the concept predated Bogardus. In the early 1900s, Robert Park and his colleagues at Chicago were curious about the origins of prejudice as a new arena of social science research. The urgency around this research was at least partially a result of external factors. Rapid immigration from abroad and migration from within the country were commingling previously separated ethnic and racial groups. America's largest cities, in particular, were experiencing an accelerating urbanization that pushed together diverse groups into ever densifying geographic spaces. Rising prejudice, even violence, were challenges that needed solutions.

Park and his colleagues believed that, at its root, prejudice was the expression of an individual's desire for distance from other groups. He challenged his colleagues and students like Bogardus to develop a way to measure such desires, at the individual or group level. Bogardus took up the challenge and administered the first social distance survey in 1926.[2] Quite influential, it eventually was incorporated into the General Social Survey, a nationally projectable, longitudinal study of Americans' attitudes and perspectives in the social sciences.

Research has tended to show that among demographic traits, racial and ethnic differences produce the strongest expressed preferences and observed behavior. One way of measuring aversion to other groups is through analysis of people's personal relationships.[3] James Cook, Miller McPherson, and Lynn Smith-Lovin, for example, examined differences over time in the degree to which Americans share having close confiding relations with members of other groups.[4] They compared survey responses from 1985 with those from 2004 and found that "there was more contact between individuals with different races, religions, and gender in 2004 than there was in 1985. . . . The absolute rate of racial matching decreased from .95 to .90. This is a substantively significant change, but one that still leaves the vast majority of ties within race." Over the nineteen-year period, that is, the proportion of close relationships that were with others of one's own race had declined from 95 percent to 90 percent.

When I first came across research findings like these, I was stunned, because they did not jibe with my own experiences. Given what I had observed in my parents' friendships, I wondered whether results would differ in settings like the professional, white-collar workplace. That interest led me to Herminia Ibarra, who was among the first to analyze the social and professional relationships of women and minorities in predominantly white, male organizations.

Ibarra's work showed that women and minorities were inclined toward more gender and ethnic diversity in their connections than their white and male peers.[5] This led to the insight that although the diversity of the setting was a key influence, there were differences in relationship patterns within the same organization. In short, the tendency remained to stay within the group.

Ibarra's work raised questions for me about how the presence or dearth of cross-race relationships might influence the work of finance professionals. Would the general tendency of relations to stay within one's own group influence the ability to provide financial services in an increasingly multiracial, multiethnic business environment? In the remainder of this chapter, I share the story of Wells Fargo and its efforts to respond to an increasingly diverse commercial lending marketplace.

## SOCIAL SEGREGATION, PERSONAL NETWORKS, GENTRIFICATION

My fieldwork with Wells Fargo in Compton, California, began with a recommendation. "I think there's some neat stuff going on at Wells

Fargo that would make a very cool case study," offered Catharine Carrales, one of my MBA students. "Cat" had spent the previous summer
working in Wells Fargo's Los Angeles–based commercial banking group.

I did not initially see the overlap. In my sense of things, large-scale,
nationally branded bank chains like Wells Fargo were not involved in
serving lower-income or immigrant consumers. I carried the belief that
minorities building wealth in metropolises like Los Angeles tended to
rely on explicitly minority-serving institutions or informal sources of
capital (check cashing, payday lending, and alternative financial services providers). Ultimately, I was intrigued by a project that might
challenge my assumptions.

In 2002, Carrales and I flew to Los Angeles to learn about Wells
Fargo's interest in lending among the city's growing and highly diverse
immigrant and ethnic enclaves. In what might be termed the "mainstream" market, a number of financial services firms were competing,
including large, interstate banks like Bank of America and Citigroup.
Their clients—owners of small- and medium-size enterprises—were
generally well acquainted with debt capital and tended to "shop" their
business needs to various lending units until they found a deal with
the most attractive rates and terms. Clients also tended to belong to
the same local civic, business, or social groups as their loan officers
and—relevant to this chapter—they were overwhelmingly middle-
aged, white, and male.

In a concept known by scholars as racial and ethnic matching,[6] the
loan officers who called on these clients were generally white, middle-
aged, and male as well. This "traditional" market had relatively few
asymmetries, as all parties shared similar educational and professional
backgrounds and overlapping social networks. Thus, rivalry among
firms was high.

In what I will term the "developing" portion of the market—
immigrants, ethnic minorities, and women—there was greater uncertainty. While these groups were clearly engaging in entrepreneurial
pursuits, uncertainty about their market potential arose from the circumscribed, confined networks of loan officers: white male lenders
tended to serve white male business owners. They knew fewer of this
burgeoning class of entrepreneurs personally, and knew little about
the markets they served.

At issue was the fact that, if left unaddressed, the cultural and ethnic
mismatch between the lending professionals and the potential lending

clients in highly diverse communities like Los Angeles would contribute to a loss of prospective revenue for Wells Fargo.

## A BANK STRETCHING FROM SEA TO SEA

Founded in California in 1852, Wells Fargo eventually became one of the nation's largest banks—a well-known, even iconic brand. Despite its global reach, Wells Fargo preferred to manage its business lines in a geographically decentralized fashion, even cascading down to the local level in what was described as a "pushed down" decision-making style. When we arrived at their offices in Los Angeles, Paul Watson, executive vice president in Wholesale Banking, and Todd Hollander, executive vice president in the Business Banking Group (BBG), explained that the majority of retail (mortgage) and small business loan decisions were made at the neighborhood level.

As part of that local focus, Hollander spoke of the bank's drive to court Latino business owners actively and directly. Each officer peppered his assessment with evidence of the Latino market's potential— exploding projected growth rates and correspondingly high purchasing power—and the resulting business demands this would create. It soon became clear that competitive pressures were at least one component of the bank's eagerness to tap this market.

Watson spoke of the opportunity for Wells Fargo to establish itself as a financial lender of choice among Latino consumers, and within the Latino business market in California and beyond. Both men emphasized that this goal would depend on their team's ability to relate personally to Latino clientele. To that end, Hollander had recruited commercial loan officer Albert Gomez.

The Los Angeles BBG was diversifying its lending teams as a strategic move to ensure the bank's hold on the rapidly growing ethnic markets in their geographic footprint. Although not mentioned directly, Hollander likely saw the implicit investment in Gomez's career as a lender. He recognized Gomez's latent potential to build a robust loan book, especially in the fast-growing market of Latino entrepreneurs in the area. It was also unstated that this would be considerably more difficult to achieve with an all-white, all-Anglo lending team.

## ALBERT GOMEZ AND COETHNIC
## LENDING STRATEGIES

In the summer of 2000, Albert Gomez had to decide whether to press forward in recommending a substantial construction loan to potential clients, Raphael and Minerva Salinas.[7] The Salinases intended to use the loan to upgrade their business manufacturing capabilities in response to a sizable unmet demand for their products. If approved, it would be the largest loan the family had ever received. Gomez had gone to great lengths to cultivate a trusting relationship with the Salinases over the previous three years, and he now had to overcome a number of issues to make them "loan ready" in the view of his bank's loan review committee.

Gomez was preparing to recommend approval of the Salinases' request for a $4.25 million construction loan to build a new, state-of-the-art tostada- and tortilla-processing facility. Unlike others within Wells Fargo, Gomez had no doubts about the family's ability to build the business and service the debt, but he did share concerns about some of the loan's irregularities.

As Gomez drove us to meet the Salinases at their facility, our conversation became more candid. The Salinases' plant was based in the largely Latino community of South Gate, and Gomez commented that we would likely not be impressed with what we would see—neither in the neighborhood nor in the plant.

He explained that the area might make peer loan officers uncomfortable, and that the plant would not immediately suggest an underlying business capable of servicing such a sizable loan. This was especially the case if one could not see beyond the area's gritty trappings to the massive magnitude of pent-up demand that businesses like the Salinases' served. Gomez related how biases had prevented a former loan officer from seeing its potential and, as a result, the Salinases' business had almost slipped through Wells Fargo's hands. Over the past few years, however, the Salinases had developed a deep confidence in both Gomez and his colleague John Murillo, the manager of Wells Fargo's local South Gate retail branch.

Gomez explained that the Salinases' loan, like others, involved developing a "pitch" for his senior credit officer, Hollander. The primary question he would need to defend was whether the Salinases would be able to meet debt service—i.e., cover their new loan payments. Gomez recognized a strong likelihood that others within Wells Fargo's BBG unit would view the potential loan as "just too risky." As we listened, I could hear in Gomez's narrative that he possessed the underlying cultural knowledge that allowed him to see what others would miss and to recognize economic value where others could not.

Gomez was explaining what a business scholar would term "tacit knowledge" that allowed him to assess the relevant liabilities and effectively turn uncertainty into calculated and even prudent risk. He also perfectly exemplified what is known as "character-based lending," in which lenders make decisions using information gleaned from their personal relationships with potential clients, rather than from purely algorithmic, arms-length, quantitative assessments.

## WHO WERE THE SALINASES AND WHY THIS BUSINESS?

Since Raphael and Minerva Salinas started their company in 1981, it had grown to more than fifty employees, working in three shifts over a twenty-four-hour period, six days a week. At the time of the building loan request, annual revenues were approximately $5.1 million and the Salinas family retained a handsome equity share, at nearly 25 percent. Even after their healthy salaries, net income over the past three years had averaged approximately 10 percent of revenues. Not only was their plant running at full capacity, but Gomez also estimated that the national corn tostada and tortilla chip market was growing at a rate approximating 6 percent.

Following our arrival and introduction to the Salinases, we were ushered into the company's modest administrative office. I marveled at how small it was. The space was no more than six by seven feet and, with five of us, the room was tight. As with almost all of my interviews, I began: "So, when did you first decide to found a . . . [tostada manufacturer]?" All questions and answers were translated from English to Spanish and back again by Carrales.

Raphael Salinas was first struck by the idea to build his company soon after he emigrated from Mexico in 1976. Previously, Salinas had worked for PepsiCo's Mexico subsidiary in a variety of capacities— sales, marketing, and accounting. However, when he first arrived to the United States, Salinas had trouble finding work, due in part to his lack of formal education. Though he did not possess a degree, there were no limits to his drive and ingenuity. Salinas astutely took note of the many Los Angeles neighborhoods with high concentrations of Mexican immigrants who were seeking goods that were familiar, hard-to-find reminders of home. He brokered a relationship with a local wholesaler and began selling tostadas and tortillas door to door. Raphael knew the product, he understood the consumer, and he had the necessary selling skills. Yet he surprised even himself when he began earning $1,000 net profit from just one day's work, usually a Sunday.

## LAUNCHING A MANUFACTURING FIRM

Over time, Raphael Salinas became less content with his role of intermediary selling agent to the sizable, yet untapped, tostada and tortilla market in South Los Angeles. Although he was doing well financially, he intuitively understood the concept of power in value chains and recognized the greater degree of opportunity for profit and decision-making authority he would have as a product manufacturer rather than as a distributor. From a personal standpoint, the Salinas family had always practiced frugality. This lifestyle ultimately allowed the couple to save enough money to start their own independent corn chip manufacturing plant. Their initial step was the purchase of a small parcel of property in the community of South Gate.

South Gate is a legally separate city within the Los Angeles metropolitan area that is 3 percent white and 95 percent Latino.[8] Nearly two out of five workers are employed in manufacturing (37 percent), and the average household income in 2012 was $41,851, lower than the state's then average of approximately $47,500.[9]

I suspect that in addition to language and cultural barriers, perceived crime and income profiles only magnified uncertainties among many lenders, including Gomez's colleagues. It is difficult to assess risks in neighborhoods that you are afraid to drive through.

Initial results from the Salinases' new manufacturing operation were promising. As Raphael had guessed from his on-the-ground sales, demand exceeded supply for tostada and tortilla chips. By the early 1980s, recently arrived Mexican immigrants had few choices to satisfy their demand for the food products that they regularly ate in their home country. Concurrently, the Mexican food craze had just begun to diffuse to the non-Latino population. The couple was aware that few mainstream supermarkets stocked items that they personally would find appealing, and for this reason, the Salinases recognized their best avenue for distribution would be the smaller, local grocers operating in ethnically Latino neighborhoods. On the product side, they sought to differentiate themselves by developing products with authentic taste and ingredients. Suggestive of their strong religious beliefs, they named their brand *El Paraiso*, referring to Paradise or Heaven.

## EARLY GOOD DEEDS AND LASTING REPERCUSSIONS

Success can create unique problems, and one that I had encountered in previous fieldwork with family-run businesses also beset the Salinases. For the first several years, there were few formal separations between family and business finances and, given the Salinases' commercial success and their visible trappings of wealth, it became increasingly difficult to turn away requests for financial assistance from less fortunate relatives and friends. More than a few times, the Salinases cosigned and even paid notes on personal loans for automobiles and home mortgages that had cumulatively amounted to the substantial sum of $378,000.

As I had seen in other fieldwork with small business owners, some of those loans had not been paid on time. It was often only later, when hosting cosigners applied for a loan themselves, that these delinquencies came to light, leaving the cosigners with a blemished credit history and the denial of their own loan request. By taking on the risk of cosigning loans for others, the Salinases became legally responsible, and these bad loans followed them.

## UNDERSERVED, BUT NOTICED

Although we recognized that there was still unmet market demand at the time of our field visit, the tostada company had other competitive challenges. Foremost was a "rollup," or effort to acquire and consolidate independent tortilla and tostada chip manufacturers in the Los Angeles market, by the multinational Mexican conglomerate Gruma (S.A. de C.V. Gruma).

In part, Gruma's competitive advantages accrued from aggressive use of marketing dollars to ensure prime shelf space for its products. The company paid the substantial slotting fees demanded by larger national retailers whenever a company requested an expansion through the addition of new products (known as stock-keeping units, or SKUs).

For grocers, slotting fees are essentially a protective insurance for SKUs that have yet to show market appeal.[10] A *Forbes* article from 2002 gave a sense of their potential magnitude:

> For a new product, the standard price of admission to the shelves is a slotting fee—up to $25,000 per item for a regional cluster of stores. (A California food producer says he met with a buyer at a chain grocer who demanded $250,000 for ten stores and wouldn't even take a meeting until he received a $100,000 check.) Small manufacturers hate paying upfront money; it can put them out of business before they've even started.[11]

The Salinases decided against paying slotting fees, as their new business simply could not afford the added financial burden. Given their target market, and the tendency of national-chain grocers to operate outside of lower-income, urban neighborhoods, slotting fees did not immediately present a great threat. In any event, the Salinases believed that demand for their products, as opposed to monetary payments, should command shelf space. To a large degree, it was a blind trust influenced by their religious devotion.

## AUTHENTICITY IN THE SUPPLY CHAIN

Working with suppliers was difficult in the early stages of the Salinases' business. Many, if not most, of California's tostada and tortilla chip makers did not manufacture their own dough, or *masa*, for their products; instead, they mainly sourced it from Gruma, which sold a corn flour called *Maseca*. However, the Salinases were not impressed with the Gruma product. Moreover, they recognized that sourcing from a competitor would make their business vulnerable to Gruma's pricing decisions. The Salinases illustrated, once again, an intuitive understanding of value chains and that a greater degree of verticality—or control over expanded portions of the manufacturing process—was the only way to ensure that consumers would receive the highest-quality end product.

The couple experimented until they developed a formula that provided a taste very similar to the homemade tostadas they thought would appeal to recently immigrated Mexicans. They sourced ingredients, produced the fresh *masa* on premises, fried the corn tortillas in 100 percent vegetable oil (instead of the more commonly used lard), and sold their product in different sizes of crunchy, round, corn tostadas.

## FAMILY VALUES

As was often the case in firms based in ethnic enclaves, the Salinases were not only managing a coethnic customer and store strategy, but they were also enjoying a deep hiring relationship within the local area. All their employees were first-generation Latino immigrants, mostly Mexican, who lived in the surrounding South Gate community. Most workers earned minimum and slightly above minimum wages. Many had worked for the family since the early start-up years. As I had seen before with family-run firms, the Salinases eschewed employing professional managers. Along with their now grown daughters, Raphael and Minerva managed day-to-day operations even as the company's scope grew considerably. This simple, unceremonious management approach lent a family atmosphere to the business, creating close and informal relationships between the workers and the owners. There were benefits and liabilities to this approach.

## THE RELATIONSHIP BUILDERS: ALBERT GOMEZ AND JOHN MURILLO

Todd Hollander told us that some at Wells Fargo talked about Albert Gomez as a potential future star in the Business Banking Group. Within his short tenure, he had distinguished himself as one of the bank's top ten commercial loan officers, building a book of traditional (white) and "development" (Latino) clients over time. Later that day, after we left the Salinases and drove back to the Wells Fargo offices, Gomez shared the story of how he first became a loan officer.

Early on, he worked as an analyst at a small community bank to put himself through the University of Southern California. Although his work paid the bills, his dreams were of law school. Gomez's admitted ability to shrug off rejection was partly due to his having been turned down by law schools not once or twice, but four times. Eventually concluding that the law would not lead him to the success he craved, Gomez reexamined his goals and decided to dedicate himself to the business development, revenue-generating side of banking. Because his analyst position offered limited career potential, he began applying for commercial loan officer jobs. Again, he encountered difficulties.

Gomez realized that while his interviews seemed to go well, he never received a callback that resulted in a job offer. Gomez then shared a fascinating story: He promised himself he would not let a lack of assertiveness derail his career plans; instead, at his next interview, he would leverage his salesmanship skills, demand immediate feedback, and ask, right there and then, whether he would be offered the job.

As it happened, Gomez's next interview was with Wells Fargo. True to his promise, Gomez asked for feedback. "You've done a great job presenting your credentials, and I like your enthusiasm. If it were up to me, I would hire you," the interviewer assured him. He was taken aback when Gomez asked straight out whether he would be offered the job. The interviewer explained, "Unfortunately, I'm not in a position to make the final hiring decision. As I said, you're a good candidate."

Refusing to be put off, Gomez began suggesting alternatives: "Is the hiring manager available? Could he join us? Is there a competitive exam I could take?" Gomez made one final attempt.

"How about this," he suggested, "let me join the bank conditionally and you can make your decision after I complete three months of satisfactory performance. You won't regret it." Gomez's doggedness and drive seemed to resonate with his interviewer. By the time Gomez left and arrived home, he had a message from Wells Fargo inviting him to join the organization. This was quite a story, and one that I noted never included mention of his ethnic background as being a challenge to finding his way into the lending field. I wondered if he didn't think it a "safe space" to share this perception, or whether he felt that way at all.

Gomez related how his colleague John Murillo began his relationship with the Salinas family. When Murillo was named manager of the South Gate "store" (Wells Fargo terminology for a retail branch), he paid a courtesy visit to introduce himself to all the businesses that banked at his store. Murillo eventually came to call, unannounced, at the Salinases' facility.

Murillo was welcomed warmly by Raphael and Minerva, and his initial impression was that, although located on a street that some of his colleagues would find intimidating, theirs was a healthy and growing business. He began discussions with the family about how the bank might be able to assist them with a portfolio of products. He suspected they could benefit from working capital lines of credit and cash and treasury management products—all products the family had never been offered by the previous South Gate manager.

As he slowly built a trusting relationship, Murillo's suspicions about the business's economic potential were confirmed. He found that the Salinases owned their manufacturing plant outright (assessed value, $1.8 million), along with two small apartment complexes in South Gate assessed at $287,000 and $217,000. The family had a small fleet of seven panel delivery trucks. All business expansions had been funded through the firm's cash flow, and there were no existing loans on these assets. This suggested to Murillo both an ability to service debt and potential collateralizable assets.

Albert Gomez's alliance with Murillo in serving the Salinas family was not unexpected. Based on my own personal experience and what I had learned from Ibarra's work, it was my expectation that Gomez's networks would not only reach Latino and non-Latino communities but also span across levels and functions of Wells Fargo. Indeed, Murillo met Albert Gomez at an informal Wells Fargo get-together to discuss expansion of the bank's presence in the Latino community.

Murillo's first impressions of Gomez were that he was a charismatic, determined young banker who appeared bent on success. He specifically noted that Gomez hadn't avoided or cut ties in the Latino community. Like himself, Gomez wanted to create a distinctive client niche by meeting the financial needs of Latino business owners.

Both Gomez and Murillo recognized the value of their shared experiences as first-generation immigrants—their biculturalism, bilingualism, and ease in moving between Latino and non-Latino communities. They understood and respected Mexican culture, sensitivities, and challenges. They saw in each other a coethnic, complementary partner, and it was not long before the two men decided to collaborate in targeting prospective clients.

Shortly after, Gomez joined Murillo in visiting the Salinases, now seeking a commercial loan to purchase property and expand their manufacturing capacity. Murillo hoped that he and Gomez could determine whether Wells Fargo would be able to meet the Salinases' request.

The Salinas family greeted Gomez with their usual warmth, and during their talk, Raphael took the opportunity to inform Gomez that Murillo's predecessor—also a recently immigrated Mexican American—had turned down their first request for a business loan. Of course, Gomez already knew the story, but Raphael's sharing of it underscored how injurious it had been, especially when he related that the manager had added insult by saying he would not lend the Salinases "a penny."

Even with these slights, Murillo's excellent service held sway, and the Salinases continued their banking relationship with Wells Fargo. The meeting with Gomez was a new chapter, and one that could benefit Wells Fargo beyond a single loan should the couple engage more of the bank's services and products over time.

A bank with a large Latino customer base could better maximize the efficiency of its infrastructure by increasing the amount of revenue per customer and thus spend less on the costly enterprise of gaining new customers. The upshot was that if Wells Fargo secured a Latino customer's business, then the bank had less worry about that customer trading off or switching to another financial institution for temporary discounts or sales gimmicks. This characteristic confirmed an anecdotal comment I had heard from other loan officers: Minorities were less likely to "shop around" or negotiate their financial needs, and once a relationship was established, they tended to be more loyal than their fully assimilated counterparts. This appeared to be true for the Salinases, even after being broadly insulted.

## ROUNDING OUT THE CASE

As we continued our trip back to the Wells Fargo offices, Gomez spoke about the specifics of the Salinases' loan request and recounted some of the issues: "The amount of the request, $4.25 million, was not extravagant given the business's recent annual revenues of approximately $5.1 million."

Gomez's hesitance stemmed from a number of factors, beginning with cultural differences. He explained that "many [Latino] applicants might have limited experience with traditional banks. In their countries of origin, many carried a legacy of mistrust toward government institutions and even large financial institutions controlled by the government.

"It would follow," Gomez continued, "that when these families immigrated to the States, they were extremely reluctant to open bank accounts. It is an ingrained issue of mistrust that clouds the value a banking relationship could provide. The end result is that many recent immigrants build up very little positive credit history."

Gomez also touched on the Salinases' penchant for cosigning for relatives.

"This, again," he argued, "is a cultural trait, a form of personal authenticity. Over the years," Gomez sadly admitted, "I've seen multiple examples of tarnished, even wrecked credit histories from individuals practicing loyalty to family and community."

Still another issue was in the Salinases' accounting. The practice of tax minimization was very common among small business owners, Latino or otherwise, and it was heightened to some degree by suspicions of the government. As a result, a multitude of accountants and "enrolled agents" specializing in income minimization techniques populated Latino neighborhoods. (Enrolled agents are accounting professionals entitled to represent individuals to the IRS.)

Like loan cosigning, tax minimization was a practice I had seen previously. For many small business owners, there were short-term incentives to inflate their expenses, lower their net income, and thus pay lower taxes. For many, this practice would become an issue once they attempted to apply for a commercial loan. In addition to personal credit histories, the loan underwriting process considers a historical analysis of income and cash flow to the business. Over time, reporting limited or no income to the IRS meant that these businesses would not be deemed creditworthy when they pursued loans from financial institutions. Like many, the Salinases had not realized that implication when they began lowering their business taxes.

The Salinases had long used an enrolled agent, Ms. Guzman, to prepare their business and personal tax returns. Guzman's strategy had been to minimize the Salinases' income to the degree that they would owe almost no taxes. The Salinases' business had funded a lux lifestyle that was dramatically different from their hardscrabble beginnings. Gomez knew that their visible wealth was evidence of the business's actual, rather than reported, cash flow—and an indicator of possible tax evasion, raising the risk of potential legal action by the IRS.

## MAKING THE LOAN: THE SALINAS FAMILY AND WELLS FARGO'S LENDING PRACTICES

As we talked with Gomez, we learned about the process of "building" the Salinases into a more palatable loan applicant. Gomez's first priority had been to help them straighten out their accounting practices, retrospectively and going forward.

In considering whether to extend loans (and in recognition of the "liability of newness"), banks generally insist that a company have three years of financial information or audited financial statements before they will extend capital. If audited reports show limited profits, or do not suggest a business that can support debt service, then banks tend to reject loans. Lenders are certainly aware of tax minimization, but are understandably wary of making loans that may have default risks or cast the bank as a known party to fraud.

The Salinas family, with little awareness of credit and net income, tax issues, or audited financial statements, required approximately one year of intense consultation with Gomez before he was able to help qualify them for a commercial line of credit.

After months of patient discussions about how tax minimization limits a business's access to capital—and ultimately ensures a smaller, less-capitalized operation—the Salinases agreed to hire professional accountants recommended by Murillo and Gomez. The accountants helped establish a strong financial foundation in the books of the business and eventually prepared the CPA-reviewed financial statements necessary for Gomez to have even a hope of extending a commercial loan.

Over time, the family also agreed to hire corporate attorneys to create a more sophisticated corporate structure that would limit the family's liabilities and risks should the company go bankrupt or be sued for past tax indiscretions.

After a second year of close collaboration, the Salinases were able to apply and qualify for a line of credit, which they used to meet working capital requirements, fund a small capital expansion of their existing plant, and purchase almost all the real estate on the block where they were located. It was a large victory for Murillo, Gomez, and the Salinases.

Given the growing demand for their products and their progress in rationalizing their business accounting practices, Raphael began scouting for real estate to enable the company to expand operations from five to seventeen production lines and, in turn, more than triple current revenues. Beyond that, the expansion would help secure additional clients, such as mainstream supermarket chains whose recent demands exceeded the business's operating capacity.

A third year passed before Raphael found a suitable property. Now, with a specific location in mind, Raphael asked Gomez and Murillo about a construction loan. Gomez reminded us that, at this point, the family had secured three loans plus an initial line of credit from Wells Fargo. Without delinquencies or other issues, Gomez was prepared to support the loan request and submit it to his superiors.

He shared with us the Salinases' well-thought-out reasons for their request: Raphael believed his business had tapped only a fraction of Los Angeles's Latino market. Based on distribution, Gomez estimated only 5 percent penetration of potential neighborhoods. With inventory currently turning over on a daily basis, the Salinas family believed continued strong demand would enable the new facility to operate at 100 percent capacity.

Furthermore, since the property was located only a few blocks from their existing operations, the company would be able to retain most (if not all) of its employees. This level of employee retention seemed a bit suspect to me, given the state-of-the-art manufacturing operation being discussed. I was not sure whether Gomez had concerned himself with questions of the business's long-term managerial needs and capabilities. Beyond debt service, few lenders worried about these elements.

While lauding Gomez's and Murillo's efforts to groom the Salinases into a strong loan prospect, I mentioned the multiyear, multiprofessional, forensic accounting and legal cost of their efforts. Gomez acknowledged that their sustained effort had made the Salinases an attractive client for any bank, but believed that the time invested would secure the family's loyalty well past this loan. He admitted that the exhaustive "selling costs" might have put off less determined lending officers.

## OUTLINING THE PITCH

Back at the Wells Fargo offices, Gomez sketched a back-of-the-envelope analysis of how an evaluation of the Salinases' finances showed that they could, in fact, meet Wells Fargo's debt coverage ratios. Even so, he knew that the case for the Salinases' loan would be spotty, using the traditional loan-scoring methods.

Commercial loans generally are based on four primary financial considerations. First, commercial loan officers research business credit to ensure the business applicant and the business's guarantors possess criteria reflecting good repayment history. They look at reports that reflect any lawsuits, bankruptcies, foreclosures, tax liens, judgments, or the like. They also consider personal credit, as measured by a FICO score of 680 or more. The Salinases had no continuing legal issues, but their FICO scores were not above the hurdle, again because of cosigning for others.

Second, loan officers calculate interest coverage ratios to determine the extent to which recurring profits are sufficiently available to service the applicant's existing and proposed debt. It appeared that, with a more accurate accounting system, the Salinases would have little difficulty with their primary sources of repayment; however, the accounting paperwork had to be reconstructed to support this factor.

Third, loan officers consider collateral if the primary source of repayment is not sufficient to meet the loan payments. Generally, this involves examining other liquid company assets, including accounts receivable, inventory, equipment, or real estate that could be used as collateral and sold, if needed. The Salinases had few accounts receivable, and the equipment and land they held would tend to benefit only someone in a related business, or who was comfortable owning land in South Gate.

Fourth, lenders consider the owner's net worth outside of the business, as well as the personal liquid assets or real estate that guarantors can contribute. The Salinases certainly had amassed considerable personal assets, with face values that totaled into the millions. However, if a bank were to seize them in a legal action, they would be sold for pennies of their current assessed values. The weaknesses of the Salinases' business accounting and the family's credit score problems left a less than overwhelmingly affirmative case for making the loan.

In sum, this meant that Gomez also needed to be sensitive to the conditions of the loan itself. He outlined the loan's key terms. First, in terms of pricing, Gomez assumed an interest on the loan based on the average prime interest rate in 2000 of 9.18 percent. Second, he assumed that the life of the new building loan would be twenty years, and that this would encompass the loan term. Third, he accounted for the $1.3 million of existing loans that would be rolled into the new commercial mortgage loan, aggregating to a $5.5 million loan. Interest would be compounded on a quarterly basis and interest charged on the outstanding loan balance at the beginning of each quarter. For depreciation, he assumed straight-line amortization of the new plant over the twenty-year term. Fourth, his analysis provided the Salinases a residual personal income that could service the loan easily, it seemed.

Gomez's analysis appeared thorough. We discussed the loan's other inherent uncertainties, many without answers: What if the projected demand did not materialize or, worse, Gruma stepped up its efforts to squeeze smaller players out of the market? What if the local authorities stretched out the approval and permit process, causing major delays that affected revenues? What if the Salinases decided to retire and turn the business over to their daughters? Were the daughters ready to manage the business as effectively?

We discussed the nonfinancial and career-related risks. It had taken Gomez some time to get his senior credit officers to recognize the company's potential and to back the expansion loan. Gomez acknowledged that his "reputation was on the line." His long-term efforts would seem time well spent if the loan proved serviceable—and foolish, blind devotion to ethnicity if it went poorly. Because cultivation of the Salinases had been so dependent on bicultural understanding, Gomez was making his ethnicity salient to his colleagues. His reputation for production and objectivity hung in the balance.

These questions were at the top of Gomez's mind. He commented again on the Wells Fargo retail manager who had coldly denied the Salinases' application for a business loan without a second thought. Was that manager, also a first-generation immigrant, the wiser one?

## THE POSTSCRIPT

The Wells Fargo lending story is one of a financial institution attempting to expand its market, recognizing the reality of ethnically and racially bound social networks. It is also the story of the Salinases confronting the financing challenges of immigrant entrepreneurs. Likewise, it is the story of John Murillo and Albert Gomez, young Latino managers trying to advance their careers in a massive banking institution. Wells Fargo ultimately granted the loan, and from all indications, the Salinas family had no problem servicing their debt. They have continued to build their business as well as their range of the bank's financial services products.

A few years later, I caught a story that Wells Fargo Bank, the nation's largest mortgage lender, agreed to pay $175 million in a settlement with the Justice Department for steering Black and Latino borrowers into costlier subprime mortgages while white borrowers with similar credit profiles received "regular" loans. Wells Fargo admitted no wrongdoing but did note that it would cease lending through independent brokers.[12] The notion that Latino borrowers were more loyal and less likely to "shop" their loan requests among competing banks came back to me.

The story of Wells Fargo's efforts in South Los Angeles offers a lesson on the promise of enterprising units within larger firms. The endeavors of smaller, entrepreneurial players featured in other chapters are indeed no less exciting. They have a David-versus-Goliath appeal. However, what if Goliath was also working to innovate in community development? New approaches to immigrant markets among national firms like Wells Fargo have the potential of diffusing to momentous scale.

# CHAPTER SIX

# A Sense of Place

*Interplay of Geography and Capability*

WE KNOW the centrality and power of *location* in the real estate business. Two homes that seem virtually the same—each 2,200 square feet, of similar design, bedrooms, bathrooms, and lot size, located in the same city, built the same year[1]—can have dramatically different purchase prices, even if only short distances apart. Of course, we know many visible and measurable elements can influence price: access to amenities like parks, proximity to mass transit, recent trajectory of resales, percentage of rental properties in the neighborhood. However, some less geographic, social factors also play a role. For current or would-be parents, for example, a frequently considered factor is the perceived quality of the local public schools, even at the neighborhood level. Because of the considerable influence of these perceptions on initial price, appreciation, and potential resale, even home purchasers who do not have children attend to the zoning of local public schools.

Over time, I've come to understand the central role of housing equity as an explanatory factor for differences in wealth accumulation between racial groups, and that these differences are frequently compounded over time through appreciation in housing values and inheritances.[2] Initially, I had believed that the primary source of wealth differences was behavioral. Some people are spenders. Some are savers. I would have told you that if individual households would simply behave conservatively with their resources, anyone could achieve significant wealth accumulation.

In my eyes, there were readily observable, risky, and counterproductive spending behaviors, especially in our consumption-driven culture. Years later, as a researcher, I began to recognize that there were nonbehavioral, less observable factors, such as inequity in wage rates for comparable jobs, labor market ghettos, and segregation in housing, that influenced differences in starting points and the rate of wealth growth. As I began to take a more nuanced view, I questioned whether characterizing wealth disparities as purely accruing from behavior was perhaps "convenient" and "unexamined."

The sociologist Charles Tilly coined the term "durable inequalities" to describe differences created and reinforced in social systems.[3] For me, the surprising element in Tilly's work was the degree to which these differences "lock in" inequalities that influence where we learn, where we work, and where we live.

Recognizing the deep anxiety among consumers about home purchases, developers have long sensed latent demand for differentiators across property offerings, and they have skillfully offered features that suggest the promise of price appreciation. Although these certainly include aesthetic novelties, they also encompass amenities that help to create collective belonging among residents—a "sense of place."[4]

For many developers, these enhancements involve providing features like community pools and clubhouses, fences and gated communities, planned unit developments (PUDs), private communities, and private streets. These collective assets become selling points that provide reassurance of increased home appreciation over time in the "right" kind of communities.

As I gradually began to wade through the ample econometric work done on the question of how neighborhood amenities influence housing values, I came to understand that seemingly frivolous choices could have very real economic value. For example, a consortium of researchers analyzed the relative appreciation of similar, homogenous homes located inside and outside of gated communities or on privately owned streets in St. Louis between 1978 and 1998:

Consider pricing a "standard" house, defined as a 3-bedroom, 2½ bath home built in 1925 with a detached garage and 2,500 square feet of space on a 0.20-acre lot. The expected sales price for this house, if selling during the summer of 1998 . . . would be approximately $235,000 in an open, public subdivision not governed by a home-owner's association. If the same house were located within a subdivision governed by a homeowner's association, the expected price would be $275,000. Finally, if the same house were located within a private gated subdivision, the expected sales price would be about $296,000. These are clearly economically significant differences.[5]

From a theoretical standpoint, the authors develop and apply the concept of "defensible spaces" to explain their results. The term was first coined by the urban planner Oscar Newman in the early 1970s. Newman developed the notion that in planned, gated communities and on private streets, residents "maintained, controlled, and identified with those areas that were clearly demarcated as their own."[6]

The concept of defensible spaces, of course, raises the question "defending from what?" In an article titled "Security Is the Draw at Gated Communities," Marcelle Fischler reported on her interviews with residents of gated communities in suburban New York.[7] Fischler found that worries about crime were a primary concern. The mayor of North Hills, the community featured in the article, summed it up this way: "I love the lifestyle, the feeling of safety. You walk around your entire complex anytime of day or night."

Perception is the key variable in this calculus. Fischler reported that, over time, crime was actually down in the area, whether inside or outside a gated community. Given the larger context of racial residential segregation, it is difficult to separate these messages from racial tropes and fear appeals. Whether or not these communities actually defended residents from crime, it appears that they did offer a sense of association and maybe even camaraderie. Over the years, these factors drove home equity valuations higher for homeowners purchasing in gated communities.

As I continued exploring the influence of neighborhood characteristics on equity value in my dissertation research, I began to appreciate that the choice *not* to live in a gated or planned community could mean "leaving money on the table." Knowing that seemingly insignificant amenities can significantly sway the appreciation of housing stock, how would my wife and I factor these considerations into our own decisions as we chose where to live? Put differently, how would our knowledge of social policy and impact influence our own housing and investment choices?

## LOCATION AND PERSONAL CHOICES

As I reviewed the literature for my research, these notions became more than theoretical. We were moving to start work at my university with a one-year-old daughter and another child due soon. We knew that the quality of the neighborhood schools, as measured by student outputs like test scores, would be an important consideration. On the other hand, as an ethnically diverse family, we were sensitive to the ethnic makeup of the school district.

Considering my ongoing research on neighborhood segregation, we wondered whether individual schools might show signs of unevenness. Sure enough, we found that they did. In line with expectations developed by my research, what we found was a relatively high degree of racial and income segregation across school districts, as well as marked differences in test scores.

Given our values around diversity, and the fact that a few neighborhoods would be considerably closer to my job, we were faced with alternatives that did not optimize all of our desires. We eventually pinpointed two communities of primary interest. The elementary schools located in both these neighborhoods were of similar size and student-teacher ratios and were located less than three miles from the university where we would both be spending a great deal of our time.

Poring through background data provided by the school system, we learned that the two elementary schools were actually quite proximal, so the travel question was moot.

Another indicator we looked at was the percentage of students who passed the Virginia Standards of Learning (SOL) tests. On this academic measure, Johnson scored below the state and the City of Charlottesville, while Venable performed comparably better.

We were faced with a dilemma. Both schools fit our desire to place our children within a diverse student body, racially and economically. They were similar in a number of important ways, and their profiles suggested that our children would attend school with some students who faced challenges and some who were advantaged. However, one appeared to offer the potential of a better start academically.

One of the challenges of having deep, research-based knowledge about how continuing segregation diminishes opportunities is a recognition of how your own choices might influence others. This was one occasion when there was some semblance of conflict between espoused values and lived ones. We were a couple deeply aware that individual choices, such as where to purchase a home, would certainly have an impact on our children, and very likely on others as well. Did we have a responsibility beyond our own family?

In the remainder of this chapter, I will focus on a financial institution whose efforts have influenced the economic fortunes of the geographic areas in which it operates. The example I share turns the lens toward a provocative question: How might the presence and services of a financial institution improve the lives of the unbanked *and* the values of real estate owners?

## AWARDS AS FACILITATORS OF CONNECTION

I first learned of the Latino Community Credit Union (LCCU) at the announcement of the winners of the Opportunity Finance Network (OFN), Wells Fargo/Wachovia NEXT Award in 2007. NEXT recognition, funded by the MacArthur Foundation and Wells Fargo, was designed to spotlight innovative, "new leadership" community development financial institutions (CDFIs), as opposed to the long-standing, large CDFIs that regularly received recognition for their efforts. More than just a "feel-good" acknowledgment, the award bestowed on the CDFI and its leadership both funding and recognition that could lead to media coverage, which in turn would certainly lead to follow-on funding. The notion behind the award was that it could catapult a nascent, emerging CDFI into the realm of the industry's leading organizations.

The 2007 OFN conference—the first of many I attended—took place in Miami. The NEXT award announcement featured a visual extravaganza of elaborate corporate marketing, complete with glossy videos of the award finalists, followed by a suspenseful, countdown-style reveal of the winner. The first-prize winner, LCCU, received a financial package totaling $5.5 million.

The LCCU's narrative provides a case study on financial innovation and spillover impact, specifically on surrounding community real estate values.

## AN EXUBERANT RECEPTION

I remember I was quite taken with the LCCU's representatives' acceptance speeches. As the award was announced, the audible eruption that followed was no less emotionally exuberant than for an Oscar or Grammy award. As CEO Luis Pastor took the stage to accept the award, he invited all of his team to join him, nearly half a dozen people in total. My sense was that this level of exuberance was atypical. It was certainly quite different from previous awards ceremonies I had attended in the finance industry, which tended toward perfunctory, prepared speeches by a single executive, a formal thank-you, a handshake, and a posed photo op.

## A CREDIT UNION FOUNDED TO STOP CRIME: THE LATINO COMMUNITY CREDIT UNION

North Carolina had a large and rapidly growing Latino population. I learned that, prior to my research, the rapid growth was due, in part, to an unskilled labor shortage that had begun in the mid-1980s. As manufacturing slowed and jobs shifted into services and construction industries, demand grew for the jobs left behind. As news of these supply gaps began to diffuse through social networks, immigrants began to move from entry point cities, like San Antonio or Los Angeles, to the southeastern United States. Employers came to recognize that native-born workers held "reservation" wage rates markedly higher than those demanded by immigrant workers.[8]

Immigrants were attractive to employers because they were perceived to be cheaper, more productive hires. In 2000, one North Carolina study captured their reasoning: "Time and time again, [employers] revealed their deeply held conviction that Hispanic workers—most notably Mexicans—have an excellent work ethic."[9]

The demand for these workers became so pronounced that North Carolina's employers began to recruit immigrant workers through the informal social networks of current workers and through advertisements placed in Spanish newspapers in cities like Houston and El Paso. These labor market demands fueled the growth of the local Latino population.

The organization that I would come to know as the LCCU was founded by a consortium of nonprofits: El Centro Hispano, the North Carolina State Employees' Credit Union (SECU), Self-Help Credit Union, and the North Carolina Minority Support Center. The impetus for its founding stemmed not only from the region's increasing immigrant population but also from a trend of violent crime. Many Latino immigrants—often carrying large sums of cash on their person—had become particularly vulnerable to muggings and robberies, especially on or around paydays when they would cash their checks.[10]

"There was a criminal element that knew that immigrants kept their money at home, under their mattresses, in coffee cans in the freezer, or in boxes in a closet," said John Herrera, a Latino community activist and early LCCU board member, "and they found that it was very easy to invade their homes and rob them. They knew that immigrants, because they feared the police, did not report these crimes."[11]

It became increasingly clear that one response to the problem could be a financial institution to serve the needs of the largely underbanked immigrant population—a proposition in contrast to many financial institutions, which are more often driven to innovate by the potential for economic returns. There was a growing sense of a need for a credit union for the immigrant population.

As the community in Durham, North Carolina, began to strategize a response, Self-Help Credit Union, one of the city's strongest voices in community development, concluded that it was not sufficiently equipped to take a leadership role in establishing the new depository. At least one reason was that Self-Help's strong, visible social and branding connection to Durham's low-income African American and white population was perceived as a barrier. Latino and immigrant populations did not see the institution as a welcoming one, or one for people like themselves. Even in retail banking, a sense of place matters.

Although they would not directly service this new consumer franchise, Self-Help's leadership agreed to lend personnel and logistic support to the effort. El Centro Hispano, a Durham nonprofit, helped recruit a membership base, maintained payroll services, and offered staff support, all funded by the North Carolina Minority Support

Center. The North Carolina State Employees Credit Union provided on-the-job training to the LCCU's initial team of employees, as well as operational and technical support. In addition to the four founding entities, the LCCU was capitalized with deposits from sixty-five institutions, including Duke University, Central Carolina Bank, and Bank of America. Its first branch in Durham opened in 2000.

LCCU's leadership recognized their pivotal role in bringing about lasting change beyond the customary range of credit union products and services. The institution offered financial education classes and no-cost educational seminars, funded by the National Endowment for Financial Education and the American Express Foundation, among others. Lessons were practical and broad-based, ranging from the how-tos of opening a savings account to buying a home and preparing taxes.

One innovation was the feature film *Angelica's Dreams*. Produced in 2007 with a grant from the Community Development Financial Institutions Fund, the film was a component of the LCCU's home-buyer education program and was screened locally as well as at independent film festivals in major U.S. cities. In 2010, the credit union released another targeted, feature-length film, *Roberto's Dreams*, about an immigrant couple's hope of starting a business. Its release coincided with a new CU product offering—microbusiness loans to expand or start a small enterprise.

In my conversations with Luis Pastor and his team, I gained a sense that there was a heightened energy given to expanding the LCCU's business in terms of members, number of locations, and range of services. Nevertheless, the executive team could not avoid becoming involved in larger, overarching policy matters because of the organization's expansion in a state dealing with rapid demographic change.

One example of this "shadow activism" led to death threats. In 2005, under federal pressure to tighten licensing laws, North Carolina required a social security number before it would issue a driver's license.[12] As a consequence, undocumented immigrants could not legally obtain a driver's license or drive a car.

Pastor and his team debated issuing credit cards to members as a way of countering these restrictions. Pastor recalled asking, "If we offer credit cards, should we add the card-holder's picture and signature digitally printed on the front? For credit union members who did not, or would not, be able to hold drivers' licenses, the cards could have the added benefit of avoiding public embarrassment when shop-keepers ask for photo identification."

He also shared that there had been considerable anti-immigrant backlash against the LCCU within the broader community, and he showed us a copy of a hate letter they had received: "Crime does not pay," the anonymous author began. "All you illegal immigrants have disrespected every law in America. Now you want to be rewarded for invading this country."

The remarkable letter goes on to describe the impact on American citizens: "*Millions* and *Millions* of U.S.A. citizens go hungry and families broken up because of cheap labor *slaves* sneaked in here and underminded citizen jobs causes a lot of heartache and pains [emphasis original]." The writer was mirroring a labor market study that described employers' rising preference for immigrant workers.

Pastor shared that the letter was just one of many. As I read it, I recognized how the simple act of providing financial services and a photo on a credit card could thrust an organization into larger political skirmishes.

Soon after launch, there was a sense that the need for an institution like the LCCU was also felt outside of Durham, and the organization quickly began to scale. In a decade of operation, the LCCU expanded to ten branches and 53,000 members, becoming one of the fastest-growing credit unions in the United States. Less than a year after the opening of the LCCU's Charlotte branch, the Charlotte-Mecklenburg police announced a 22.6 percent drop in reported armed robberies against Latinos. (This estimate was likely underreported.)

As the LCCU grew, key elements of the business model remained stable, including low fees ($10 to open a savings account); relatively minimal identification requirements (accepted from any country); and a range of financial products responsive to the evolving needs of clientele, such as depository accounts, several types of small consumer loans, credit builder loans, and remittance services.

In all of its locations, the organization welcomed Latino immigrant clientele by conducting business in Spanish by default—a courtesy designed to give the CU a more accessible ambience. According to Pastor and his team, the credit union's success in making clientele feel comfortable within its doors might have been the most important reason for the LCCU's fast growth. As the number of branches and members grew, so did the credit union's celebrity. In 2013, cofounder

John Herrera was honored at the White House as an "Immigrant Innovator Champion of Change."[13]

Plaudits for their work abounded, but as I learned more about the organization, I became increasingly interested in understanding the impact of their efforts, given the centrality of the discussion about immigration, segregation, and housing values. I wanted to know how its presence in the community influenced crime rates and how these in turn influenced housing appreciation. In the next section, I will report the results of those statistical analyses.

## THE INFLUENCE OF IMMIGRANT-SERVING CREDIT UNIONS ON HOUSING VALUES

Given the LCCU's rapid growth, multiple branches, and diversity of locations, I felt there was an opportunity to generate knowledge of best practices for financial services providers in other geographic locations that were considering whether to serve a fast-growing Latino population. However, I soon recognized an opportunity for another analysis altogether. We had the makings of what economists term a "natural experiment" that would allow us to examine the impact of the LCCU branches on their surrounding communities and turn the question on its head: Did the presence of the LCCU benefit the community as a whole, even non-Latinos?

During our team's background research, we found precious little statistically based research that illustrated the impact of financial institutions on nonfinancial outcomes like crime. We were convinced that the surprising reason for starting the LCCU would provide the basis for a novel analysis.

In an effort to shed light on the issue, a university colleague trained in economics, Kulwant Rai, joined me on this project. He set out to collect data that would allow us to undertake a multivariate analysis examining the cities where the LCCU branches had opened and the subsequent levels of reported robberies.

Apart from studying the relationship between robbery and violent crime and Latino- and immigrant-serving CU branches, we were also interested in understanding the follow-on effect of lowered crime on property values and the value of real estate longitudinally. Finally, we set out to determine whether, given the LCCU's rapid growth, it was taking on undue risks in its operations.

## THE ANALYTICAL APPROACH

As Kulwant and I started to assess the impact of the LCCU's branches on crime in their surrounding locale, we determined our first step would need to be comparing the number of reported robberies before the opening of a LCCU branch with the reported number after the opening. We developed the statistical model with a time-period lag to measure the effects of a branch after two years of operation. We reasoned that the effect of a new credit union branch would not be instantaneous and that any resulting drop in crime would occur after a period of time during which the newly operating branch penetrated the target population. This would take into account the time it took for the LCCU's services to diffuse, as customers opened accounts and built banking habits (and the corresponding time it would take for criminals to realize that formerly profiled targets were less attractive victims). Specifically, we were testing the hypothesis that Latinos and immigrants living in the LCCU service areas would, over time, become less likely to carry large amounts of cash or stash their savings within their homes.

To perform this analysis, we employed a research method known in economics literature as difference-in-difference methodology, which allows one to examine relative impact across places and over similar time chronologies. For example, we found that there were 1,131 robberies in Durham in 1999. In 2002, two years after the opening of the LCCU's first office in Durham, the number of robberies declined to 968. That is, over the three-year analysis period, the number of robberies declined by 163, or 14.4 percent.

This decrease, while promising, is insufficient as a sign of demonstrated impact. We recognized the need to adjust this fact for larger trends. Speaking analytically, we questioned whether robberies were falling across the entire state of North Carolina during the same period and, if so, whether they were falling at a similar rate. If that were the case, it would suggest the LCCU's presence might have had little real impact on the rate of robberies, and that the decline was the result of a larger statewide trend. To adjust for this possibility, we computed the mean number of robberies for all counties except Durham. Using these counties as a control group, we found that average robberies per county in North Carolina increased slightly, from 109 to 113 during the same period, 1999–2002, a 3.6 percent increase. Had Durham followed the larger pattern across the state, the number of robberies would have increased to 1,171 in 2002.

We concluded that Durham experienced a relative downtrend in robberies when compared to other North Carolina counties. Of course, there could be many other factors influencing the decline, such as region of the state, differences in underlying economies, education, policing, or others. Our finding was blunt at best, and we sought ways to increase our confidence.

We knew that after opening its first Durham location, the LCCU began increasing its presence in other counties. In 2001, the credit union opened its second office, in Charlotte, and a year later cut the ribbon on its third office, in Raleigh. In 2003, the LCCU opened its fourth and fifth offices in Greensboro and Fayetteville. Now, with five branches operating in different parts of the state, serving thousands of members, we could revisit the analysis to see if the finding for the initial branch applied to the others. To do this, we computed the difference-in-difference estimates for each of these counties.[14]

When we examined the five counties in which there were LCCU branches, we found that, with one exception—Guilford County, which had a 3.1 percent increase—all counties experienced the same relative decline in the number of robberies, ranging from 14.1 to 14.4 percent.

We recognized that these analyses were, again, rough and preliminary. Specifically, they did not include other factors that might influence the rate of robberies and violent crime. To adjust for this possibility, we analyzed the number of robberies in a multivariate fixed-effect regression framework using panel data for each county in North Carolina over a far longer period, 1980–2008. We included a few key factors: the time-lagged number of robberies, the number of sworn officers per thousand residents, the county's Latino population, and a variable intended to measure the impact of an LCCU branch opening (also known as a "dummy" variable).

At this point, I should share a bit of our logic concerning these variables. We considered that using the lag in the number of robberies was warranted under the assumption that the number of active criminals would not vary from one year to the next unless they were arrested, charged, and ultimately incarcerated. The number of sworn police officers per thousand residents was an included variable because we reasoned that relative increases in the number of law enforcement agents should deter criminals (and the impact of police presence would be relative to population size). We also included a control variable for the size of each county's Latino population to determine the impact of overall growth or retraction in the size of the local population.

The results of our statistical model are presented in table 6.1. The multivariate regression had impressive explanatory power, indicating that 98 percent of the variation in number of robberies was explained by variations in the variables used in our model.

We also noted some counterintuitive findings. For example, the number of sworn officers per thousand residents was statistically insignificant, implying that differences in their number did not significantly influence the number of robberies per county. The variable that measured the time lag in the number of robberies was highly statistically significant. The impact of the size of the Latino population was also positive and highly significant, perhaps implying that criminals were indeed targeting Latino populations.

Our analysis involved another question: Would the opening of an LCCU branch have a statistically significant impact on robberies and violent crime in these counties and, if so, in what direction and at what magnitude? We found that the dummy variable that captured

TABLE 6.1
Regression of Robberies for Counties in North Carolina (1998–2008)

|  | Robberies |
| --- | --- |
| Intercept | 60.96 *** |
|  | (0.00) |
| Robberies (t–1) | 0.47 *** |
|  | (0.00) |
| Latino population | 0.002 *** |
|  | (0.00) |
| Sworn officers per 1,000 | –0.61 *** |
|  | (0.71) |
| LCCU dummy | –57,23 *** |
|  | (0.00) |
| Fixed effects for counties |  |
| R2 | 0.98 |

P-values are given in parentheses below coefficient estimates. ***, **, * denote significance at the 1 percent, 5 percent, or 10 percent level, respectively.

the opening of an LCCU branch was statistically significant, implying that the LCCU branch openings led to declines in the number of
robberies.

We were also interested in examining what might be called second-
order effects—that is, would increases in violent crime slow or depress
increases in real estate property values? We hypothesized that households living in proximity to intermittent sparks of violent crime would
desire to move elsewhere, and that those considering purchasing in
these areas would review local statistics to determine prevailing crime
rates. Taken together and in large numbers, these factors could reduce
home prices.

## AN INVERSE RELATIONSHIP: HIGHER
## PROPERTY VALUES = MORE CRIME?

Once again, we reasoned that any relationship between crime and
property values would take time to be revealed in altered behavior on
the part of home purchasers. Ultimately, we believed that our lagged-
time methodology would account for increases or decreases in crime
rates, and their relationship to property values. If we assumed that
the incidence and perception of crime risk influences the interests of
potential buyers—and thus, home price appreciation—we could also
assume other factors, such as population growth and expenditures on
roads and public transportation.

Our sense was that increases in population would positively correlate with appreciation in property values, indicating a rising demand
for housing. The per capita income of an area would also positively
correlate with property values, as higher levels of income suggested
greater buying power.

We also knew that families make choices across neighborhoods
based on amenities, such as access to major roadways and, in some
cases, mass transportation. Additionally, we knew that public expen-
diture on roadways and transportation is frequently associated with
other public amenities such as parks, schools, and libraries. While there
could be others, we felt that these would collectively serve as a viable
impact estimation strategy, based on data availability and the need for a
model to account for all of these factors simultaneously. We employed
a modeling approach known as a random effects regression model.

We used this method because it allows us to account for unmeasured differences in each county, as well as the variation among counties with respect to real estate values.

In sum, our approach was to statistically examine the yearly taxable real estate values (TREV) of all counties of North Carolina from 1998 to 2008 based on the factors we had hypothesized as having possible influence on values: the time-lagged number of robberies, population size, per capita income, public roadway expenditures (PRE), and a variable capturing the overall upward or downward trend in housing values. We used a prior year time lag because we anticipated that property values would respond to changes in each of these variables with some degree of recency.

As seen in table 6.2, all of the variables we hypothesized are highly statistically significant, and the overall statistical model has striking explanatory power. Our model and its variables account for 98 percent of all variation in North Carolina property values during the study

TABLE 6.2

Regression of Taxable Real Estate Value for Counties in North Carolina (1998–2008)

|  | Taxable real estate value ($000) |
| --- | --- |
| Intercept | 191,000,000*** |
|  | (0.00) |
| Robberies (t–1) | –7,460*** |
|  | (0.00) |
| Population (t–1) | 110*** |
|  | (0.00) |
| Per capita income (t–1) | 275*** |
|  | (0.71) |
| Trend | –100,719 *** |
|  | (0.00) |
| Transportation expenditure | 0.026 *** |
|  | (0.00) |
| Random effects |  |
| R2 | 0.98 |

*Note:* P-values are given in parentheses below coefficient estimates. ***, **, * denote significance at the 1 percent, 5 percent, or 10 percent level, respectively.

period. The analysis indicates that the variables representing population size, per capita income, and transportation expenditures positively affect the value of real estate, while the number of robberies depresses the value of real estate (both with a one-year lag). We were surprised to find that, controlling for all of these factors, the overall trend for real estate values during the study period was negative.

Taken together, these findings appear to indicate that the opening of a Latino-serving LCCU branch accompanies a decline in robberies. To put this into perspective, for the years 2001 to 2008, the findings show an approximate 4.2 percent decrease per year in the average number of robberies committed in counties where the LCCU established a branch location. In addition, our analysis implies that LCCU branch openings positively contributed to the appreciation of property values in proximal neighborhoods. The reported decreased incidence of robberies resulted in a nearly 3.8 percent average annual increase in property value (2001 to 2008) for the counties in which the LCCU established branches.

The data on robberies and property values strongly suggest that, by 2008, LCCU establishments had contributed to the appreciation of $9.8 billion in taxable real estate value. These findings imply that explicitly targeting the unbanked for service produces benefits not only for the unbanked households but also for law enforcement (through reduced policing load) and the community at large (through public safety, property appreciation). By focusing on higher property values, we measured one specific benefit to the general population, but we could well imagine others, such as heightened community engagement and civic affiliation as well as less income insecurity.

## OKAY, BUT IS IT PRUDENTLY MANAGED?

There was still one nagging unanswered question: Was the LCCU financially sound? If a financial institution deploying a mission-based model is not financially viable, then we would anticipate that replicating its practices would be unlikely. Diffusion across the sector would be highly improbable. Given the LCCU's rapid growth rate, we were particularly interested in whether the organization was taking on undue risks.

We decided that the best way to approach this question was to develop a peer group of similar financial institutions established at the same time (2000) and then examine their progress and financial health over time. We identified five peer credit unions opened in 2000, plus one (Crow Wing Power Credit Union) established in 1999. These organizations were of similar size and capital structure at their outset.

Table 6.3 illustrates that, during the period from 2001 through 2009, the LCCU experienced relatively strong growth in key financial variables, including assets, liabilities, loans, and deposits, when compared to its peer group.

We were reminded that the LCCU had built its franchise on servicing primarily "high-risk" clients: immigrants, low-income clients, and minority members. According to its Impact Statement, this clientele comprised 97 percent of the LCCU's 53,000 members, of whom 75 percent had no prior banking experience. Given this profile, we were interested in understanding the sources of the LCCU's income. The table also illustrates that the LCCU was the second highest among the seven peer institutions in generating income and producing margin gains.

TABLE 6.3
LCCU Comparison: Margin and Income, 2009

| | Operating income | Net margin | Net interest margin | Fee income | Fee income / member |
|---|---|---|---|---|---|
| LCCU, North Carolina | 5,666 | 3,460 | 2,911 | 520 | 0.01 |
| Crow Wing Power CU, Minnesota | 1,266 | 1,264 | 1,186 | 49 | 0.01 |
| Church Koinonia FCU, Tennessee | 122 | 122 | 106 | 16 | 0.00 |
| New Mount Zion Baptist Church CU, Tennessee | 106 | 93 | 88 | 4 | 0.01 |
| Permaculture CU, New Mexico | 301 | 215 | 173 | 42 | 0.04 |
| MemberSource CU, Texas | 9,113 | 9,498 | 6,667 | 1,513 | 0.07 |
| Mount Pleasant Baptist Church FCU, Washington | 8 | 3 | 3 | 0 | 0.00 |

*Note*: Numbers in thousands of dollars

Of course, we recognized that another common concern when serving low-income members is the high risk of default and delinquency rates. We examined whether the LCCU's clients exposed the institution to higher risks compared to its peers by searching for evidence of these risks in the ratio of nonperforming assets to loans, and loan loss to loans.

We found these risk ratios were not the highest among the credit unions analyzed. The LCCU, at 2.85 percent nonperforming loans, was performing much better than New Mount Zion Baptist Church, at 12.62 percent, but worse than Crow Wing Power Company, at 0.13 percent. Therefore, at least one conclusion is that the LCCU was not overly exposed to default risk compared to its peers. For a national comparison during the period of our study, the rate of nonperforming loans for credit unions was 1.75 percent.[15]

Our review of the statistical analyses led us to conclude that the LCCU was producing average profits, in line with peers. It was not overly exposed to default risk, and it was adding members at the fastest rate among its credit union peers. Taken together, we felt it safe to conclude that the LCCU had successfully implemented an innovative banking model that provided a potentially replicable example for the business community at large in serving minority and low-income members.

I had no idea when I saw Luis Pastor exuberantly leap onto the stage at the OFN conference in 2007 that he and his team would offer both a rich narrative and an opportunity to statistically test some common questions about servicing low-income financial consumers. Just as important, they offered noteworthy confirmation that, while generating profits, their innovative efforts were beneficial to their customers, to their communities, and, in a ripple effect, to the economic fortunes of nonmember residents. They had demonstrably affected the sense of place for the LCCU's members and nonmembers alike. This was, for me, a far-reaching achievement in support of the rationale for expanded, rather than exclusive, models of financial services.

## OUR SENSE OF PLACE

As to our home search, we chose a home in Charlottesville a short walk from the University of Virginia's Rotunda, designed by Thomas

Jefferson. The house was nestled into a cul de sac of fewer than two dozen bungalow-style homes. There is a neighborhood association, the Kellytown Association, and there is also a history: in 1800, John H. Craven bought what was known as the Rose Hill Estate. Craven moved to the area to manage Thomas Jefferson's 540-acre Tufton farm.

Over time, the area became less of a farm and without slave labor, the land was eventually divided and sold into parcels by Craven's descendants. After the Civil War, newly freed Black families settled on the upper portion of this strip, establishing mini-neighborhoods that are now known as Kellytown and Tinsleytown. Our neighborhood is racially integrated, though overwhelmingly filled with academics. Two of our three children were born while living in this home, and all of our children have attended the high-quality and diverse neighborhood public schools (including Venable Elementary). We've also enjoyed the knowledge that the land we live on was once the property of newly freed men and women.

# CHAPTER SEVEN

# What Ethnic Hairstyling and Credit Unions Have in Common

A FEW years ago, I needed to look for a new barbershop. One obvious step—to perform a web search—might provide some sense of the operators in town, but would have one big limitation. I couldn't screen for an important feature: whether the establishment was what I would call a "Black-serving" barbershop. I knew from personal experience that often the places where we get our haircuts are segregated along racial and ethnic lines.[1]

This is a practice based on preferences. All licensed barbers and cosmetologists in Virginia have to pass both a written and a practical exam, demonstrating both knowledge and ability to cut hair within a broad range of hair types and styles that cut across ethnicities.[2] Put differently, there is only one license issued, and it does not vary by race or ethnicity.

The "color line" in barbering has existed in the United States at least since the mid-1800s.[3] In the antebellum period, one of the accepted occupations for both free and enslaved Blacks was barbering and hair care. In fact, many enslaved barbers gained their freedom through the wages they earned cutting the hair of Blacks and whites.

After the Civil War, many became entrepreneurs in the barbering trade because—unlike unionized, relatively well-compensated trades such as blacksmithing, carpentry, and construction—there were relatively few barriers to entry. In many cities, Black barbers gained a reputation for providing competent, comfortable service, and these barbers found demand among white patrons.[4]

As these tastes among whites developed over time, some of the more economically successful and politically powerful Black entrepreneurs in cities like Atlanta, Richmond, and Durham were proprietors of barbershops. What is notable about these entrepreneurs is that although they were Black, and their staffs also were primarily Black, Black patrons were not served in their establishments. One prominent example of this dichotomy is Zora Neal Hurston. Years before she became one of the preeminent authors of the Harlem Renaissance, Hurston earned money as a manicurist for white politicians, bankers, and members of the press who patronized a popular, Black-owned, Washington, D.C., barbershop.[5]

So, more than a century after the introduction of color-line barbering, why was I seeking a Black barbershop? Was I practicing discrimination? Surely. My personal belief is that segregation—residential and social—is a pernicious institution that causes serious harm. Why, then, was I seeking a "Black" barbershop?

Some scholars would argue that expressed preferences for same-race providers in personal services are not unusual, and that they may be a historical legacy. In helping to explain preferences for same-race providers, in personal services and indeed banking services, I will share the story of a credit union that built its business by serving the needs of recently immigrated Asian customers. The Northeast Community Federal Credit Union (NCFCU), located in San Francisco, was the subject of a memorable fieldwork visit.

## NCFCU: SERVING THE "SINKS" IN THE CITY BY THE BAY

Through my networks, I had been asking around for a leading Asian-serving financial institution that had faced challenges because of acculturation and outmigration from cities. NCFCU, a San Francisco community development credit union (CDCU) and its CEO, Lily Lo, were commonly suggested. My team and I visited Lo at a critical point in the organization's development and found that the NCFCU story offered a richer and deeper set of insights than I had hoped.

Our visit took place over a few sunny days in May 2011, and we interviewed Lo as she moved through the city, taking buses and walking, her preferred modes of travel.[6] We had a chance to listen and experience just a bit of her world. Sometimes it is helpful to be reminded with facts-on-the-ground confirmation about things you understand but do not fully "know" until you see and experience them.

I knew then and still know that there was considerable Asian within-group inequality in America. Our research at the time confirmed what I had suspected: pockets of concentrated poverty in California's Asian population. Organizations like NCFCU committed to working with recently immigrated, low-income populations, despite the fact that they could alternatively choose to serve the executive class populations just a few miles away in fast-growth technology firms, many staffed and led by Asians. This field visit was a helpful reminder that there are significant challenges in many communities, even those that abut Silicon Valley.

## CHINESE IN SAN FRANCISCO: A STRUGGLE FOR INCLUSION

In the mid-1800s, the discovery of gold made California the undisputed go-to destination for migrants from the eastern part of the country and for immigrants from around the world seeking wealth. A good number of the latter came from China.[7] As with many early migratory patterns, early settlers were primarily men without families, which created an early gender imbalance among ethnic Chinese in the area.

In terms of status, Chinese immigrants were essentially of the same social position as African Americans (some of whom were ex-slaves), Native Americans, and other recent European immigrants like Italians and Irish. As they grew in number, the threat of economic competition with incumbent residents led to legislation to impede Chinese economic progress, much like Jim Crow laws in the South. By 1870, San Francisco had passed anti-Chinese ordinances to curtail housing and employment options.[8] Chinese were even barred from California's fishing industry; given the city's bayside location, this was an economically crippling limitation.[9] As with many newly immigrated groups that find blocked mobility, some early Chinese immigrants opened restaurants, dry goods stores, or laundries, and these firms primarily targeted and served white customers.[10]

There was treatment that today I can only describe as terrorism. For example, in 1873, the city passed the "Queue Ordinance." Chinese immigrant men, especially those from the Manchu region, wore their hair in long braids, or pigtails, called "queues." The practice was not only culturally supported, but was even part of Manchu law. Soon after passage of the ordinance, gangs would attack Chinese men wearing queues, cut them off, and parade around with them as trophies. In China, cutting off someone's queue was illegal and, from a personal standpoint, would result in great disgrace for the victim.[11]

Because of legal covenants restricting their access to residential areas and the fear of violence, an enclave in the neighborhoods of North Beach and Telegraph Hill began to be known as "Chinatown." Many of its residents were from the province of Canton—also known as Guangdong.

As Chinatown grew, organizations were founded with the explicit mission of supporting residents who, understandably, were feeling under siege, economically and socially. As early as 1859, the "Chinese School" operated in Chinatown, establishing segregated education in response to the prohibition against Chinese children attending San Francisco's public schools with white students.

In 1882, the Chinese Exclusion Act dictated a ten-year freeze on Chinese immigration and prohibited Chinese from becoming naturalized citizens.[12] To limit reentry into the United States, in 1888, the Scott Act forbade the return of Chinese laborers who left the country to visit China or travel elsewhere abroad. This law was challenged in the Supreme Court in *Chae Chan Ping v. United States* but was upheld in 1889.

Introduced by a California congressman, the Geary Act of 1892 instituted another ten-year freeze on Chinese immigration and required all Chinese to carry a certificate of residence. If they were found without these documents, they could be arrested or even deported. (One means by which to obtain the certificate required the testimony of "at least one credible white witness" that a Chinese individual was a confirmed resident.)[13]

These discriminatory acts were repealed in 1943; however, quotas were established specifying that no more than 105 visas per year would be granted to ethnic Chinese of any nationality.[14] More than twenty years later, President Lyndon Johnson signed the Hart-Cellar

Immigration Act of 1965, releasing Chinese desiring to immigrate to the United States from long-standing barriers and quotas.[15] With formerly closed entry now open, Chinese migration to the United States grew rapidly; many immigrants settled in San Francisco, and when they arrived, many chose Chinatown, at least initially.

As time went on, some Chinese were able to move to the city's outlying suburbs, while Chinatown itself continued to flourish, at least in population density. Beginning in the late 1970s and continuing through the 1990s, there was a clear movement away from San Francisco's traditional "gateway neighborhoods" to the city's outlying areas.[16]

As acculturation increased and segregation by ethnicity declined, Chinatown was no longer the business or social magnet for many of San Francisco's ethnic Chinese. During this transitional period in which a growing proportion of ethnic Chinese settled into surrounding suburbs, Chinatown nevertheless remained an important location for "cultural" consumption and identity. Although many suburban dwellers left because they preferred not to pay the high cost of living in their historic neighborhood, their Chinese identity remained an important part of their lives, and they returned regularly for cultural festivals, Chinese holidays, grocery shopping, banking, and other services (even hairstyling).

A key element of Chinatown's development was its banking and financial services presence, which allowed recent immigrants to build savings, take on mortgages, and get business loans. This financial presence cannot be overlooked as a key element of Chinatown's eventual draw for non-Chinese. As housing prices rose across San Francisco, home buyers who, years earlier, would have felt uncomfortable in an ethnic Chinese neighborhood began to find reasons to buy homes there. And as interest from affluent home buyers accelerated during the 1970s, so did worries about sustaining affordable housing for incumbent families. Chinatown was noteworthy in deterring displacement and gentrification by using subsidized housing, tenant protections, and community-based organizing.[17]

## A STROLL THROUGH THE NEIGHBORHOOD

An accountant by profession, Lily Lo was born in Indonesia; in 1974, her family immigrated to the United States. Like many of her staff, Lo is ethnically Chinese. She first gained experience at a credit union when she was hired to manage the Lee Federal Credit Union, which served members of the Lee Family Association, of which her husband was a member.

The San Francisco Lee Federal Credit Union had been chartered in 1964. To be a member, a person must have or be descended from someone with the surname Lee. By 2010, the San Francisco Lee Family Credit Union had grown to $12 million in assets and nearly nine hundred members. Although there were other Chinese surname associations and credit unions in San Francisco, its basis for membership was still novel:

> When it comes to field of membership, the Lee Federal Credit Union may be one of a kind. Unlike community chartered credit unions open to members in a wide geographic area or credit unions that have a burgeoning list of select employee groups, Lee FCU is open only to members whose surname is Lee. Forget about film director Spike Lee being a member, or the family of the late singer Peggy Lee or rocker Tommy Lee. Even descendants of Confederate Gen. Robert E. Lee and Henry David Lee of Lee jeans fame don't qualify. The only Lees at this credit union must have the Chinese surname of Lee or be related to one of those Lees.[18]

San Francisco has a high incidence of financial institutions, and not far from the NCFCU headquarters was Chinatown's Grant Avenue, with a cluster of major interstate banks.[19] Their large, ornate brandings were interspersed among the colorful awnings of small shops selling memorabilia for tourists and exotic foods like whole roasted ducks. As we walked, Lo mentioned that while these banks were proximal, they were not necessarily competition because of differences in mission and service.

To a significant degree, the NCFCU's membership was composed of low-income families, recently immigrated, with modest English skills. Some had nascent or nonexistent past relationships with financial institutions, and others had poor credit or none at all. "These banks don't want my clients," she mentioned as we walked past one institution that often referred borrowers who did not meet its standards to the nearby NCFCU. This was a direct reference to the economic inequality within San Francisco's Asian and Chinese communities.

During our walk, Lo recalled a story, related by a mentor, that helped shape her dedication to credit unions in general, and to the mission of the NCFCU in particular. "A young man wants to start a business, so he goes to his uncle and asks him for money. The young man's uncle wants to help his nephew, but he says, 'That money is my life's savings, to support me when I am old. I can't give that to you.' But if the uncle puts his money in a credit union with the others in the community, then the nephew can get a loan for his business from the credit union, and in this way, the uncle can help his nephew."

"I was making good money [before coming to credit unions]," Lo explained, "but I wasn't happy with what I was doing. Working here, helping people, teaching them how to balance a checkbook, that made me feel good about myself."

Hiring ethnic Chinese had been an effective NCFCU strategy because many members did not speak English well and required the services of staff who were both bilingual and familiar with their cultural preferences. Some members were even illiterate, and needed the credit union to extend services beyond general retail banking. For example, it offered assistance in preparing annual tax returns, at multiple sites, through the government's Volunteer Income Tax Assistance (VITA) program.[20] With a reservoir of established trust, it was not uncommon for VITA volunteers to field questions on topics such as immigration or obtaining a marriage license, in addition to tax issues. Lo recognized that, for some, NCFCU was a "way station" for members in transition. It was not unusual for members to move on to larger, branded, "mainstream" banks after rebuilding their credit and developing good banking habits at NCFCU.

This was one of the overarching themes in many ethnic-serving financial institutions. Given their mission to provide products to those often overlooked, these institutions knowingly operated their branches in communities that many of their customers would eventually leave. Acculturation and suburbanization were, in many ways, good things—indicators of rising income and wealth—but could also fuel eagerness for more sophisticated products that were not offered by early financial providers. For the NCFCU team and similar organizations, remaining relevant and consistent with their mission was a continuing challenge.

## MEETING A FOUNDER

Although it had opened its first office in the heart of Chinatown, NCFCU board president Michael Chan liked to say that the idea to start the organization came from the streets of Washington, D.C. In the late 1970s, when he was a local real estate developer and president of Asian, Inc., a nonprofit organization, Chan was active in representing the concerns of Asian American communities to national policy makers.

On one trip to Washington, Chan picked up a brochure about starting a community development credit union, and he immediately recognized that such an institution would be valuable. There were plenty of banks in Chinatown, but as Lily Lo had explained, many of them bypassed immigrant and low-income account holders who did not qualify for credit from a mainstream bank. Chan envisioned that a community development credit union could fill that lending gap and target the unbanked.

Back home, he collected two hundred deposit pledges before NCFCU was chartered in 1981. Chan explained: "There is no concept of a credit union in China, but culturally, there were similar institutions in the Asian-American community such as Korean *kye* clubs and Chinese *hui* lending circles.[21] Asian, Inc., already supported trade associations in Chinatown, but the credit union was a way to help individuals, those who worked in printing shops, groceries, restaurants."

A Community Services Administration and Community Development Block Grant provided capital for operating expenses, including hiring the credit union's first manager. "In the first month, we had only $24,000 in deposits," recalled Chan, "because at the time, credit unions were not allowed to collect funds before receiving their charter."

From these modest beginnings, the credit union initially offered basic passbook savings accounts and small signature loans.[22] Certificates of deposit (CDs) followed, and by 1983, NCFCU also made small business loans. In 1988, the credit union achieved financial self-sufficiency, and second mortgage loans were added to the product mix; these were generally taken out by families to finance their children's education or to provide capital for small businesses. The credit union began originating first mortgages for real estate purchases in 1997.

Chan had an "internal desire to achieve and not fail. I like seeing something grow, and I like helping the diversity of people." As the initiator of NCFCU's strategic activities, Chan acknowledged that Lo's practical, managerial sense had been important to "temper [his] pursuit of [too many] things." I have noted elsewhere that this tension to "double-down" on social impact had to be consistently balanced against the reality of the balance sheet. Financial institutions operating in development settings needed vigilance about the risks and relevant areas of expertise and capability.

## EXTENDING SERVICES BEYOND COETHNICS: A BRANCH IN THE TENDERLOIN?

By the late 1990s, NCFCU management recognized that the credit union had many Asian members living in the Tenderloin neighborhood of downtown San Francisco. Should NCFCU consider an expansion by opening a branch in the Tenderloin and engage the area's non-Chinese population? At the time, the Tenderloin was nearly devoid of regulated financial institutions.

There were many reasons to doubt the wisdom of moving into the Tenderloin and risking the unique strategic approach and financial health of a financial institution collectively owned by its member base. At first glance, this move would appear a mismatch. Gary Kamiya, writing in *San Francisco* magazine, described the Tenderloin's unique profile:

It is the strangest neighborhood in the metropolis—maybe the strangest on the planet. In the midst of one of the most affluent cities in the world, it is a 40-square-block island of poverty and squalor. Its streets teem with the people the Chamber of Commerce does not want you to see: the ragged, the mentally ill, the addicted, the paroled, and the homeless. While all big cities have such denizens, they are usually scattered here and there—not clustered right next to the most valuable real estate in town. . . . Make a wrong turn coming out of the Hilton Hotel, and in a few seconds you feel like you're in the South Bronx—or Calcutta.[23]

The comparative histories of Chinatown and the Tenderloin are, in some ways, an illustration of the importance of community-based social capital and resource mobilization.[24] Until the 1970s, the Tenderloin was more of a location than a community because it was bereft of neighborhood institutions or organized civic groups. People lived in the many single-resident hotels and were either working-class or elderly on a fixed income. Traditional families with children were uncommon. In the 1970s, efforts by the city to clear out the tenant hotels to build more profitable tourist hotels and commercial real estate were met with forceful resistance from Tenderloin residents, spurring organized protests by groups of housing activists, community organizers, and early gay-rights advocates.

It was also around this time that the Tenderloin experienced an influx of immigrants from Southeast Asia, including Vietnamese, Laotians, and Cambodians, many of whom were ethnically Chinese. This wave of immigrants arrived with families in tow, and they chose the Tenderloin despite its unsavory reputation because of the relatively inexpensive housing prices; by this point, the area was one of the most affordable districts in San Francisco. The arrival of immigrant families, the rise of anti-developer/pro-tenant sentiments, and the establishment of neighborhood groups and a local newspaper, the *Tenderloin Times*, provided the area the makings of a cohesive communal identity for the first time—a community some might see as an oppositional one. [25]

By the late 1990s, San Francisco politically opened its arms to immigrant and LGBT populations, as did a growing cadre of the area's technology firms, venture capitalists, and banking institutions. The economic and technological changes considerably altered the composition of neighborhoods in the city. The demand for labor to staff those industries was an important element of the city's continued growth and progress. However, as highly educated and well-compensated workers flocked to San Francisco, concerns about gentrification turned into outright protests. The city became progressively less affordable for low-income workers and their families, creating concerns of displacement. The Tenderloin remained one of the few localities that didn't quickly and completely gentrify, at least in comparison to other areas.

At least one reason for the slow pace of development, or protection from gentrification, may have been that many homes in the Tenderloin would require considerable alteration to meet the standards and "must-haves" of affluent buyers.

Randy Shaw, executive director of the Tenderloin Housing Clinic, summed up residents' opposition to gentrification in structural terms: "It is impossible for the Tenderloin ever to be gentrified." His reason? The housing stock. "The gentry don't want to live in places without kitchens or bathrooms."[26]

Poor-quality housing stock that was resistant to conversion would mean relatively few mortgage loans. This, combined with an income composition that leaned toward low-income workers or residents living on social security or disability income, would make the area especially unattractive as a place for a credit union to seek new members.

Despite deterrents, NCFCU's leadership remained open to the notion of a Tenderloin branch, and they approached Patelco—a much older, larger credit union also looking at the area—about forming a partnership.[27] The two credit unions agreed that NCFCU would move forward, with support from Patelco, in marketing the branch to attract new members and nonmember deposits onto NCFCU's balance sheet. The CDFI Fund of the U.S. Treasury also awarded $720,000 in support of the branch—$320,000 in grant funding and $400,000 in deposits. The Tenderloin branch opened in 1999 with space in the Tenderloin Neighborhood Development Corporation (TNDC).

As time went on, the NCFCU team learned a great deal about serving its new clientele, which encompassed veterans, low-income residents, the mentally ill, and the elderly. A number of those living in nearby Mercy Housing were elderly Chinese, and social workers at the property often called upon NCFCU's staff to translate for them in a range of situations, including matters that had nothing to do with financial services. In our interview, Lo said that she believed NCFCU's services had helped change the behaviors of Tenderloin branch members and area residents. Membership required just one form of identification and no address, which effectively allowed homeless people to join. NCFCU required a deposit of just $5 to open a savings account, and foreign identification could be used.

In recognizing some of the challenges of Tenderloin residents, NCFCU also decided to limit cash withdrawals to $50 per day at its branches, although members could withdraw up to $500 from a "share branch" at no cost to themselves because NCFCU paid the transactions fees.[28] "Our members don't need to carry more cash than that," Lo explained.

The credit union began offering direct-deposit services in 1999, meaning that members living on disability, social security, or welfare could avoid paying the fees charged by check cashers as well as avoid the dangers of carrying large amounts of cash on their person.

When we visited the Tenderloin branch, Lo recalled one member who was recently out of rehab, employed, and using NCFCU's direct-deposit services. Lo beamed when she told others about how this man accomplished something he had never thought he was capable of prior to his relationship with the credit union—the purchase of an automobile. However, he too had "graduated" and was now being served by a larger bank. During our visit, Lo explained why the expansion to the Tenderloin had been a mission-driven risk. It turned out that although it was not a coethnic neighborhood, the Tenderloin had many of the constituent elements of the credit union's Chinatown membership. Both areas were populated by lower-income, challenged populations, and within each locality, there were unique, nuanced issues that needed to addressed (e.g., intimacy, trust, culture, range of services).

## SOUTH OF MARKET?

After seeing steady business in the Tenderloin for more than six years, NCFCU looked to SoMa, or South of Market, an area adjacent to the Tenderloin (which was also known as North of Market). An LGBT enclave since the 1960s, SoMa began gentrifying in the 1980s as the spread of AIDS prompted the City of San Francisco to close bathhouses and to regulate bars that had previously been social hubs for the gay community. The opening of the Moscone Convention Center brought new traffic to SoMa, and the San Francisco Museum of Modern Art, opened in 1995, became a magnet for galleries and other art spaces, including the Yerba Buena Center for the Arts.

After 2000, technology companies began opening headquarters in the area as warehouses and loft spaces were transformed into sleek offices. NCFCU had been offered a potential branch site in Plaza Apartments, San Francisco's first "green" low-income housing facility, located at the southern end of SoMa, bordering the Mission district and the Tenderloin. The Ford Foundation had extended $100,000 in grant funding to outfit the storefront that would serve as the new credit union branch. At the time, urban revitalization was also reaching the district as upscale restaurants and trendy art spaces slowly spread south. By opening a SoMa branch, Lo reasoned, the credit union could serve the area's restaurant workers as well as immigrant populations and the residents of nearby Plaza Apartments.

As we continued our walking interview, we encountered crowds doing their end-of-the-day shopping at the open-air grocery markets lining the streets. Lo explained that in the late afternoon and early evening, the streets of Chinatown swelled with people who came to the district to purchase groceries. They made this trek before heading home because Chinatown's vendors were known to have lower prices than other retailers, and, as important, their selection was culturally relevant to Asian shoppers. The markets also provided important social connections for Chinese who did not live in the neighborhood but who stopped to shop for dinner before boarding the Bay Area Rapid Transit (BART) trains or buses back to the suburbs. Lo was again illustrating the importance of understanding the particular needs of her members, and how this critical cultural recognition was informed by coethnic knowledge and sensitivity.

As we walked, Lo also shopped. Her gaze rested for a moment on the prickly-looking dragon fruit stacked in rows. The rest of us were unfamiliar with the fruit, and Lo told us the spiny pinkish rind concealed sweetness and soft, white meat, but one would never guess that without first cutting into the fruit. With her eye on the colorful array of vendors' wares as we wove our way through the shoppers, Lo discussed recent conversations she had had with Chan about the potential new branch in rapidly gentrifying SoMa. Both Lo and Chan were eager to serve the low-income SoMa community; however, there were concerns. The credit union's expansion into the Tenderloin had shown early indicators of membership growth. Lo felt that the challenge in a SoMa branch wouldn't be a technical one, or based on her team's competence. Rather, she worried about a change in the NCFCU business model by moving away from their traditional lower-income, immigrant, and largely underserved clientele.

"In Chinatown and the Tenderloin, we know our borrowers. We translate for them, help them write checks. In a community like ours, you can't necessarily underwrite by the standards of the big banks," she said, referring to the greater use of relationship banking practices. She wondered whether her staff would be able to establish the same rapport with SoMa clients who would likely be Spanish-speaking. All NCFCU staff members were bilingual, but they spoke Cantonese, not Spanish. If she did not have the proper team at the time, could she find the right staff to meet the needs of this new target population?

Lo and her board of directors faced a difficult choice, even with grant funds in hand. As a nonprofit financial institution, the credit union was partially reliant upon grant funding from philanthropies and government agencies to underwrite new ventures. Would a SoMa branch attract the steady stream of members NCFCU had seen in

Chinatown and the Tenderloin? Or would the gritty neighborhood make potential members wary of transacting their finances in an office located there?

The daunting list of risks was contrasted with the issue of mission. Lo knew there was a need for regulated financial institutions in the district, but did the potential to bring in SoMa's unbanked population pose too great a threat to NCFCU's existing membership? As NCFCU considered the options, SoMa's gentrification was proceeding with far less protest than other areas of San Francisco, in part because it had far fewer residents and community organizations to give voice to incumbent interests. A failed location could imperil the operations of the credit union as a whole, putting the financial stability of its 1,600 current members at risk. For Lo, these variables brought to mind her mentor's story of the young man seeking funds from his uncle. Would this action risk losing the funds of a number of "uncles"? Because most members were from lower-income families, such a loss would be particularly painful.

In the end, NCFCU did open a branch in SoMa, on Howard Street, just a short walk from an Intercontinental Hotel and the largest convention center in San Francisco, the Moscone Center. Nearby, outdoor cafes, a children's museum, art galleries, and wine bars draw a cross section of the population. As SoMa continued to gentrify, the NCFCU team successfully met the service needs of both the area's incumbent Latino population and the incoming, more educated and affluent residents.

## COLOR-LINE BARBERS AND
## MINORITY DEPOSITORIES

I first became aware of the work of the economist Gary Dymski through his writing about the decline of retail banking in his book *The Bank Merger Wave: The Economic Causes and Social Consequences of Financial Consolidation.*[29]

I began looking for other citations of his work and came across a series of papers that examined Asian American– and Black-serving banks in Los Angeles. Dymski termed these *ethnobanks* and defined them as "banks that are owned or controlled by members of ethnic minority groups and which primarily provide financial services to ethnic businesses and residents."[30]

Dymski describes an informational asymmetry in which banks, as providers of credit, avoid serving low-income, immigrant, and ethnic neighborhoods because the costs of figuring out how to evaluate creditworthiness are too high (not to mention the costs of servicing savings and checking accounts). Dymski tied the rise of ethnobanks, at least partially, to the decline of "mainstream" banks in low-income areas. For me, Dymski's work posited a "mainstream exit" phenomenon. There is an unstated implication in his work that without the exit of the mainstream banks, it is unlikely that ethnobanks would arise.

My work has taken an alternative thesis that has only a small quibble with Dymski: Might there be a desire on the part of consumers—and yes, entrepreneurs—to create a "sense of place" in retail banking, in which they preferred being served by coethnics? Does the experience of operating as a minority in a larger environment with racial hostility create a preference for a place where intimacy and trust would be important? Would this be especially true if the experience involved something as important as the management of finances and the creation of wealth?

In listening to the executives from NCFCU, I had questions I was too polite to ask: How long do you believe banks of this type can last? In the face of technological innovation, will trust built through personal interactions and the management of symbols still be a competitive advantage? Since Asian Americans have the highest household incomes in the nation, won't there be competition for those dollars over time? Won't traditional, mainstream banks compete for their business?

It seems to me the fortunes, and indeed the economic sustainability, of ethnobanks is predicated on the interaction of a number of variables that are not always accounted for in models of how banks compete: immigration, assimilation, and the persistence of residential segregation. First, a steady flow of immigrants has been a structural factor buoying the customer base of similar institutions. This base may be composed of low-income households with relatively unsophisticated financial needs. As long as these institutions can serve as the "safe space" that helps customers navigate unfamiliar territory, they will continue to have an advantage with recently arrived populations.

Second, the importance of ethnic identity—becoming American, yet continuing to be ethnically *Chinese* American—will be an important factor in allowing the banks to expand and grow as their customers' education and household incomes increase. I see either a strong social or charitable motivation for this to happen, in which consumers value either (1) maintaining relationships with institutions that were important to their parents or (2) supporting an institution that provides services to those less fortunate, who share an ethnicity.

The third factor is spatial. As long as ethnic groups live within distinct and separate neighborhoods, minority-serving institutions will be able to use their physical proximity as a barrier to entry.

In most urban areas, neighborhood demography will undoubtedly continue to shift. Would NCFCU's leadership be prepared to follow its customers intergenerationally? That is, as the children of its current clientele grew to need banking services, would the services they desired, such as electronic banking and brokerage services, be competitive with the offerings of other banks? Essentially, credit unions and banks like these increasingly will have to serve two customer bases—one composed of recent immigrants, and one composed of the relatively affluent and assimilated. I can imagine that the technological capabilities needed to serve these disparate markets and their disparate needs would lower overall efficiency, but ultimately that could be compensated for by volume.

Yet even that model has an embedded assumption—that the mainstream banks would not compete outright for ethnic Chinese consumers. If traditional financial institutions could offer services in a convenient fashion, and more cheaply, it is likely they could puncture the ethnic envelope that is the foundation of NCFCU and ethnobanks like it.

# Croissants and Corridors to Wealth Creation

CHARLES LOUIS Fleischmann, an immigrant from what is today the Czech Republic, arrived in Cincinnati, Ohio, in 1865. Dissatisfied with the quality of the bread he found there, he and his brothers created a yeast company and an eponymous brand. Fleischmann's company eventually became the world's largest yeast producer.

At around the same time, a German immigrant and professional baker named Christian Mueller began making egg noodles in his New Jersey kitchen. Peddling them house to house from a wicker basket, he eventually began selling his product to local restaurants.[1] By 2013, Mueller's was the third-largest pasta manufacturer in the United States.[2]

More than a hundred years later, following a well-worn entrepreneurial path, Håkan Swahn, a Swedish immigrant, opened Manhattan's highly acclaimed Nordic restaurant Aquavit. Featuring a broad selection of its distinctively flavored namesake spirit, the restaurant promoted its devotion to serving high-end, authentic, Swedish cuisine. Toward that end, in 1995, Aquavit's founders hired a new chef. Under Marcus Samuelsson's direction, it was not long before the restaurant began to receive increasing public recognition, as well as a number of prestigious national and international awards.[3]

Samuelsson had, in some ways, an unlikely personal story. Kassahun Tsegie, the boy who would become Marcus Samuelsson, was born in Ethiopia. His mother died when he was three, and Swedes from the city of Gothenburg subsequently adopted him. It was from his adoptive family that he developed his knowledge of the Scandinavian palate, cooking techniques, and culture that would allow him to interpret Swedish gastronomy in an authentic fashion.

Yet Samuelsson remained an African. Years after leaving Aquavit, Samuelsson would open other restaurants in New York City's Harlem, London, and Gothenburg. All of these ventures required an ability to deliver a dining experience that offered authenticity and innovation in African, African American, and Scandinavian cuisine. Mirroring Samuelsson's own personal journey, his menus reflected adaption and perhaps assimilation. He became known for a unique capacity to transform the old into fresh new realities.

Samuelsson's experience as an immigrant had not impeded him. It may well have been the assist that gave him the capacity both to recognize the elements that his customers would find comforting, reassuring, even challenging, and to balance them expertly in a way that would lead those customers to willingly pay premium prices at his risk-taking establishments.

## THE CREATIVE COMPLEXITY OF FOOD BUSINESSES

Food service and food production are two of the more common industries for entrepreneurial pursuit. At least one reason is that food-related entrepreneurs have to overcome relatively fewer barriers to entry than, say, a manufacturing firm.

Not surprisingly, in the United States, food-related businesses have become a common career path for many immigrant entrepreneurs, in part as a result of repeating waves of immigration and corresponding cycles of assimilation. For each new wave of immigrants, this duality creates a tension between the pull of memories of the "old country" and the opportunities for a "new life" in a new place. Initial forays into entrepreneurship offer products and foods that, for some, provide a longed-for "taste of home"; for others, an opportunity to "experience" another culture; or for still others, as in restaurants like Samuelsson's Red Rooster or Swahn's Aquavit, an altogether novel fusion of cultural tastes.

For firms that offer authenticity, in terms of a mother culture, the service delivery process can be complicated, with many elements in production encompassing referents, cues, or symbolic ties to the ethnic group or experience being commercially offered. Hard-to-find ingredients, cooking techniques, physical space and decor, even ethnic-appropriate servers who assist in what can become an almost performative service effort, can all provide the perception of an authentic dining experience.

Many entrepreneurs have recognized that there are those who see value in traveling into recognizable ethnic neighborhoods when they want to enjoy ethnic cuisine. The experience of eating Italian food, prepared by Italian chefs, and served by ethnic Italian staff, in a city's historic Italian neighborhood, allows diners to effectively travel to Italy without a passport.

There are other ways to experience what seem to be the authentic tastes of faraway locales. For example, at least one primary reason that consumers purchase packaged goods produced by Goya Foods is that they assume these products are authentically Spanish. In part, this is because of the company's Spanish-referent branding. It is also because of the Spanish ethnicity of the firm's immigrant founders. Begun in 1936, today Goya is the country's largest Latino-owned firm. The idea that consumption of an ethnic meal can happen in a consumer's home is the basis of Goya's business model as a processed foods manufacturer.

## ENCLAVE ECONOMIES, ETHNIC PRODUCTS

Segregation-social and residential-has been a strong theoretical and thematic element throughout my research. The basic concept is not foreign to business scholars, with whom the notion of location and density among related firms (termed "clusters") is cited as a strong factor influencing the growth of firms and industries.

Michael Porter, one of the most authoritative scholars on clusters, defines them as

> geographic concentrations of interconnected companies and institutions. . . . Clusters encompass an array of linked industries and other

entities important to competition. . . . [They] extend downstream to channels and customers and laterally to manufacturers of complementary products and to companies in industries related by skills, technologies or related inputs.[4]

In what is arguably an ethnically explicit extension of the clusters concept, the term "ethnic enclaves" was coined to define distinct geographic areas, segmented by race or ethnicity, that establish an interlinked set of suppliers, firms, and entrepreneurs sharing a business, social, and cultural connection.

The sales of what are known as "ethnic cultural products" have long had a place in entrepreneurial literature, especially as they relate to ethnic minority entrepreneurs.[5] By leveraging social networks and relationships, ethnic entrepreneurs may take several courses of action. They can:

1. Target their products to insiders and rely on shared social networks and relations (coethnic entrepreneurship)
2. Target their products to groups of outsiders (interethnic entrepreneurship)
3. Attempt to service both types of groups, which may have attendant risks in maintaining a level of authenticity that would please both groups

There are two generalized notions here. The first is that consumers of ethnic products—whether sold by coethnics, such as Chinese consumers served by Asian grocers, or inter-ethnics, such as Black consumers shopping for Goya products—are seeking an "authenticity," albeit in different configuration. Second, ethnic identity and cultural knowledge create a barrier to an outsider's entry into the market niche, especially when there is a high degree of cultural content in the product and service offerings. This authenticity does not extend, for example, to Uncle Ben, who was the advertising character and namesake of the nation's leading rice brand made by the food conglomerate Mars. Since he's a fictional character, Uncle Ben has been updated over the years to reflect more modern sensibilities, in his depiction and background. The term "uncle" was often used to refer to older Black slaves in the south, and needn't reflect any biological relation.

There is also a conceptual and operational distinction between ethnic entrepreneurship and ethnic enclave entrepreneurship. Ethnic entrepreneurship involves firms that leverage their knowledge and relationships to market products to a recognized group with a common cultural heritage or origin. The primary distinction between the two is geographical: enclave entrepreneurs rely to a greater degree on proximity (and segregation).

Among ethnic entrepreneurs, a subset operates within segregated neighborhoods—ethnic enclave entrepreneurs. They often rely on establishing and maintaining deep relationships within their group, and their circumscribed location provides physical boundaries and social proximity that simultaneously protect and limit their market. Geographic density and segregation allow these firms to reach suppliers, consumers, and even employees in less time and with far lower search costs than firms that need to cover greater social and physical distance.

While in some ways a defensive factor, the "closed market" of the ethnic enclave can also impede the establishment of external relationships that would be beneficial. As societal tastes change and the demography of neighborhoods shifts, entrepreneurs with businesses built to serve a local, coethnic market may find their customer base shrinking or moving out altogether. The survival of these firms will rest on their ability to adapt to conditions when their shared ethnicity no longer plays a role in facilitating commercial activity.

To illustrate, I will share the narrative of a food manufacturing firm deploying "ethnic entrepreneurial" strategies. Relevant to the themes of this book, I will focus on its interactions with a unique equity capital provider.

## A DIFFERENT TYPE OF INVESTMENT FIRM: PACIFIC COMMUNITY VENTURES

Matt Innamorati, one of my former MBA students, was skeptical, though extremely polite, when he first approached me after class: "This whole arena of 'social' finance, I just don't get it." In truth, I have often found the "social" modifier a sticking point. As we discussed his skepticism, rather than try to change his mind, I made an offer: "Why don't you study a business I recently learned about, and if possible, let's turn it into a case study?"

I wasn't entirely sure whether there was something valuable in the firm I had in mind. Once Innamorati agreed, we turned our attention to the founders and leadership of Pacific Community Ventures (PCV), a community development venture capital (CDVC) firm located in San Francisco.

California's "City by the Bay" was the launching locale for a number of what would become iconic, influential firms in the early venture equity industry, and Federal Street was home to a growing cluster of venture capital (VC) firms, including PCV. Yet, as we would soon find out, PCV was different in a number of ways.

The first difference was an institutional one, and the second was its purpose for being. Pacific Community Ventures, Inc., was, for the most part, a nonprofit organization established in 1999. Second, PCV was founded not to explicitly create substantial wealth, but to respond to California's growing occupational, income, and wealth inequality— a problem in which, some have argued, the private equity (PE) industry has played a substantial role.

PCV was founded by former technology insiders who believed that private sector business solutions and funding could create, support, and expand firms that would, in turn, help ameliorate income and wealth gaps—with the added benefit of creating jobs. Although initially founded as a nonprofit, in 2007 PCV established a for-profit subsidiary, Pacific Community Management, to administer an investment fund. Through this structure, a separate yet affiliated entity, Pacific Community Ventures, LLC, was set up to manage equity funds. By the time of our visit in 2010, PCV was managing more than $60 million in three different funds. In addition to equity investments, PCV offered extensive social impact technical assistance to its portfolio companies through its nonprofit entity, PCV Insight. As a comprehensive entity, PCV was also a certified CDFI by the U.S. Treasury (specifically, a CDVC firm).

## A NOTION FOR VENTURING SPROUTS IN NORTHERN CALIFORNIA

Although Californians typically enjoyed median household incomes significantly higher than those of other states, the state was also known for having a high cost of living, and this was especially true of San Francisco.

The city had low rates of homeownership, with just 37.6 percent of the population owning a home in 2010. Statewide, California had a home-ownership rate of 54.6 percent in 2010.[6] This tightening housing market contributed to a pattern of residential displacement.

These shifts underscored the direct interplay of occupation, educational attainment, housing, and wealth that was playing out in urban centers that had previously been abandoned. I would argue that San Francisco's experiences are only harbingers of trends that are now being experienced in every major urban center.

Because of expanding growth in fields like technology, consulting, and finance, San Francisco was becoming a prime illustration of how industrial clustering in knowledge-intensive and professional services industries was creating inequalities and contributing to an ever-growing "have" and "have-not" imbalance—socially, occupationally, residentially, and educationally.

## VENTURE CAPITAL AS A POVERTY-ALLEVIATION TOOL?

Two pieces of federal legislation contributed to the growth of equity venture firms. First, the Small Business Investment Company (SBIC), a program initiative of the Small Business Administration (SBA), provided a new form of financial assistance designed to spur small business development. And second, the Economic Recovery Tax Act of 1981 (ERTA) was enacted (also known as the Kemp-Roth Tax Cut).[7]

The SBIC program established federally matched and guaranteed funds which allowed privately owned and managed investment funds to make equity and debt investments in qualifying small businesses. Since investing directly with individual firms is not in its mandate or capability set, the SBA matches funds and provides guarantees to qualified investment firms, and these firms, in turn, directly invest in opportunities that meet their particular areas of expertise.

The ERTA's primary lever was that it lowered capital gains taxes from 28 percent to 20 percent, thus making high-risk investments far more attractive. Coupled with the concurrent growth of technology firms in the Bay Area, the legislation ushered in a robust period for the private equity industry.

Although intended as a broad-based program to provide capital to a diversity of firms, between 2000 and 2005, an estimated 60 percent of venture funds deployed nationally were in biotechnology and other technology-related sectors and were concentrated in thirty-five zip codes in Silicon Valley, Orange County, and San Diego.[8] The only issue that clustering presented was that enterprises in other locales and industries were often outside the notice of venture capital firms. Given the emphasis on knowledge-intensive, knowledge-driven industries, businesses that provided jobs for entry-level and lesser-skilled populations were not as attractive to investors.

In response, a new notion took hold—a novel type of venture firm that recognized both the value of the VC investing model and its deployed limitations in application and impact. The vision was a new breed of equity firm that, at its core, was dedicated to improving thorny social problems like rising inequality.

PCV was cofounded by Penelope Douglas, a self-described "general manager," and Bud Colligan, a former software entrepreneur. Both were drawn to the community development venture capital (CDVC) model because of its potential to make a social impact.

Douglas, who would become PCV's first CEO, brought to the firm a rich professional background that included posts at banking giant Wells Fargo and the multinational professional services firm Ernst and Young. She also had worked at the healthy-beverage company Odwalla, whose social bent was evident in its three key operating principles: make great juice, do good things for the community, and build a business with heart.

During its first year of operation, PCV recruited six advisers to work with six small businesses on plans for growth and attenuating social ills. PCV's first fund was capitalized with $5 million from Wells Fargo. Combined with other commitments from Cathay Bank, Greater Bay Bancorp, Provenex (the Rockefeller Foundation), and Silicon Valley Bank, the fund's capitalization amounted to $6,250,000. PCV's first fund, Fund I, focused on early-stage companies with annual sales of $250,000 to $3 million.

Halfway through the firm's first year, Douglas hired a consultant to evaluate the fledgling organization. With results in hand, PCV's leadership found themselves facing a choice: PCV could engage in socially responsible investment (SRI) focused on entrepreneur development, or focus on creating jobs and wealth-building opportunities. The leadership team rejected this one-or-the-other choice, believing instead that the optimum deals would encompass both elements. Based on experience, Douglas and her colleagues began to develop a view that, at the margin, there were sometimes compromises that had to be made. By 2001, they had committed to the notion that, in times of direct conflict and forced choice, they would lean toward job creation and wealth building over developing a new cadre of socially motivated entrepreneurs.

The team came to a key decision that investing in small to medium enterprises (SMEs) was a proximal way to provide high-quality, stable jobs for people living in low- to moderate-income (LMI) areas. They believed that a high-quality job was the first step on the path out of poverty, and that SMEs were pivotal to transforming underserved communities because they were job creators with deep ties to local communities, making them less likely to move jobs elsewhere. PCV's portfolio of invested firms reflected a strategy for transitioning people into the financial mainstream. And as part of the terms of their investments, PCV negotiated "equity set-asides" to ensure that employees had the opportunity to financially benefit at the time of the portfolio firm's sale (also known as "the exit").

## SOURCING FROM DIVERSE INVESTORS

One of the cornerstone concepts of this book is the ability of many of our featured firms to access and assemble pools of capital with varying goals, such as market rate returns, job growth, minority managers, women managers, or environmental sustainability. This is a challenging task that comes with careful expectation management and sometimes complexities associated with responding to social impact measurement.

In 2003, PCV received its first award from the Community Development Financial Institutions (CDFI) Fund in the amount of $1 million intended to capitalize its second fund, PCV Investment Partners, LLC II. The first fund had achieved two objectives: it launched PCV into the entrepreneurial community, and it provided a learning platform. With the second fund, Douglas and the team altered their target investment parameters to include larger businesses that could achieve both job creation and community wealth development. The inclusion of CDFI Fund capital also enabled Douglas's team to source investments from philanthropic sources, allowing PCV to further invest in businesses that provided quality employment to residents of low-income communities.

In 2004, PCV was awarded a three-year, $1.5 million contract from the California State Treasurer's Office to expand its business advisory services. In all stages of growth, PCV focused on brick-and-mortar companies that required lengthier developmental periods before a successful sale of the firm than was the custom with technology-based firms typically sought by more traditional VC firms without SRI objectives.

## NOVEL APPROACH, NOVEL TEAM

PCV's leadership talent came from the usual set of backgrounds—founders of entrepreneurial firms, members of venture capital firms, and executives in financial services. However, some had credentials that differed from the expected.

Eduardo Rallo was a managing partner of Pacific Community Management, which oversaw PCV's for-profit venture funds. With an MBA from Harvard, Rallo's background fit the more traditional model, with experience in private equity as well as ownership of a chain of pharmacies and a restaurant management group.

On the team's social impact side, Beth Sirull served as executive director of Pacific Community Ventures. With an MBA and a master's in public policy, she came to her job with fifteen years of experience as a consultant on market research and strategy. Interestingly, she was also establishing herself as a "personal growth guru" and had authored a book on work-life balance. Sirull led PCV's policy arm, InSight, and sought to influence investment and public policy across a client list that included the Annie E. Casey Foundation, CalPERS, and the Rockefeller Foundation.

Adam See joined PCV in 2008 as director of development and marketing. With an MBA from the University of California, Berkeley, See had extensive experience in social enterprises and the nonprofit world, as well as more traditional banking experience at Interbank Group, an investment and management firm.

A duality or, depending on your perspective, a productive tension emerged within the firm. Under PCV's umbrella coexisted fixed sister organizations, each with related but distinct missions. Not only did this duality create a continuing internal dialogue, but it also led to the establishment of complementary sets of networks and nonoverlapping relationships. One question I had during our field visit was whether this duality would strengthen or dilute the identity or brand that each organization would have been able to build were they stand-alone organizations.

## INNOVATING THROUGH SOCIAL IMPACT INVESTMENT AND ADVICE

PCV's unique proposition was to provide a suite of products and services to businesses operating in—or employing people living in— low- to moderate-income areas.[9] However, it operated by a continuous "left-hand, right-hand" approach, deploying investment capital through its for-profit entity and providing advice and counsel through its nonprofit.

At the time of our visit, Douglas noted PCV's sizable footprint, with equity investments throughout California, although concentrated in the Bay Area, Los Angeles, San Diego, and the Central Valley. As PCV evolved through its various funds and expanded scale of operations, it shifted its investment strategy away from early-stage and start-up firms to more mature organizations, with an emphasis on providing resources suited to the needs of later-stage firms.

As we interviewed him over lunch, Rallo gave us a better sense of PCV's portfolio firms. In terms of size, PCV's typical equity investment ranged from $1 million to $5 million. The firm was inclined to focus on a few fundamental elements: a proven management team, strong revenue growth, near or recent profitability, and a portion of its workforce drawn from low- to moderate-income communities.[10] From an industry standpoint, PCV tended to make investments in relatively low-capital-intensive manufacturing, consumer and business services, and a limited set of other sectors with significant potential for social impact, such as sustainable and green businesses, alternative energy, health and wellness, trade schools, and for-profit education.

## STRUCTURE OF THE FUNDING VEHICLE

PCV's general partners had negotiated with limited partner investors (LPs) for a typical fee structure consisting of a 2.75 percent management fee and 20 percent carried interest.[11] When Rallo spoke about the fund's performance from a purely economic investment standpoint, he talked about investment opportunities that could produce internal rates of return (IRRs) in the top quartile of venture funds.[12]

When we asked about what PCV offered to potential portfolio entrepreneurs, Rallo reeled off a broad range of financing needs, including growth equity, management-led buyouts, liquidity for family-owned or closely held companies, wealth creation for next-generation managers/owners, recapitalization/restructuring to enable growth, and venture capital.

When pressed, Rallo acknowledged that private equity was already a very competitive industry even without the extra constraint of achieving a social return. A fundamental challenge was one of balance—determining how to mediate trade-offs between financial and social returns when evaluating potential investments, and deciding where to invest among a set of potentially socially impactful alternatives. He was clear that, first and foremost, the long-term success of PCV depended upon delivering a competitive financial return to stimulate follow-on investments from LPs.

Rallo reiterated that wealth building was central to PCV's business model. "[We have] a track record of working with our portfolio companies to implement innovative employee ownership programs that increase productivity, retention, and morale, which then translates to better economic results for all parties."

PCV required portfolio companies to set aside 1 to 5 percent of total equity for employees. Timbuk2, a former PCV portfolio company, was a successful example of employee stock ownership. At the time of PCV's exit, Timbuk2 employees received $1 million overall, which equaled roughly two years' salary, 70 percent of which was invested in managed retirement accounts. This was significant compensation for low-income employees, many of whom did not even have checking accounts prior to employment.

In the same vein, Rallo shared some impressive metrics. Collectively, in terms of hourly employees, PCV's firms employed 2,430 workers. One hundred percent of its firms hired workers from low- to moderate-income communities and paid a higher-than-average wage for entry-level employees; 89 percent offered health insurance; 67 percent provided retirement plans (401(k) accounts, IRAs) or profit-sharing programs; and 100 percent of the firms offered skills-based training.[13]

One of the challenges of a dual mission company like PCV was explaining, or even marketing, their unique value proposition to key stakeholders or funders who, like my student Matt Innamorati, were skeptical about social finance.

Echoing through our conversations was the tension of developing new organizations with two explicit missions—financial return versus creating economic opportunity in underserved areas. As PCV principals talked about expanding their impact to a third bottom line—environmental sustainability—I wondered whether three missions might make it challenging for the fund to achieve rates of return comparable to firms without social investment screens.

## ALTERING THE POLICY DISCOURSE

At the time of our visit, PCV was becoming a thought leader in the nascent area of impact investing. It published research to influence the discourse in equities and to support their particular form of equity investing. In 2003, PCV's first white paper, "The Challenges and Opportunities of Investing in Low-Income Communities,"[14] detailed the lessons of the firm's first five years of operation. In 2006, "Development Investment Capital: Three Steps to Establishing an Asset Class for Investing in Underserved Markets"[15] asserted that development investment capital must become a *bona fide* asset class within private equity for two reasons: to meet the needs of growing business in LMI areas and to provide incentives for investors.

Beyond financing, PCV's leadership recognized that quantifying social impact would be critical to keeping the flow of funds streaming to efforts like theirs, so Douglas championed diligent measurement of the social impact of private equity investing and wrote extensively on the subject. Douglas and her team had anticipated a question I had long asked: What constitutes social performance?

## CROISSANTS IN CALIFORNIA'S CRIME CAPITAL

When we inquired about an exemplar PCV investment, Rallo related the unlikely story of Galaxy Desserts—unknowingly, a firm with whose products I was already familiar.

For years, my family had been purchasing croissants from Williams Sonoma as a traditional part of our Thanksgiving Day meal. The soft, pillowy, buttery, yeasty-smelling croissants were a luxury, and were priced at a premium. Galaxy Desserts developed, manufactured, and marketed gourmet desserts and pastries for retail, food service, and catalog sales throughout the United States,[16] including my family's annual purchase.

As he shared the details, Rallo acknowledged that food service was outside of the expected set of industries private equity firms usually focus on, and that there were operational and financial difficulties associated with investments that might require short turnarounds to exit profitably. He added that it was within PCV's circle of interest primarily because of the tendency of food industry firms to hire, staff, and promote lower-skilled workers. Galaxy had recently experienced both financial successes and challenges, and Rallo shared that he had questioned whether it would be able to meet its projected growth.

## RICHMOND AND THE *PATISSIERS*

Paul Levitan, Galaxy's president and CEO, and Jean-Yves Charon, its master pastry chef, cofounded the company in 1998 through a merger of their previously existing businesses. Levitan came into the food business in 1991 when, after graduating from Stanford Graduate School of Business, he bought a small dessert company in San Francisco.

Charon had grown up in France and worked as a manager for *Brioche Dorée Paris*, opening stores in London, Paris, Canada, and New York City. In 1983, Charon moved to San Francisco, working as a pastry chef before starting his own company, Paris Delights.

The eventual partners met at an industry trade show and, after a series of discussions, decided to combine their existing businesses and to restructure as Galaxy Desserts. The company grew rapidly and secured customer relationships with some of the country's largest retailers. In 1999, Galaxy's revenues were $1.5 million; by 2006, revenue had grown to approximately $8.5 million. This was a healthy small business, but it was still tiny in the realm of institutional dessert companies.

One of the first surprises about Galaxy was its plant location—especially given its positioning as a purveyor of high-quality, French-inspired desserts. Richmond, twenty miles north of the Bay Area, was a relatively low-income community, with approximately one-third of its population foreign born.[17] At the time it was being considered for investment, Galaxy employed 125 people, largely drawn from the local community.

Richmond was considered the most dangerous city in California and the eighth most dangerous city in the country in 2004.[18] It appeared that this was, indeed, the type of job-starved neighborhood in which PCV sought to have an impact. However, Rallo also spoke about the obvious risks of operating a business in a high property- and violent-crime neighborhood.

## BEYOND BAKING: THE GALAXY BUSINESS MODEL

The company's product and customer sales mix changed as it grew. Its largest customer, which represented 21.9 percent of total sales in 2005, switched dessert suppliers the following year, leaving a large gap in Galaxy's revenue as well as a surplus in production capacity. Rallo recognized this as a potential reoccurring risk for many small businesses, one that had a direct influence on overall long-term viability.

Galaxy marketed its products through four channels: retail, food service, catalog, and internet sales. In terms of retail alone, its products could be found in more than three thousand U.S. locations, with a majority of its products sold as private label and marketed under various retailers' house brands. Approximately one-third of the company's products were sold under the Galaxy brand. My assumption is that most Galaxy customers were not of French descent, yet the knowledge that Charon is a trained French chef was, and is, an important selling variable. The notion of product authenticity remains prominently featured on the company's website: "Experience the taste of France in your own home."[19]

At the time, the typical per-unit price for a Galaxy dessert was between $2.99 and $3.99, with a targeted in-store bakery margin of at least 50 percent.[20] Rallo told us that although he was initially impressed by these premium prices, more recently he had become concerned that margins would decrease as the market became oversaturated with high-end baked goods. Regarding their own Galaxy-branded desserts and their sale to end consumers rather than institutions, Rallo called out the challenge of overcoming consumers' allegiance to their local neighborhood bakeries. In addition, local bakeries typically priced their products lower than Galaxy's and, since they were often baked every morning, they were generally fresher.

Levitan and Charon co-led Galaxy's sales efforts; however, neither of them had either management or sales experience at a large, institutional food production operation. The task ahead would require new muscles. Understanding and managing the key sales growth drivers would be an important transitional step.

Galaxy's 36,000-square-foot facility was divided into dedicated areas, including a cold room for refrigerated products, a space for croissant preparation, a baking area, a sanitation room, a freezer section, an R&D test kitchen lab, and a quality assurance office and lab. During our visit, it appeared that a substantial amount of floor space was unused. In one way, this represented a potential benefit in Galaxy's ability to increase capacity without the costly requirements of relocating; yet the unused space could be a drain on profits when viewed as excess overhead expense. If the firm's revenue growth softened, the investment in space would be seen *post hoc* as a sign of hubris and unnecessary spending.

Galaxy's dual market strategy also presented a strategic dilemma. Rallo commented on the trade-offs of simultaneously pursuing both a branded and a private-label product strategy, noting that the development of a recognizable Galaxy brand would increase the firm's overall value (and PCV's eventual return at sale). On one hand, in a world of limited marketing resources, devoting the lion's share to a strong brand strategy would come at the cost of short-term profits. On the other hand, pursuing a private-label strategy would satisfy capacity but limit Galaxy's differentiation among commodity bakeries and hinder long-term brand appreciation.

As they reflected on key moments in the firm's growth, Charon and Levitan mentioned Oprah Winfrey's 2002 discovery of Galaxy's croissants, which she named as one of her "Favorite Things" during a Thanksgiving week broadcast.[21] Recognition by arguably the leading celebrity guru on the planet led the team to prepare an ample supply in anticipation of market demand; however, despite their efforts, they were ultimately unable to meet the outsized demand for their croissants. Receiving what by all accounts was a great honor only served to underscore limitations in the firm's product supply, customer response management, and manufacturing systems.

## CLEARING PCV'S SOCIAL RETURN
## REQUIREMENTS

"First of all, the entrepreneur must be aligned with PCV's social philosophy before we will even consider an investment," Rallo explained,
stressing that the potential for social impact was a component of the
due diligence process. In their initial review, Galaxy had received a passing score of 37 out of a maximum of 60. PCV's analysis noted Galaxy's
strong performance in five areas: (1) employing a predominantly full-
time workforce; (2) setting aside a small percentage of equity to pay
low-income employees in the event of a liquidity event; (3) hiring from
within and providing advancement opportunities for hourly employees; (4) providing health and retirement benefits to all employees after
six months of employment; (5) donating imperfect products to its local
food bank.

In keeping with PCV's consultancy emphasis, the review also noted
areas of potential improvement, which included increasing the average
hourly wage; increasing payment of health care premiums; and providing a greater degree of employee training.

As for the first area of needed improvement, at the time of PCV's
investment, Galaxy paid an average wage of $9.39 per hour, which
was lower than the local community's average living wage and below
the average ($13.56) paid by other recently acquired PCV portfolio
companies.

Second, enrollment rates for health care were low because Galaxy
covered only 75 percent of health premiums. The uncovered portion
translated to $200 to $300 in out-of-pocket expenses for employees—20
percent of average gross monthly wages—not a small amount for a low-
income family to save or set aside. And third, there was limited employee
training available, with the exception of on-the-job shadowing.

PCV believed it could assist in each of these areas. However, all
of them presented material trade-offs. For one thing, addressing any
improvement area would raise the firm's costs and, unless offset by
increased productivity, could be viewed as a constraint on profitability.

Galaxy Desserts was a concrete example of the type of dilemma
PCV faced in its social benefit form of investing. Some could argue
that merely providing full-time jobs with an opportunity for benefits in
California's murder capital would be sufficient. Even at its size, Galaxy

had become a relatively prominent employer in an area characterized by high unemployment.

## DEAL TERMS

When consummated, the ultimate deal structure included a participating preferred equity offering of approximately $3 million, and Rallo expected a post-money valuation to be in the range of $6 million to $9 million. The proceeds would be used to purchase new automated production equipment, build out storage space, hire sales and marketing personnel, fund working capital, pay off existing debt and banking fees, and repurchase all outstanding series B preferred stock of the previous third-party institutional investors.

At the point of investment, Rallo expected Galaxy would not need any additional rounds of financing and PCV would exit the investment in five years at a cash flow multiple comparable to that of recent market transactions.

## GALAXY EXITS

In the months that followed our field visit, Matt Innamorati worked with me to draft the teaching case study before his May 2011 graduation. That summer, I flew out to San Francisco to road test the newly written draft before an audience of one hundred Darden alumni, many of whom worked in private equity or funded ventures. Sirull and Rallo were in the room, though they were not introduced or identified. The PCV team had the opportunity to listen to the audience debate the merits of the PCV approach, and the potential risks and opportunities of the Galaxy investment, without having anyone know they were present. After surreptitiously listening to the discussion, which included a wealth of questions and criticism, I introduced Sirull and Rallo to the surprised group. The two graciously said a few words and mentioned that they were elated to hear their challenges discussed in real time and to be featured in a study by a leading business school.

I periodically conduct web searches to update my knowledge of the firms I have featured in my cases. In April 2012, I found the following (abbreviated) announcement on the website of boutique investment banking firm C.W. Downer:

## US: FRANCE'S PASQUIER ACQUIRES GALAXY DESSERTS

**By Stuart Todd, 5 April 2012**—French bakery group Brioche Pasquier has confirmed that it has acquired California-based Galaxy Desserts which specialises in desserts and cakes with a French flavour.

The value of the transaction has not been disclosed. It is Pasquier's first acquisition in the US.

Based in Richmond, Galaxy Desserts . . . generates an annual turnover of close to EUR20m.

The founders will continue to manage Galaxy Desserts in association with the director of Pasquier's international division, Fabrice Sciumbata.

Pasquier employs 3,000 staff and operates from 16 plants. Apart from its base in France, it is present in several European countries such as Spain, Belgium, Germany and the UK.

Its 2011 turnover was EUR545m.[22]

The press release confirmed that PCV had indeed exited its investment within five years of the original investment offer, and that Galaxy was generating something in the order of $26.3 million in revenues. For perspective, in 2007, the last full year of sales prior to the investment, Galaxy had $11.8 million in annual sales, suggesting a 17.3 percent annual growth rate—above PCV and Galaxy's projections. Since this was an acquisition by a private firm, the actual sale price was not disclosed. However, on the basis of the sales data, I estimate a sales price somewhere in the $27 to $33 million range based on multiples of sales and cash flow. Assuming that PCV's investment represented between 30 and 45 percent of the firm's equity at the time of sale, PCV could have received from as little as $8.1 million to as much as $14.9 million for what was approximately a $2.7 million stake.

A bit later, I found an interview with Charon featured by the World Economic Forum, in which he discussed best practices in building entrepreneurial ecosystems. Charon noted the split marketing strategy as a tension point, but also as a key element of the firm's success.

Building our croissant business with Williams-Sonoma has been great for both sides. We certainly could not have done it without them. In fact, Oprah discovered our croissants in the Williams-Sonoma catalogue, and we were fortunate that the orders resulting from our Oprah appearances all came through the Williams-Sonoma infrastructure. We would have had an incredibly hard time trying to handle that type of volume ourselves. . . .

In 2006, we began working with two national retailers on private label programmes, each starting with our Butter Croissants. We executed so well, and both launches were so successful, that we expanded to multiple SKUs with both. Like we did with Williams-Sonoma, we were able to collaborate on ideas with these key strategic customers. . . . The volume, which resulted from our private label customers, helped us to automate some of our processes, making us a better manufacturer.

I have continued to teach this case study over the years, and although over time more students are familiar with the concepts of investing for social change, there are still a healthy number of skeptics. Even students who generally support the notion recognize the inherent tensions in the joint approach and the complementarity provided by the nonprofit advising / for-profit funding structure.

I have also followed PCV as they have continued to publish a broad array of policy briefs on employment, impact investing, and social measurement. I've noticed that they have expanded outside of California and also provide healthy amounts of loan capital.

As for Galaxy Desserts, one thing that has always stood out to me about the company's marketing approach is the lack of an explicit appeal to consumers based on the location of their production facilities. Unlike Ben and Jerry's, The Body Shop, or other firms that prominently tout their social impact goals and achievements, I have never found any consumer-facing mention of the largely immigrant, low-income workforce at Galaxy's Richmond plant. My sense is that they have always been comfortable with this fact being known in some circles, but that their extensive, high-end product line—mousse cakes, tarts, cheesecake, crème brûlée, and croissants—is the undisputed hero in their marketing campaigns, as opposed to visuals of the frequently brown people who labor to make them. This is not a criticism. I appreciate their clarity in branding—French pastries, well made.

# CHAPTER NINE

# Targeted Private Equity I

*Neighborhood Integration, Black Capitalism, and the Inception of Minority Private Equity*

NOT LONG before I began kindergarten, my parents purchased their first home in the relatively new neighborhood of Dale City, Virginia, because of its proximity to Washington, D.C.—and, important to my parents—. Since their purchase was a new construction, a number of other military officers with young families were also moving in at the same time. Colin and Alma Powell—and their son, Michael, who was my age—lived just over the backyard fence and up the hill.

For my parents, the integrated community was an important factor in deciding where to bring up their two young children. And yet, in some ways, this represented a "walk of faith"—both had grown up in segregated neighborhoods. They believed that integration was good social policy, and so believed in this notion that their intent was to find a home and a school system for my sister and me that would allow them to test the possibilities.

Integrated housing was not easily found outside of military bases, even for recently returned Vietnam veterans. For families like the Powells and mine, this problem was addressed head-on when, in 1963, Secretary of Defense Robert McNamara issued his directive to ensure immediate nondiscrimination in housing and schools, including off-base residential housing: "I am fully aware that the Defense Department is not a philanthropic foundation or a social welfare institution," McNamara wrote in 1969. "But the Department does not intend to let our Negro servicemen and their families continue to suffer the injustices and indignities they have in the past."[1]

This type of sentiment coming from the Defense Department's leadership strengthened my parents' commitment to the notion of integration. The military was able to apply economic force behind the policy by requiring that the owners of off-base real estate leased by the military agree to a racial nondiscrimination clause. Any property owner that declined to agree to the policy would not be able to lease to servicemen at all, of any race.[2]

As I read Secretary McNamara's words now, they seem especially direct and powerful. That an organization in the executive branch would designate the immediate implementation of social policy, and require full compliance, is audacious in ways that few government agencies or businesses would attempt today.

Despite extensive criticism and public controversy, McNamara pressed on. In 1967, only a few years after his 1963 directive, McNamara followed with another direct order: All posts with five hundred or more servicemen were required to survey the available housing within their geographic footprint to ensure that there was no evidence of racial discrimination. Further still, the directive required installations to use the economic pressure of the military to force integration in communities that abutted those bases. McNamara's directives underscore the important role of government policy, and sometimes explicitly social policy, in shaping our economic lives.

## RICHARD NIXON, BLACK CAPITALISM, AND THE IMPETUS FOR MINORITY BUSINESS DEVELOPMENT

Around the time that my family and the Powells were settling into our neighborhood, Richard Nixon was coming into office. One of Nixon's campaign promises had been to promote a program he called Black Capitalism.

Nixon believed that one way to improve social conditions in segregated Black neighborhoods was to provide them with technical assistance, loan guarantees, and capital to expand established businesses and spur the creation of new ones.[3] Prominent economists and civil rights leaders at the time seized on one of the policy's more controversial underlying assumptions: A focus on building businesses in "segregated" Black neighborhoods, rather than developing Black businesses in "integrated areas" (or, by extension, the hiring of Blacks into white-owned firms). The prevailing notion was that Blacks would be likely to hire employees from within their own neighborhoods, which in turn would lower rates of unemployment and poverty.

The distinction here is that this policy's impact would be absorbed and experienced in "segregated" areas. It was a subtle yet clearly alternative notion.

A *New York Times* review of Theodore Cross's book on Black Capitalism captured the critique:

> By focusing on "the ghetto" and making most of his tax incentives ghetto-specific, Cross virtually defines the permitted theater of success for the talented black. . . . What of the black man who wants to open a store in Westchester? Of the community corporation that wants to invest in New Jersey real estate? Come back another day; to succeed in Cross' system, you'll have to stay in the ghetto.[4]

In 1969, *Harvard Business Review* published an article, "The Limits of Black Capitalism," by Frederick Sturdivant, a professor at Harvard Business School. Sturdivant was not a fan:

> There are three alternatives in dealing with the problem of the black slums of this nation: 1) Try to disperse their population—that is, achieve total integration. 2) "Isolate" the ghettos from the rest of society, with the provision of certain resources and an encouragement to develop into prosperous, peaceful and semi-autonomous entities. 3) Try to improve the social and economic welfare of ghettos and increase interaction with "outside" communities, with a view to eventual elimination of the conditions of deprivation prevailing in the ghettos.[5]

Sturdivant went on to argue that the first option was socially and politically impossible to implement, while he felt the second option smacked of "apartheid" and was antithetical to the values of the nation (of course, this option was Black capitalism). Sturdivant believed that "the third alternative holds the only promise. . . . I believe that efficiency and self-determination are not mutually exclusive."[6]

Reading about the Black Capitalism movement half a century later, my own sense is that its theory of economic change could produce short-term gains in minority employment and create wealth for a small base of minority entrepreneurs, but would ultimately be unsustainable. At best, it would be a partial strategy, combined with efforts to integrate into the larger economy.

## CREATING A DOMESTIC DEVELOPMENT AGENCY

On March 6, 1969, just forty-five days after being sworn into office, President Nixon made good on his campaign promise by using his executive powers to create the Office of Minority Business Enterprise (OMBE) in the Department of Commerce (Executive Order 11458), to be staffed by experts in banking, business, agriculture, and philanthropy.[7]

Later that year, Secretary of Commerce Maurice Stans announced the establishment of the Minority Enterprise Small Business Investment Company (MESBIC) program, an initiative to provide minority business owners access to equity capital. The program was funded through a public-private partnership, with support coming from the Small Business Administration (SBA) and eighteen corporations that had each agreed to provide $150,000.

"The potential venture capital available to minority businessmen can run into a billion or more dollars when the MESBIC program is fully implemented," Stans said. "Business recognizes that this is a practical and effective means by which it can help to meet the capital and financial needs of minority people who are anxious to operate their own businesses and who need this kind of assistance."[8]

Although they were private companies, MESBIC companies were licensed and regulated by the SBA, and were an outgrowth of the already existing Small Business Investment Company (SBIC) Act of 1958.

In the Nixon administration's view, the MESBIC program extended equity through firms catering to African American, Asian, Eskimo, Hispanic, or Native American entrepreneurs. The goal was to provide capital and advice ("smart money") to those who had been historically excluded from access to mainstream venture capital (VC) or SBIC funding.

In its early years, the program had some prominent failures and successes. The very first chartered MESBIC, Arcata Investments, announced closure after fewer than three years of operation. Its sponsoring company, Arcata National, explained the failure this way:

> During the first year of operation, many investments, in retrospect, were more socially than economically motivated. The urge to produce tangible results quickly to win over support . . . tended to erode good business judgment. . . . Had we applied from the outset tough-minded and complete evaluations of each business opportunity, we probably would have seen less investments and that many fewer failures.[9]

In contrast, North Street Capital Corporation, funded by consumer goods conglomerate General Foods, was one profitable example. Begun in 1971 with a $150,000 investment, by 1986 it had placed more than $2.6 million in portfolio firms founded and managed by more than forty minority entrepreneurs. Fifteen years after its founding, the estimated value of North Street's portfolio was $35 million.

## A COLLEAGUE'S INTRODUCTION TO TARGETED PRIVATE EQUITY

In 2000, I began a seminal project on private equity firms that focused their investments on minority business owners. Robert Bruner, a senior colleague, invited me to join him in a research study on the extent and manner of private equity investing in depressed and overlooked markets. Bruner was a well-known and highly respected finance scholar. I should also mention that, for me, Bruner's racial and professional identity was an unspoken but important factor. For a white finance scholar to engage in research work of this type would suggest to others a legitimate academic inquiry, and that these research pursuits would not be, well, "ghetto-ized."

Before the project, I knew little about VC or private equity (PE) firms, other than they seemed to occupy a rarified space within the world of finance. I knew that a VC's value was predicated on the notion of what sociologists term "brokerage"—individuals who can "bridge" relationships through their ability to interact with two disparate and otherwise disconnected groups.

Venture capital and PE firms create value by connecting with entrepreneurs who were seeking capital, assisting them with advice, guiding their growth, and eventually helping with the sale of their firms (the "exit"). VC firms also connected sources of investment capital with entrepreneurial firms looking for investors.

I found that this form of investing had many features in common with my work on community development finance. One of the prominent similarities was the critical role of ethnic and racial segregation. In community development, residential segregation by race and ethnicity is an issue of concern; in PE, it is social and professional segregation by gender, race, and ethnicity.

I came to learn about a set of "classic" firms, which were the early players in the minority-targeted PE sphere. These included, among others, Opportunity Capital (Fremont, California), TSG Capital (Stamford, Connecticut), and Syncom Venture Partners (Silver Spring, Maryland). Founded decades ago, these firms had established long and impressive track records.

There was also a more recent "emerging" cadre of firms, measured by both length of time in business and the age of their founders. These companies were receiving considerable attention because they appeared to represent a new vanguard in the minority-focused PE arena. Each had been able to raise significant amounts of funds in what seemed to be a very short time; among them were ICV Partners (New York), Altos Ventures (Menlo Park, California), and Ascend Ventures (New York).

I will share the narrative of Syncom Ventures, an early descendant of Secretary Stans's MESBIC program. Like other similar firms, it encountered the array of opportunities, constraints, and considerations that are embedded in the social and racial contexts in which the firm was founded and evolved.

## THE "CLASSIC": THE STORY OF SYNCOM VENTURES

Syndicated Communications, or Syncom, dates to 1977, when a group of investors—including the Cooperative Assistance Fund, Ford Foundation, Opportunity Funding Corporation, and Presbyterian Economic Development Corporation—petitioned Herbert P. Wilkins to found a new venture capital fund. Wilkins was a successful financial and management consultant and a graduate of Harvard Business School (1970).

The nascent fund's objective was to seek investments in early-stage, high-growth companies that met at least one of the following criteria: (1) business models conceptualized by ethnic minorities; (2) firms managed by minorities; or (3) firms that targeted minority, underserved markets. This three-part investing focus was relatively common among MESBICs and would become influential over time. One could envision businesses that met all three criteria, and some that would only meet one. My own observation is that this fuzziness in intent has, at times, been a benefit to these investment firms, allowing them the flexibility to pursue multiple business opportunities in relatively smaller market spaces.

Although most venture capital firms were organized as partnerships of limited duration, Syncom was initially created as a corporation, with a total capitalization of about $1.75 million. As president and CEO, Wilkins focused his energy on building companies and mentoring entrepreneurs, and he spent the first several months of his tenure studying the market for available deals, devising a business plan, and figuring out how to raise more capital.

Early on, Wilkins hired Terry Jones. As a senior financial analyst with the Communications Research Center (Washington, D.C.), Jones had extensive knowledge of opportunities in the communications industry. Jones had both bachelor's and master's degrees in electrical engineering and, like Wilkins, had earned his MBA from Harvard. In addition to work as a practicing engineer, there were other elements of Jones's resume that would add value to the firm: his experience with the Booker T. Washington Foundation and work focused on securing minority-owned cable franchises in major cities.

I suspect investors eyebrows raised about the competence of minority businesses or those who invested in them (remember that the launch of this equity firm is happening at the same time that Andrew Brimmer questioned minority depository instititutions, mentioned in chapter 3). At the time, the venture capital industry was not only geographically localized, it was demographically comprised of white, male managers. In addition, VCs were generally graduates of a small number of educational institutions; importantly for Syncom, the Harvard Business School was one of them. Jones and Wilkins each brought recognizable, elite educational and professional credentials to the new firm. They had attended the "right" schools and worked in the "right" companies. They also shared a passion for developing opportunities in markets others overlooked.

Recognizing the need to grow beyond the initial capitalization, Wilkins and Jones's approach to raising funds was to join the SBA's MESBIC program and simultaneously seek additional capital from private-sector investors. Wilkins's private-sector funding efforts were unsuccessful. Although he had the proper credentials, he was an unknown entity within the circles of limited partners who typically funded venture capitalists. In 1978, Wilkins and Jones applied for a MESBIC license via a subsidiary firm they created, called Syncom Capital Corporation (SCC).

The MESBIC program provided a means to jumpstart Syncom's activities by providing leveraged capital. The partners were able to raise an additional $3 to $4 million for each $1.3 million in private funds that had capitalized SCC. One of the program's benefits was that it could provide capital multipliers that would encourage investors to provide seed funding to investment teams like Wilkins and Jones.

The incentive of matching funds would allow firms to increase their capital base relatively rapidly. Without regard to racial minorities, many venture capital practitioners considered the SBIC program to be a great vehicle for getting involved in the VC business because of the general scarcity of capital at the time. Some went on to become iconic venture capital funds, including Draper & Johnson and Sutter Hill, which both began as SBICs.[10]

## THE MEDIUM IS THE MESSAGE[11]

Wilkins, Jones, and their team sought to develop a differentiated business strategy. Since the firm targeted early-stage, high-growth opportunities in underserved markets, they felt it important to build a capability in investments within the media and telecommunications industries. With relatively limited competition in their investment niche, Syncom executives figured this level of specialization would help them identify undervalued opportunities faster and target investors with an appetite for media deals. Jones's prior work experience with minority-owned cable franchises provided a solid knowledge base for the investment team; however, there was an enabling change in government policy that accelerated demand in their niche.

During the early 1970s, the broadcast communications industry began to receive increased scrutiny for its relative lack of ethnic and racial representation. Because broadcasting was the dominant source for America's public information, the industry's regulator, the Federal Communications Commission (FCC), had an interest in a diversity of voices on the airwaves.

Recognizing that the broadcast airwaves are a publicly held property, the FCC required broadcasters to provide regular reports on the ethnic and racial diversity of their staffs; it specifically requested data on seven job categories, from officials and managers through labor and service workers. Not surprisingly, studies of the industry at the time showed particularly low levels of representation—for example, less than 3 percent minority representation among officials and managers—in 1970.[12]

In 1976, FCC chairman Richard Wiley modified these reporting requirements by exempting broadcasting firms with fewer than eleven employees. At the time, firms with fewer than eleven employees represented 32 percent of the industry and 47 percent of its entry-level jobs.[13]

Although the rationale was to eliminate unduly burdensome procedures, that decision received considerable opposition from civil rights and religious groups, including the NAACP, the National Catholic Communications Association, and the National Organization for Women. In 1977, the U.S. Court of Appeals struck down the FCC's rules as "arbitrary and capricious."[14] If the reporting requirements were limited to firms with eleven employees or more, then a substantial segment of the industry's employment would not be included.

The following year (February 1978), in another effort to increase diversity in the industry, the FCC announced its intention to increase the number of minority-owned radio and television stations; in the late 1970s, only 1 percent of stations were owned by minorities. In May, the FCC, by unanimous vote, approved two policy mechanisms to facilitate diversity, detailed in a Policy Statement on Minority Ownership of Broadcast Facilities.

First, any owner who sold his or her station to a minority would not have to pay taxes on any capital gains from the sale. Second, any existing broadcast owner in danger of losing the station's broadcast license would be allowed to sell to a minority at a "distressed" price (a distressed sale being a relatively attractive alternative to outright loss of license).[15] Although this policy was launched during the Carter administration, it mirrored the Nixon administration's belief that the way to influence diversity within the broadcast industry was to create more minority managers. Both Black capitalism and the FCC's minority ownership initiative rely on the underlying assumption that increasing diversity can be achieved through ownership, rather than through monitoring and encouraging existing, white-owned or white-managed firms to integrate.

About the time Syncom was obtaining its MESBIC license, only one of the 8,196 television licenses in the United States was held by Blacks, and none by Latinos.[16] Undaunted, Syncom's executives recognized that as more minorities pursued broadcast licenses, they would need capital to complete potential sales. Wilkins, Jones, and their team envisioned Syncom as a niche innovator, creating opportunities for minorities to participate in the media and communications industries as owners and professionals.

The FCC's new policy had opened a demand space, and Syncom's partners were confident they had a competitive advantage over "mainstream" VC competitors. Because of social and racial segregation, they felt that most white investment teams would not be familiar with the social networks, culture, and dynamics of minority communities. They understood their competitive edge not only in locating the best potential minority media entrepreneurs, but also, as important, in establishing bonds of trust that could be of significant benefit during a firm's acquisition and financing process. Their notion was based on a harsh reality. Even among professionals with elite education and corporate experience, relationships were still racially circumscribed. Class matters, but so does race.

## BREAKING INTO BROADCASTING

The FCC's diversification initiative gave Syncom an incentive to target a large portion of their initial investments to radio broadcasting and television cable systems.

Some underlying features of broadcasting made investing unique. One was the regulated control of the number of firms in the industry. Since access to media airwaves required a license, and there was a finite number of licenses available, Syncom's managers knew that companies' asset values would be influenced by scarcity. Even though a station's management might underperform, an assessment of its valuation had to take into account the value of its underlying geographic market access and reach. Scarcity also meant there would likely be a number of purchasers for a station at some future point, so it would be more appropriate to construct financial models that encouraged sale rather than the expectation of debt service.

The Syncom team also considered that not all broadcast media were equally attractive. The company limited its investment in television stations because of the large capital requirements involved in building television franchises. Instead, Syncom pursued opportunities in building and developing new issues of both FM and AM radio stations.[17] The team was particularly attracted to FM radio, partly because of low entry valuations but also because they believed it to be the future of radio broadcasting.

Syncom's team became aware of a fascinating natural experiment. In their experience, there was a "color gap" in radio advertising sales revenues. Advertisers tended to support a station owned and managed by white broadcasters, even when the station offered a Black programming format. When Black-format stations were sold to minority managers, advertising support often diminished, even disappeared. To some, this phenomenon was due to the result of stereotypes about the skills of minority managers, even those operating Black-format stations. Another theory, which I tend to endorse, saw this "race discount" as a function of social networks. White station owners, despite format, would be more likely to have established comfortable relationships with advertisers, many of whom would also be white. This type of value, accruing from social relationships, is one example of what sociologists term "social capital."

To analyze an investment opportunity in FM broadcasting, Syncom typically ignored the capital size of the deal; Syncom's managers believed they could always find the capital to finance a good opportunity. Instead, they concentrated on understanding a station's business model—its operating model and position in its target market. Wilkins wrote about the team's close attention to the credentials, experience, and abilities of a station's potential management staff, a factor that they considered almost as important as the underlying value of the station itself.

One early entrepreneur who faced probing questions from the Syncom team was Cathy Hughes, the general sales manager of Howard University's radio station, WHUR. She had approached Wilkins and Jones to discuss her interest in station ownership. Their meeting inaugurated a long-term business relationship that saw Syncom provide the initial seed funding for Hughes's company, Almic Broadcasting, later renamed Radio One.

Over the years, they challenged, cajoled, and encouraged Hughes to expand her business through the acquisition and management of a growing group of stations—a strategy grounded in purchasing small, underperforming stations in urban markets and then focusing the format on the tastes of the local minority population, such as rhythm and blues, talk, or politics.[18] Theirs was a strong, multifaceted relationship; Wilkins and Jones were Hughes's investors, advisers, and mentors, as well as her friends. When Radio One went on to offer an initial public offering (IPO) in 1999, Hughes became the first Black woman to lead a publicly traded firm.[19]

This type of close, confiding relationship with portfolio managers was a key element of the Syncom business approach, and it promoted substantial trust among its largely minority base of potential portfolio entrepreneurs.

## "GRADUATING" FROM THE SBIC PROGRAM

While the SBIC program offered a helpful head start, the Syncom founders would eventually find the program's policies limiting, as several restrictive guidelines curtailed where they could invest, how much equity exposure they could assume, and how much return was possible through exits.

First, the program tended to have greater applicability to businesses in mature, rather than nascent, industries. The structure of many SBIC instruments favored businesses with established, relatively predictable returns.[20]

Second, the SBA seemed to prefer financing the most socially or economically disadvantaged entrepreneurs. This was at odds with Syncom's target market and the firm's support for attractive investments that had been overlooked or underpriced by the larger set of investors (predominantly nonminority).

Third, MESBIC managers were generally restricted from taking controlling positions in portfolio companies except as protection mechanisms for damaged investments. And fourth, they usually realized liquidity events via debt repayments by their portfolio companies and sales of warrants, instead of through strategic sales or public equity offerings. This meant that MESBICs could not fully benefit from a substantial amount of their invested capital since, typically, the largest potential investment realization for any private equity firm occurred through the eventual sale of an invested firm. The lack of a strategic sale or IPO option was considerably limiting, especially for a firm that was financing broadcast media purchases.[21]

Because of SBA restrictions, Syncom's partners made a decision that presented substantial risks but potentially offered great opportunity for the minority-controlled venture capital community: raise a fund from exclusively private sources. After an intense three-year marketing effort, the partners succeeded in forming Syndicated Communications Venture Partners II, also known as Syncom II. Founded in 1990, Syncom II was capitalized at about $35 million and featured the traditional limited partnership structure.

This organizational evolution also meant a structural change for Syncom, as it would no longer operate as a corporation, but as a partnership. This was the typical structure for private equity and venture capital firms, which seek capital from what are called limited partners (LPs), usually institutional investors like pension funds and high-net-worth individuals. Investor funds are then held in time-determined limited partnerships, which typically last six to ten years. During the limited partnership, the general partners (GPs) find, vet, and make investments in firms that are likely to be sold or become public companies at a later date (ideally, within the period of the partnership). Any profits from the sale or IPO would be split between the GPs (the investment professionals) and the limited partner investors, often distributed by allocating 20 percent to the GPs and the remainder to the LPs.

Syncom's partners consistently encountered legitimacy and reputational barriers in attracting interest from institutional investors. First, one common concern was their lack of "sufficient experience" or a "track record." As the venture capital industry was a relatively small club at the time, few minorities would be able to present a record of past investments.

Second, some investors cited the mediocre or poor returns of other SBA-funded groups as a reason for not committing capital. The Syncom team believed the poor performance of early MESBIC funds applied a "broad brush" that unfairly tainted new investments with similar objectives. Syncom had to overcome a widely held perception that a minority-focused, niche fund was somewhat less profit oriented and would tend, as did the failed Arcata Investments, to focus on "socially conscious" programs.

Third, other potential investors expressed interest but preferred to wait until Syncom had completed liquidation of its previous funds—an approach that Syncom's managers objected to because they felt they would be "leaving a lot of potential upside on the table."

Wilkins reflected on the subtle perceptual differences he felt Syncom had to overcome: "Venture investing is a very personal business, and so if you think that the people you're considering investing in are inferior, you will not believe they will make it, so you won't invest. Many institutions are not investing in minority-controlled funds or portfolio companies because they are blinded by racism."

For me, this represents one of the classic errors in what may be called "social" or "impact" investing. The reason many people consider these phrases to be fluffy oxymorons is that, frequently, there is ambiguity in the intended goals and objectives at the outset. It seems that some MESBIC funders saw their investments as charitable. In other words, they would influence change with capital, but not by personally engaging with the funding recipients. The key underlying issue is that they did not see minority entrepreneurs as being able to mount competitive firms that would produce returns. I am speculating, of course, but it seems that some envisioned minorities operating in exclusively minority environments, in separate places. The proposed capital would be used to help minorities create their own firms, as long as the existing social structure—a segregated one—was maintained.

Wilkins and Jones began to contemplate ways to create a more favorable and receptive environment, either for the next fundraising round or when firms with a similar focus tried to follow Syncom's lead in expanding beyond the MESBIC program.

Early in 1991, Wilkins and Jones developed what they believed was a novel line of attack. Wilkins called JoAnn Price, president of the National Association of Investment Companies (NAIC), a professional association of funders pursuing opportunities in the same set of niches as Syncom. Most of its investment managers were Black.

Wilkins told Price of his belief that the industry would benefit from the creation of a fund of funds (FOF)—allowing LPs to invest in a market basket of investment funds rather than in individual securities. The FOF could act as an intermediary representative of the industry, advocating for the niche itself rather than for an individual team of managers, or GPs.

Price agreed that the plan would provide a broad base of organizational support, quantitative data, and institutional legitimacy that would benefit many attempting to raise capital. Potential investors curious about investing with minority-led firms could outsource some of the due diligence by using the FOF to research the best teams and to allocate capital accordingly.

Interested LPs would gain an additional level of diversification by investing in a group of vetted GPs, rather than an individual team. The FOF could provide an intermediary step for LPs who might be interested in "testing the market." Wilkins's pitch was that through an initial, exploratory investment in a minority-targeted FOF, LP investors would gain exposure to talented, diverse GPs, and the knowledge, comfort, and familiarity gained through the experience would encourage them to make larger commitments to individual investment teams.

Not long after, JoAnn Price left her position as NAIC president to start Fairview Capital. While benefiting many, the FOF's strategy paid dividends to Syncom as well. Five years later, when Syncom's partners began raising their third round of funds for Syndicated Communications Venture Partners III, LP, Fairview Capital contributed $18 million.


## ENTERING THE CABLE TELEVISION SPACE

Having recognized fundamental structural differences between radio broadcasting and cable systems, Syncom's partners crisscrossed the country looking for cable deals they could finance. Unlike radio broadcasting, in which the correlation between high audience ratings and revenues was not always positive for minority-owned properties, success in cable systems appeared to be independent of advertisers because of subscription fees. Syncom executives believed that by focusing on the operational details of building an individual cable television system, the franchises it backed would achieve financial break even faster than in radio.

TABLE 9.1
The Syncom Investment Approach

| What is the objective reality? | What is the subjective reality? | What are the hurdles and constraints? | Resolution |
|---|---|---|---|
| • Collection of all relevant facts, including macro environment, target market, and individual customer characteristics, tastes, preferences, and so forth. | • What do Syncom and other investors want vis-à-vis management's and other stakeholders' motivations? | • Defining a winning strategy—what does Syncom have to do to get what it wants?<br>• Defining funding strategy, establishing financial controls, and addressing political issues. | • Triangulation among ideal solution and alternatives, then taking a view.<br>• Resolving legal issues and negotiating deal specifics. |
| Emphasis on assessing feasibility and market conditions | ──────────────────────▶ | | Emphasis on venture development and management |

Table developed from case writer notes based on interview with Terry Jones.

During our interviews, I asked Terry Jones whether he could summarize the Syncom approach to investing. He provided a detailed answer, distilled in table 9.1.

## MANAGING THE DISCOUNTS

Unfortunately, the "race discount" in advertising prices persisted and continued to be a major problem that depressed the potential value of Syncom's portfolio. Most of the advertising dollars still went to white-owned stations that offered general programming in the same markets as Syncom's stations, even when those stations had lower ratings.[22] The success that many of Syncom's radio stations had in becoming audience-ratings-leaders did not necessarily translate into commensurate revenues. (Their firms would have had higher revenues if the owners were white and had social connections to other white business owners.)

Years later, in 1998, the FCC would release a study that confirmed Syncom's experience. When a minority owned a minority-focused radio station, it received 17 percent less in advertising revenue than when a comparable minority-focused station was white-owned.[23] Syncom's managers felt vindicated, yet they were proud they had managed to develop strategies to combat the problem rather than have it stymie their efforts to assist their client companies in achieving growth and prosperity.

Through 1991, Syncom's cumulative results confirmed a substantial impact on the minority-owned business sector. Syncom's GPs had financed more than sixty minority-controlled companies across the spectrum of media and communications. The firm had realized a compounded 18 percent return, a performance level that placed the firm in the upper quartile of the VC industry.[24]

I visited Syncom in 2002 in their Silver Spring, Maryland, offices for field interviews. By this point, Syncom was a recognized, established, institutionalized team of investors with a track record of successful investments. These included BET, Radio One, South Chicago Cable Television, Ed Dorado Communications, and Z-Spanish Radio.

At the time of interviews, they were engaged in something truly audacious. Ethiopian-born entrepreneur Noah Samara was seeking Syncom's assistance in his attempt to launch three satellite radio networks to three continents—Africa, Asia, and South America. The business was similar to XM and Sirius Satellite Radio, introduced only a few years earlier. Samara's vision was a direct-to-receiver satellite audio service that would broadcast information and entertainment directly to a consumer's personal, compact, portable receiver from a satellite in geostationary orbit.[25] He named his company WorldSpace to indicate its goal of channeling media content to parts of the world other players had overlooked or believed unreachable.

Once fully functional, the WorldSpace constellation of satellites would beam signals to three continents and deliver digital, audio, and multimedia programs to a potential audience of 4.5 billion people—roughly 80 percent of the population in developing nations. Figure 9.1 presents the intended coverage area of three satellites, once fully deployed.

Samara estimated the total cost would approach $300 million, and he and his partners had found the resources needed to achieve their aggressive goal. Preliminary estimates indicated that WorldSpace

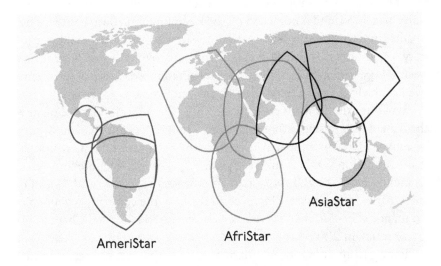

*Figure 9.1* WorldSpace global coverage.

would break even after selling approximately fifteen to twenty million receivers.

I remember thinking how bold the whole venture seemed. As they described the WorldSpace deal, the group outlined its five categories of "need": financial, regulatory, space and ground infrastructure, receiver technology, and program content.

Financially, the venture would require hundreds of millions of dollars over a five- to ten-year time frame in order to fully develop the system. The to-do list was long. Syncom had passed on the initial idea of investing, in part because the team believed that clearing all of the funding, licensing, regulatory, and technical hurdles would prove too difficult.

By the time I interviewed the Syncom team, they had made the decision to invest with Samara to a lesser extent and with a different objective. In fact, Samara was not asking them to meet the substantial price tag for development. He was far more interested in the strategic and symbolic support they could provide, which would be critical during the firm's early stages. In short, Samsara had sought out Syncom because of its demonstrated ability to navigate complicated regulatory funding and managerial waters.

The Syncom team likened WorldSpace's potential to the advent of cable television, and it homed in on the large, rapidly growing advertising market in developing countries. WorldSpace also presented an opportunity to extract first-mover advantages from its ownership of proprietary technology to power the only truly global radio broadcasting system, as well as shield it from exploitation by the satellite radio spectrum.

Syncom exited the investment in 2005, when WorldSpace company held its IPO, raising just under $250 million. From Syncom's perspective, their investment had resulted in a positive return, although Samara's vision was not fully realized. The WorldSpace satellites were launched in Africa and Asia, with an estimated 170,000 and 450,000 subscribers, respectively. However, in the end, the company was unable to meet its massive debt service requirements and filed for Chapter 11 bankruptcy in 2008.

For Syncom, it had been a daring venture that did not result in the same type of success as their radio and television financings, or their relationships with companies like Radio One, Black Entertainment Television (BET), and TV One. Syncom's managers recognized that VC is an industry fraught with long odds and certain failures, and that the overall returns of a fund depend on the likelihood of having more successes than failures.

In late 2013, Herbert Wilkins passed away. His achievements were reflected in the remembrances of entrepreneurs who had worked with Syncom. Debra L. Lee, president and CEO of BET, said, "Herb's influence in the Black and Hispanic media landscape is unmatched. He is in large measure responsible for the success of BET Networks and Radio One—two of the largest brands in the media space."

Cathy Hughes, cofounder of Radio One and TV One, offered a more personal account: "Herb was a firm lender, but he was patient, and nurturing. When I could not make my payments to Syncom, I pled with him to be patient with me, and I promised him that I would be the largest and most successful company in his portfolio. God has blessed me to make good on that promise."[26]


# GEORGE W. BUSH, THE FCC, AND MY NEIGHBOR

Colin Powell was a White House Fellow in the Office of Management and Budget during the Nixon administration, and I suspect would have been familiar with Black Capitalism, OMBE, and MESBICs. On his second day in office, President George W. Bush appointed Powell's son, and my childhood neighbor, thirty-seven-year-old Michael Powell, chairman of the Federal Communications Commission.

Powell gave one indication of how he might approach the issues of minority broadcast ownership and representation on the airwaves in a speech he gave to the California Broadcaster's Association.

> In my mind, we are right to be concerned when we see trends that suggest that minorities and women may not be enjoying the fruits of economic opportunity in this industry. We should work to find the reasons why this pronounced disparity exists, and where solutions may lie. . . . Moreover, in a competitive free market we cannot employ the same tools we once used to advance the interests of under-represented groups. . . . I would like to see more efforts to encourage private-sector initiatives. The market is inherently the domain of private actors, not public officials. . . . One way to address the problem is through investment funds specifically targeted to serve the needs of minorities and women.[27]

## THE FALSE CHOICE

For me, the suite of programs initiated under Black Capitalism had a challenging set of assumptions. It seems that during the late 1960s, there was an either-or choice about government intervention to improve social outcomes for those living in segregated, impoverished areas. Either policy should support initiatives providing economic and technical incentives to achieve greater ownership of firms within segregated spaces, or policy should support initiatives to achieve similar goals through integration in our workplaces, neighborhoods, and areas of public accommodation.

Of course, I personally experienced McNamara's experiment in forced integration by the U.S. military, and I suppose Michael Powell and I are the products of those efforts. In some cases, government intervention does indeed bring about change.

My issue with the first Black Capitalist model—interventions targeted at improving "segregated" locales rather than advancing "integrated" ones—is that I do not believe it either is born in the spirit of equality or results in that spirit. This does not mean I think initiatives to develop minority-owned, women-owned firms are not appropriate. Looking back over the decades, I think we have come to the conclusion that the either-or approach is not best; we need to leverage insightful both-and strategies if we are to effectively propel change.

# CHAPTER TEN

# Targeted Private Equity II

*The Advantages of Being a Marginal Minority*

THE SOCIOLOGIST Erving Goffman defined *total institutions* as places apart from modern societies but simultaneously situated within them. Goffman described them as "social hybrids, part residential community, part formal organization; therein lies its special interest."[1] Goffman recognized the military as a total institution—and, as a result, a natural experiment. One of those was the experiment of integration.

Because of the formal and structural controls imposed by military leadership, I grew up living on military installations around the world and in integrated civilian communities at home in the United States. The prevailing sociological research suggests that the experience would have sheltered me from other's expressions of their needs for racial distance that were common in other settings. The military system removed everyday residential, educational, and working distance between groups.

I suppose living overseas—with many classmates who, in addition to English, spoke Japanese, Filipino, Korean, or German at home—added to a comfort with social fluidity. As I've mentioned elsewhere, I didn't know how unusual this was for someone my age.

As a youngster, the syndicated airings of the *Batman* series starring Adam West and Burt Ward were among my favorite TV shows. For my friends and me, this show became destination viewing. Back then, I couldn't see the now obvious corniness, campiness, double entendres, and penchant for hyperbole. Instead, what mattered most were the action sequences that took place in every episode.

One episode was particularly memorable because of two special guests: the Green Hornet and his sidekick, Kato. At first, there was a bit of confusion about whether the Green Hornet and Kato were criminals or crime fighters, and as a result, there was a face-off battle between the two crime-fighting duos. In a battle of equals, Batman struggled with the Green Hornet while Robin fought with karate ace Kato. It was an edge-of-the-seat contest, and although I was a Batman fan, I found myself rooting for Kato. I can only guess that it was because he was a lone Asian among white crime fighters. It was inspiring for me to see a person of color who was not a criminal but a larger-than-life champion. In the adulation children feel for superheroes, I felt a kinship with Kato's insider-outsider status.

## BROKERAGE, HYBRIDITY, AND LIMINALITY

One of the more influential notions in sociology is that there are advantages to occupying social positions that link groups that are otherwise disconnected. One conception of these potential advantages is essentially medial. That is, in situations when there is only one or a few avenues of connection between groups, control of the avenue of exchange offers "structural" position and the ability to speed or slow exchange across groups.[2]

An even deeper competence is the ability to see opportunities others cannot by virtue of knowledge, experience, and connections across groups that can lead to innovations and novel ideas. This step beyond simply structural power is diverse "cultural" knowledge—the ability to understand what is and is not said that provides an individual the skills to achieve or "get things done" across disconnected domains.

The strategy and policy that led the U.S. military to integrate has spilled over into other domains, including academic institutions and corporations, albeit at a slower pace. As with the impact of the military's integration policy, these efforts have led to a small, growing cadre of women and ethnic minorities that have been educated and employed professionally in high-status institutions associated with paths to power.

In what were formally closed social spaces, the widening aperture has provided opportunities to learn and appropriate the markers and symbols of status and power with a broader population. The opportunities for this learning and relationship building include fraternities, sororities, clubs, and leadership posts during college (even secret societies), and boards, fellowships, and other associations that mark accomplishment or esteem in the professional sphere.

As these individuals progress in what are also social experiments in integration, they collect a wealth of experiences and relations— those from before entering college or corridors of corporate power, and those since. In a society so otherwise segregated, this knowledge and structural position allow for a capacity of hybridity that can be an advantage in business, and especially in the creation of new firms.

## ASCEND VENTURES INTO EDUCATION

In the summer of 2001, an old friend called to recommend an article in the *Wall Street Journal*. "Let me know what you think," she asked.

Under the title "Fund Taps Web of Firms Owned by Minorities," I read Paulette Thomas's story about the Ascend Venture Group, which had just closed a $40 million financing round.[3] "Venture capital is all about connections. Few minority-owned start-ups have had connections in mostly white, male venture capitalist circles," Thomas wrote.

What I found novel was that the article mirrored my own observations about the implications of the rising diversity in elite circles, specifically the access of women and minorities to higher education and the corridors of corporate firms. Thomas continued:

> As Ascend's four partners, all African-Americans, prowl for potential investments, they are testing the idea that ethnic minorities and women have now attained the critical mass needed to be a viable sort of *outsiders* club [emphasis added]. For although many of these businesses lack tickets into traditional venture capital networks, they belong to other tight-knit webs. "There are fairly robust and

well-connected networks of minorities in the professions," says Darryl Wash, Ascend's managing partner.

It was intriguing to learn that Wash and his partners were building Ascend with the notion that they would have competitive advantage *through* their minority status. The founders believed that we have reached a point in American elite institutions where sizable numbers of women and ethnic or racial minorities have had the opportunity to receive graduate degrees from the "right" schools (Harvard, Stanford) and to work at the "right" firms (Goldman Sachs, Credit Suisse). These new entrants would face fewer questions of industry credibility or legitimacy and might well be comfortable in the clubby corridors of finance and private equity.

Unfortunately, because there are still so few minorities populating the upper echelons of business institutions, they are especially visible. To the degree they choose to connect with other minorities—"outsiders who are also insiders"—they can leverage their positional status to gain considerably greater levels of connectivity than their white, male counterparts.

The theory was intriguing. Could underrepresented minorities embedded in networks of social and professional elites use their connections to leverage advantage and, in the process, help others who were truly excluded?

As part of our broad-based research on private equity and funding for minority entrepreneurs, my team and I traveled annually to a number of finance conferences, among them the National Association of Investment Companies (NAIC), largely composed of minorities and firms that focused on minority markets or owners. While attending in 2002, I finagled an introduction to Ascend founder Darryl Wash and his partner, Roszell Mack, who graciously agreed to participate in my field research.

Unlike the seasoned, legendary Syncom founders discussed in the prior chapter, the Ascend principals were my contemporaries but there was another differentiator. When I visited Syncom, I had felt that I was learning about past, breakthrough experiences of Black men who had faced a starkly different terrain from the one I traversed, and I knew I owed them a debt of gratitude. At the Ascend offices, there was a palpable difference: this visit had a future-forward aspect to it, filled with promise and potential.

## THE BEGINNINGS OF ASCEND VENTURES

After operating as an angel investing network for several years, in the late 1990s Darryl Wash, Roszell Mack, David Bowen, and Charles Crockett decided to pursue a formalized investment effort and establish their own firm. Given their personal and professional histories, the partners believed they had a unique, unmatched ability to access the most attractive investment opportunities within their networks.

The founding four enjoyed impressive credentials: Wash graduated from the University of California, Berkeley; Bowen from Williams College; Crockett from the University of Pennsylvania's Wharton School; and Mack from Yale University. They each began their careers at the financial powerhouse Goldman Sachs, where their professional lives initially intersected in the mid-1980s.

At about the same time, they independently left Goldman to pursue advanced education: Wash and Bowen at Stanford Graduate School of Business; Crockett at Stanford Law School; and Mack at Harvard Business School. Subsequently, the four returned to Goldman Sachs, where they forged a strong personal and professional friendship. Over time, each moved on from Goldman Sachs; yet the four remained in contact and, from time to time, met to discuss potential private investment opportunities.

A turning point came in June 1996, when Mack was presented with an opportunity to invest in a start-up Internet company, StarMedia Networks, Inc., focused on creating user communities in Latin America. One of StarMedia's founders, Jack Chen, was a business school classmate and close personal friend of Mack. Based upon Mack's enthusiasm for the deal, the group performed extensive due diligence and determined that StarMedia was indeed a very attractive investment opportunity.

The only challenge was the amount of capital the company was seeking. At the time, the Internet was in its nascent stages, and private investment opportunities in Latin America were unexplored, unknown, and uncertain. As a result, the group found only two additional investors willing to augment the capital the four were prepared to commit. In November 1996, the extended group made a seed investment in StarMedia for $0.50 a share. The original group of investors participated in every subsequent round of funding, up to the company's initial public offering (IPO) in 1999, at which time shares of StarMedia sold for $15.00.[4] The group had made a substantial gain on their investment.

Following the StarMedia deal, the investors participated in several other opportunities, and set out to develop a reputation as a team of angel investors. Between 1997 and 2000, the group formed several separate special-purpose entities for investing in technology-based companies, and by 2000 they managed more than $10 million in capital for more than eighty investors.

In our discussions, Wash shared that he had maintained enthusiasm for the development of his own firm and, by spring 1999, proposed that the group establish a formal, institutionalized venture capital (VC) firm. While Mack shared Wash's excitement at the prospect, the others were not so easily convinced. By Labor Day 1999, however, the four had committed to launching Ascend Ventures. By early 2000, all had resigned from their banking jobs and each had invested $250,000 in the new firm. The group planned to raise at least $75 million in total for their first fund and hoped to secure investments from individual investors for whom they had managed personal capital.

## SKEPTICS ABOUND: GETTING ASCEND OFF THE GROUND

Initially, the group worked out of Wash's apartment. Fundraising efforts started with a private placement memorandum:

> The Partnership will focus on early-stage technology investments. With target commitments of between $75 million and $100 million . . . the Partnership will . . . focus on investing in companies that have pre-money valuations of less than $25 million. . . . In most cases, the Partnership will continue to invest in follow-on financings of successful portfolio companies.

By March 2000, the group had begun to approach institutional investors and their network of high-net-worth individuals. The timing could not have been more perfect. The team's flagship investment, StarMedia, had just reached $70 per share and two others, Kozmo .com and Evolve Software, had filed to go public within a day of one another. The team knew that the fundraising process for first-time funds could be lengthy and challenging, but it expected to receive early support from its individual investor base and from one or two institutions with whom it had begun discussions.

There were, however, negative signs in the market that tamped down investors' appetites. On March 10, 2000, the NASDAQ composite, a proxy for the technology sector, closed at 5,048.62. One year later, in a steady decline, it was trading below 2,000. Against this backdrop, the interest of individual investors evaporated, leaving the Ascend team with only long-term institutional investors to target. And while many institutions invest through up and down cycles, the unprecedented decline gave virtually all investors pause.

Compounding the difficult market environment, Ascend seemingly lacked a number of elements important to limited partners. Despite their collective investing activity, the principals did not have a true portfolio track record, backgrounds in technology management, or significant operating experience. Skeptics believed that the firm would be unable to raise the amount of capital that would allow them to sustain their operations, and some suggested that the firm alter its approach. These suggestions included changing personnel, hiring investment professionals with operating experience, and partnering with a larger, more established (and perhaps nonminority) firm to heighten credibility. Adding to these problems, Ascend was running low on resources to pay for office space and personnel; the founders themselves had gone without salaries for a year.

After nine months of marketing, Ascend got the break it needed. Three important investors—the Goldman Sachs Group, the New York State Common Retirement Fund, and Fairview Capital Partners (led by JoAnn Price)—all committed to provide substantial capital to the new fund.

As an accommodation to these investors, Ascend hired, as a consultant, a venture partner with substantial technology and operations experience and formed a technology advisory council.[5] In March 2001, Ascend held its first closing of $40 million for Ascend Ventures and began investing.

In the aftermath of the September 11 terrorist attacks, investors once again became wary of making investment commitments. By the beginning of 2002, the Ascend team had invested in eight companies. Considering the challenges associated with fundraising, and under the watchful eye of its limited partners, Ascend stuck narrowly to its original, marketed focus—leveraging minority and women's networks to invest in early-stage applied technology companies. Ascend knew that staying "on scope" was important to the institutional investment community and that, as a new firm, it had not established the goodwill to stray too far. The partners maintained a long-term goal of broadening Ascend's investment activities, but when and how to do that were persistent questions.

## AN OPPORTUNITY IN PUBLIC EDUCATION

A few years prior, the Ascend partners had been approached with an investment opportunity in a niche industry that was ripe for growth—supplemental education services, such as tutoring and counseling.

The firm, Platform Learning, had a novel angle: a focus on urban, low-performing schools. Roszell Mack, Ascend's lead investor on educational ventures, explained that Platform's programs were targeted toward students within Title I public schools identified as "in need of improvement" under the No Child Left Behind Act.

Like Ascend's founders, Platform Learning's founders Gene Wade and Juan Torres were highly educated, credentialed minorities. Torres had graduated from Baruch College and received his Juris Doctor degree from the University of Michigan and his MBA from the University of California, Berkeley. Wade was a graduate of Morehouse College, Harvard Law School, and the University of Pennsylvania's Wharton School (MBA). Given how few racial minorities have these backgrounds, it is really no surprise that the two teams found one another.

Early in his career, Wade developed a passion for educating poor children and minorities that was motivated by reflections on his own education experiences within the inner-city schools of Roxbury, Massachusetts. He saw schools as "powerful catalysts for human economic development and as incubators of human talent for the growing technology industry."[6] Torres, who had been raised in the South Bronx, shared Wade's commitment to both education and entrepreneurship.

Only a few months after the $36 million sale of their first highly successful venture, LearnNow, Inc., the two cashed-out entrepreneurs became intrigued by the opportunity to tap into the estimated $4.1 billion public education market. They recognized dual market potential resulting from the recently signed No Child Left Behind Act: assisting failing public school districts in becoming qualified providers of supplemental education services, and providing supplemental education services directly to children. In 2003, Wade and Torres founded Platform Learning, Inc., envisioning a company that would deliver after-school, weekend, and summer tutoring programs.

## AN ENABLING EXECUTIVE ORDER: GEORGE BUSH AND NO CHILD LEFT BEHIND

Education in 2002 was an $815 billion industry, largely funded through local real estate taxes.[7] Despite per-pupil expenditures of nearly $6,700 annually, the overall performance of American students remained dismal compared to that of their foreign counterparts.[8]

Between 1965 and 2004, when Congress passed the Elementary and Secondary Education Act (ESEA), the U.S. government spent more than $242 billion to help educate disadvantaged children.[9] Yet the achievement gap between rich and poor and white and minority students remained significant.[10] Figure 10.1 shows rising ESEA expenditures and relatively flat reading scores.

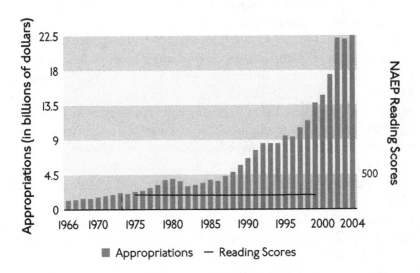

*Figure 10.1* National ESEA reading scores, 1966–2004.
*Source*: Jay R. Campbell, Catherine M. Hombo, and John Mazzeo, *NAEP 1999: Trends in Academic Progress: Three Decades of Student Performance,* National Center for Educational Statistics, August 2000, https://nces.ed.gov/nationsreportcard /pdf/main1999/2000469.pdf.

Following a yearlong bipartisan effort to bring flexibility and accountability to federal education programs, on January 8, 2002, President Bush signed into law the No Child Left Behind (NCLB) Act. Its objective was to achieve academic proficiency for 100 percent of public school students by the 2013–14 school year, with a particular focus on low-income students attending low-performing schools. One provision allowed Title I funds—money provided to school districts from the federal government based on the percentage of children eligible to receive free or reduced-price lunches—to be used for supplemental education services (SES), such as tutoring, remediation, and academic intervention.

Under NCLB, the competition for Title I funds created significant financial pressure for districts to become qualified providers of supplemental education services or find other ways to maintain control over their Title I funding. Title I fund eligibility for SES, per pupil, averaged more than $1,200 dollars annually.[11] In essence, NCLB created the need for a sizable tutoring and test-prep market, particularly for those districts with a large number of Title I schools. It fell to school districts to find ways to compete with private providers of supplemental education services.

There were two market segments for SES. The first was the private market, in which parents paid for their children to receive tutoring and test prep outside of school. The second was the public market, in which states, school districts, and government agencies funded tutoring, test prep, and other enrichment services that the NCLB required. In 2003, the private SES market was estimated at $4.3 billion.[12] This market segment offered significant opportunities, given its large size, rapid growth, and high degree of fragmentation. The market leader was Sylvan Learning Systems, which had less than 5 percent overall market share.

The public SES segment in 2002 was estimated at a healthy $4.1 billion.[13] This market was not open to for-profit organizations prior to the passage of NCLB, so the large for-profit players, including Sylvan, Kaplan, and Princeton Review, collectively made up less than 2 percent market share.[14]

Unlike its competitors, Platform Learning's strategy tapped into two income streams. First, it targeted public school districts to which the firm would provide a turnkey after-school program.[15] Second, Platform Learning would also become a qualified provider, offering supplemental education services directly to children in failing Title I schools. Not only was Platform Learning's business model unique, its market strategy was to assist school districts by addressing many of their problems simultaneously.

Platform would support underperforming districts and those that lacked the resources to develop SES capabilities by opening learning centers, training employees, and earning them designation as qualified providers. In addition, Platform would help districts implement after-school programs of a quality that directly competed with traditional for-profit players. This service was attractive to Platform's potential clients, as the majority of these schools did not have the resources or capabilities to quickly implement high-quality after-school tutoring and skill building without outside support. In this way, Platform would help districts hold onto critical Title I dollars that had begun to flow to private supplemental education service providers. This was a critical issue for school districts where, under NCLB, schools identified as "needing improvement" were barred from providing supplemental education services under NCLB.

Platform's business model was also designed to help districts train their staff on how to improve student academic performance—assistance that would simultaneously help schools meet adequate yearly progress (AYP) standards.[16] Platform initially targeted underperforming school districts that were ineligible to become qualified SES providers. Students within poor-performing districts were the most likely targets of private SES providers—and, without any practical recourse, these districts risked losing a significant portion of their Title I funding to outside providers. They would be the most amenable to Platform's services.

These trends suggested an expanding market demand with limited supply. The Platform Learning strategy seemed to provide a unique opportunity, and the founders seemed to have the requisite skills and networks to build the firm nationally.

## GETTING TO THE INVESTMENT

Unlike many decisions Ascend's investment committee faced, Platform Learning was a departure. It would be the first time the firm invested outside of applied technology, and although Platform had generated substantial revenue in its first three months of operation, it was virtually a start-up—something Ascend had publicly maintained it did not want to pursue.

Nonetheless, in the spring of 2003, the Ascend team decided to move forward with an investment in Platform Learning. The decision was made within only a few weeks, a significantly shorter time frame than Ascend's traditional four- to six-month due diligence period. Wash and Mack were champions of the Platform investment, enjoyed a long history with its founders, and had negotiated an attractive 33 percent ownership stake for Ascend's initial investment.

As the months passed since learning about the investment from Wash and Mack, I followed the progress of Platform Learning with a mixture of curiosity and, I must confess, satisfaction. Despite the strides in Black educational and professional attainment, it was still uncommon to come across Black private equity professionals or start-up entrepreneurs. The additional element of a venture that could generate profits while helping to educate children in low-income areas was as inspiring for me as it was for Platform's founders.

The company grew quickly, and by early 2005, Platform was the nation's largest SES provider.[17] However, it faced increasing and aggressive competition, which did not go unnoticed.

On April 4, 2005, I opened my morning *New York Times* to find an article titled "A Lucrative Brand of Tutoring Grows Unchecked."[18] The lede pointed out the rapid expansion of the market: "The federally-financed tutoring industry has doubled in size in each of the last two years, with the potential to become a $2 billion-a-year enterprise, market analysts say."[19]

The article also called attention to rising concerns about what constituted "quality educational services" and, in some cases, questionable marketing tactics, including offering families electronics, gift certificates, and basketball tickets for enrollment (at the time, these offerings were not illegal). The article mentioned that the City of New York had begun an investigation into these practices.

Deeper into the article, my heart dropped when I read the following: "But so far, most of the problems reported appear to reflect poor management. In March, for instance, the Chicago school system asked Platform Learning Inc. . . . to leave seven of its schools because of numerous lapses—including repeated absences by tutors—leaving hundreds of struggling students without extra help just before the Illinois Standard Achievement Test."

Just a few weeks later, the *Times* reported that congressional hearings had been held on SES tutoring, generated by concerns about the lack of industry measures and controls. A little over a year later, there was another *Times* article, "Manhattan: Tutoring Company Files for Chapter 11."[20]

Yes, I was disappointed when I read that the company was indeed Platform Learning. The story reported that New York City investigators had criticized Platform for offering to pay for school playgrounds to encourage adoption of their services.

## THE STORY FROM PLATFORM'S PERSPECTIVE

I contacted Gene Wade, Platform's CEO, and the two cofounders and I sat down for an interview in the spring of 2006. Wade and Torres said they had identified one possible and critical misstep in the matter of the firm's marketing tactics. Apparently, one regional director acknowledged that he "might have" spoken to a school principal about an incentive program that had been discussed internally at Platform but never implemented. Both Wade and Torres recalled hearing the proposal, which was similar to a competitor's incentive program and based on enrollment numbers; however, they had dismissed it as unnecessary.

In anticipation of media coverage and/or investigation, Wade and Torres, together with Platform's general counsel, agreed they should meet with Platform's employees to explore internally whether there were any actions or incidents that could validate potential competitor allegations. Platform's corporate legal counsel, Nixon Peabody LLP, was concerned that the high visibility of Platform and the industry itself would draw an equally high level of scrutiny. All agreed that through an internal investigation and audit, Platform could determine what was wrong faster than if they waited for the government's report. If the company could identify wrongdoing and take corrective action in advance of the results of any external investigations, then Platform could be protected.

The Nixon Peabody legal team determined that the external investigators mainly wanted to know how Platform had gotten so big so fast. The government's investigation focused on wrongdoing and "gray areas," such as bribery and giveaways, respectively.

In line with its strategy, Platform identified and resolved all practical issues before the New York State investigation team finished its report. Despite finding no substantial wrongdoing (that had not already been corrected), the submission of the State Criminal Investigation report, and the subsequent media coverage, severely hindered Platform's ability to sign up students in the New York metropolitan area. Additionally, in the year following the initiation of the state's investigation, the company spent more than $1 million in legal fees. Finally, a leadership transition at the U.S. Department of Education gave school districts greater authority over NCLB enforcement and exclusive control over SES operations.

Platform saw its fiscal year revenue halved, from $60 million to $30 million.

## A VOLATILE STEW: RAPID GROWTH, BIG NUMBERS, PUBLIC DOLLARS, LOOSE REGULATION

I knew that stories like Platform's rise and fall were not uncommon. I understood that "growing pains" were a common executional risk, wherein firms fail to maintain proper controls and regulations as they expand and scale rapidly to meet increasing market demand. It was clear from my interviews that no one from Platform had imagined the firm and the industry would grow so quickly.

It was also evident that no one had taken time to consider that stricter regulatory controls might be necessary in a rapidly expanding industry that was drawing on public funds. In retrospect, it seems that consideration was not given to the "optics" of the matter. There was the potentially volatile mix of private, start-up firms generating substantial revenues from the provision of services to vulnerable, lower-income students in underperforming public school systems. The specter of aggressive competition for billions of dollars, mixed with poor controls and questionable service delivery, was a recipe for scrutiny, and it does not seem at all surprising that there were eventual calls for regulation.

## A CAUTIONARY TALE?

The Ascend experience with Platform Learning seems, in some ways, a cautionary tale, or perhaps even an account of individuals with a healthy dose of hubris. First, in the aggregate, venture capital firms seldom have deals that succeed from start-up to exit or IPO. Since the industry is an unregulated, relatively opaque set of financial institutions, obtaining accurate statistics on VC success in shepherding their portfolio investments to sale or IPO is difficult. The prevailing understanding is that only a minority of investments by VC firms end with a positive outcome or exit.[21]

Perhaps the failure of the Platform Learning investment suggests something about minority-led private equity firms or ventures. I am not sure. Earlier, I made the point that the Platform and Ascend teams had the elite educational credentials that comparable teams typically assembled, if not expected. The novel element in this case was that these otherwise typical VC insiders were also minorities. When minority-led firms fail, even in industries where failure is the norm, there is often a tendency to see this as confirmation of existing stereotypes and biases—that is, even with the "proper" credentials, minorities cannot produce success.

Without regard for demography, one observation about those I have met in the venture capital and start-up industry is: They bounce back. In 2013, I came across another *New York Times* article:[22]

> *Imagine we could actually build a system of schools that . . . set up every single student who enrolled in it for success, unlike the schools we have today in higher education, where . . . most students that enter it are left with a mountain of student debt. . . .* Gene Wade thus shared his vision of an ultra-low-cost college degree for working adults. As of today, he has raised $42 million in venture capital for his new company, UniversityNow, and its two for-profit universities, Patten and New Charter [italics original].

The article also discussed Platform Learning. Wade maintained that despite the controversy, Platform Learning's employees acted properly and that his firm was a victim of "zealous investigations by school districts jealous of the federal money his company was earning."[23]

The *Times* article noted that Wade would opt entirely out of federal student aid programs in his new, accredited education ventures, instead sourcing funding from employer tuition reimbursement programs. Tuition was low, quoted in the article at between $796 and $1,316 per semester for full-time instruction in an online associate's or bachelor's degree program.

In a postscript, I learned that Ascend Ventures shut down in 2010. My understanding is that the firm had extended a considerable portion of its funds in Platform Learning and had had difficulty recovering from the investment's failure. In searching around, I discovered the founders had continued pursuits elsewhere: Wash was associated with Christina Tosi's dessert business, Milk Bar. Mack was leading his own business advisory firm, Mack & Company. Crockett was COO of Fraudnet, an ecommerce fraud prevention firm.

## A BYPRODUCT OF THE CIVIL RIGHTS MOVEMENT: LIMINALITY AND HYBRIDITY

The desegregation of American life brought the potential for access to all-white institutions by those previously excluded—women and minorities. It is not difficult to imagine that private equity firms like Ascend Venture Group would arise. One product of integration would be the creation of a class of individuals who are liminal, and while perhaps still small in the aggregates, unusually connected across groups. Their ability to understand multiple cultures and to build cross-group linkages would provide novel opportunities. They would have credentials similar to their predecessors—like those in Syncom Ventures—the new opportunity being that this socially mobile breed of entrepreneurs would be able to move within elite circles, across ethnic groups, and within networks of others who were like them. Yet this structure does not guarantee a positive outcome in the marketplace, just as it does not guarantee success for firms led by white males with elite educations and credentials.

## WHY WOULD DEMOGRAPHIC DIVERSITY MATTER?

Four decades after the founding of Syncom, the demography of the private equity industry has shown scant change in the face of considerable increases in minority education, entrepreneurship, and professional corporate experience.

> Technology investors . . . have done a poor job of integrating African-Americans, Hispanics and particularly minority women into

their ranks. Definitive numbers are hard to come by, but people in the industry, which includes some 9,300 investors, say the number of African-American and Hispanic women working as venture capitalists is a few dozen. . . . The industry is a classic good ol' boy's network that tends to draw its ranks from a homogenous pool. . . . When a job opens up, there are lines of bright, ambitious candidates who are well-connected—they know someone or are related to someone or know someone who is related to someone.[24]

Some might ask: "So, why does a demographically homogenous industry merit scrutiny?"

Yet many of us can easily understand the arguments for the inclusion of women and minorities in the electorate, in our educational and cultural institutions, and in our government agencies.

Demographically, the nation is increasingly diverse. According to a 2014 Pew Research Center study,[25] in 1960, the population of the United States was 85 percent white; by 2060, it will be only 43 percent white.[26] Over the same time period, Hispanic and Black Americans will grow to 45 percent of the 2060 population.[27]

In a number of states and an even greater number of metropolitan areas, the demography of the population is rapidly moving toward plurality, wherein no single race will represent more than 50 percent of the population. Figure 10.2 illustrates the depth of change underway.

In my fieldwork, I have found these arguments for the diversification of the private equity industry improved decision making, led to greater diversification of investments, and had the potential for positive spillovers into communities that are also rapidly diversifying in terms of jobs and wealth creation.

I have also come across arguments against efforts to diversify the field. Essentially, there is a widespread, and perhaps prevailing, set of beliefs that (1) these efforts are socially motivated, rather than based in solid investing principles; (2) diverse, qualified professionals cannot be found; or (3) investing with diverse teams is riskier.

From a public policy standpoint, there are some considerations that suggest the importance of increasing diversity in the private equity and venture capital ranks. To put it bluntly, if the funds deployed in alternative investments tend to be managed by white, male investment professionals—and if those funds tend to land in entrepreneurial firms run by white males—there are likely missed opportunities to create

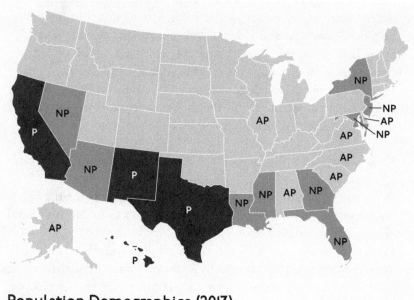

## Population Demographics (2013)

■ Plurality (P)   ■ Near Plurality (NP)
▨ Approaching Plurality (AP)

*Figure 10.2* Plurality states currently have no single racial or ethnic groups that represent more than 50 percent of the population. **Near Plurality** states have one group that represents just over 50 percent (non-hispanic whites), and **Approaching Plurality** states have one group that represents 60 percent of the population. These charts are based on Ruy Teixeira, William H. Frey, and Robert Griffin, *States of change: The Demographic Evolution of the American Electorate, 1974–2060*, Center for American Progress, 2015, 4–5, https://cdn.americanprogress .org/wp-content/uploads/2015/02/SOC-report1.pdf.

firms that aid in wealth creation and job growth for those who are not white or male.

A topic that merits more than academic interest is the notion that diversifying the base of investors will diversify the range of investments as well. The idea that diversity of investments will follow the demography of investment professionals is based on at least three long-standing, interlinked notions that have been borne out of the social science literature.

First, there is the long-standing finding from psychology that people who share similar backgrounds tend to share perspectives on a number of things, including markets and investments. Diversity—functional and demographic—in teams can lead to innovative, creative decision making.[28]

Second, there is the finding that humans tend to find comfort in settings that are familiar and tend to view the unfamiliar as risky, even dangerous.[29] This tendency to view demographic difference as perilous would influence people to avoid downside risks and seek safety in what is familiar.

Third, social relationships tend to fall within race or gender groups, rather than across those groups.[30] Inertial tendencies are recognized as a component of organizational relations, and there is ample evidence that groups tend toward hiring new members who are similar, rather than dissimilar ("homosocial reproduction").[31]

Challenges in diversifying the base of investment professionals include inertia and pressures to conform to the group's norms, as well as the downside risk associated with hiring or investing with someone who is a demographic outsider.

As an example, let us assume that an institution's chief investment officer was committed to diversifying his or her funds. A second challenge would be finding the right team. Where are diverse private equity investment teams? Who runs them? Are they qualified? How does one evaluate and judge investors operating in novel and unfamiliar markets?

That a female or ethnic-minority private equity or VC investor would have attended the same schools as white, male counterparts, and that their training would be similar, is more likely now than ever before.

In this chapter, I have provided a narrative illustrating how the field has matured since the days of Wilkins, Jones, and Syncom. The Ascend story is one of ethnic minorities with elite credentials and networks, how those networks were able to assist the firm in finding a unique investment, and how that investment performed.

# CHAPTER ELEVEN

# Building Wealth in
# Indian Country

Sleep not longer, O Choctaws and Chickasaws, in false security
and delusive hopes. Our broad domains are fast escaping from our
grasp. Every year our white intruders become more greedy, exacting,
oppressive and overbearing. Every year contentions spring up between
them and our people and when blood is shed we have to make
atonement whether right or wrong, at the cost of the lives of our
greatest chiefs, and the yielding up of large tracts of our lands. Are we
not stripped day by day of the little that remains of our ancient liberty?

TECUMSEH OF THE SHAWNEE, DEBATE AT THE
CHOCTAW AND CHICKASAW COUNCIL (1811)[1]

IN THE summer of 2013, I traveled to Shawnee, Oklahoma, to visit
one of the nation's leading American Indian–serving community development financial institutions (CDFIs), Citizen Potawatomi Community Development Corporation (CPCDC).[2]

For me, there was a little bit of personal interest. Traveling to Oklahoma would bring me near places that are important in my family's
narrative: My father was born and grew up in Tulsa; my mother and
father met at Fort Sill in Lawton.

Some scholars claim that as early as the 1600s, freedmen and
escaped slaves lived among American Indians in areas like Arkansas.[3]
In 1830, the federal government passed the Indian Removal Act and
began relocating the tribal nations east of the Mississippi to Oklahoma
and Kansas. Immediately following the Civil War, there were calls for
Blacks to move to the Kansas and Oklahoma territories and establish
free Black townships.[4] The magnitude of relocations was so significant

that, by the late 1800s, it was thought that Oklahoma might become a majority-Black state.

These histories intersect with my ancestry. My father's ancestors moved into Kansas and Oklahoma during the 1890s after being manumitted in Arkansas after the Civil War. The Fairchilds settled in the Black township of Rentiesville, in McIntosh County, one of the Oklahoma counties carved from Indian Territory. It is likely that my ancestors worked and lived around Indian peoples, and intermarriage was not uncommon, according to the historical record.[5] Unfortunately, as for many Blacks, a detailed recorded history of my family's lineage predating the Civil War is nonexistent.

Even being aware of the familial history in a region with a high likelihood of interrelations, I had not embraced the thought that I might have American Indian ancestry. Of course, I recognized that given the history of America, notions of pure, unadulterated heritage among families that did not recently immigrate here were dubious. Nevertheless, the majority of Americans define themselves by our socially constructed racial identity without regard to the reality of centuries of commingling. I have accepted this likely fictitious belief as much as any other person. Whether I personally carried Native ancestry or not, I was excited to learn about the nature of community development finance in this setting.

## VISITING SHAWNEE

The CPCDC headquarters were located at the First National Bank and Trust Company, at that time the largest tribally owned bank in the United States.[6] From our pretrip research, my team and I knew that, demographically, the Potawatomi were one of 565 federally recognized tribes, with an estimated 33,771 members nationwide.[7]

Like many tribes, the Potawatomi were displaced from their lands by expansionist encroachment. In 1838, they were pushed from Indiana to Kansas, and in 1867, they were driven into present-day Oklahoma.[8] By the early 1870s, most Potawatomi had resettled in Indian Territory near present-day Shawnee. Hoping to prevent further land losses, tribal leaders agreed to embrace U.S. citizenship, creating the basis for the Citizen Potawatomi Nation. It was not until 1948 that the U.S. government officially recognized the Citizen Potawatomi Nation (CPN) as a tribe of the Potawatomi people.

## A NATION, WITHIN AND SEPARATE

Initially, one of the daunting elements in fieldwork with the CPN was gaining a better understanding of its legal status and identification with the United States. I had come to learn that many tribes thought of themselves as distinct "nations," with their own identities and with a deeply held concept of self-governance.[9] Arguably, I was visiting sovereign territory—with a unique history, language, religion, laws, and government. It seemed that a member of the CPN would have a nuanced identity I hadn't come across before in my work.

Because of the complex and disturbing history between the United States and Indian tribes, I also felt the weight of moral concerns. In the next few paragraphs, I will provide a short list of considerations that have bearing as barriers to wealth accumulation and to the relationship between American Indians and financial institutions.

Many American Indians lived within an evolving citizenship boundary, a space "in between." The laws differed by state, and had no real consistency or logic. For example, some laws allowed American Indians to become citizens by marrying whites, or by serving in the military. In legal and practical matters, this mismatch of citizenship statuses presented some challenges, as in the ability to sign legal contracts or vote. This, of course, created a healthy sense of distance and skepticism toward white-controlled institutions, which extended to banks and other financial institutions.

The Indian Citizenship Act of 1924 granted full citizenship and limited government infringement on their tribal rights. Even so, many states continued to erect various nuisance barriers until the early 1960s, thereby perpetuating the traditional distinction of American Indians, indigenous people, as included and simultaneously apart.

These notions of dual identity were echoed in the Indian Reorganization Act of 1934, a legislative "about-face" in many ways, with features that reversed reeducation and assimilation on the basis of respect for distinct Native cultures. It provided the initial opportunity for tribes to organize as businesses or corporations and to build commercial enterprises that would assist in economic self-sufficiency.[10] This statute provided both American citizenship and self-government. However, given the productive quality and isolated location of the majority of Indian land, few tribes were able to establish both self-government and economic viability. Nevertheless, legally and federally recognized tribes took action to establish their rights to self-govern and to codify the sovereign-nation-within-a-nation pattern of relations with the United States.

## THE LINGERING IMPACT OF HISTORY AND CONTEXT

As I have mentioned elsewhere, the way individuals are first familiarized with financial institutions can have long-lived effects. A commonly held belief is that financial behavior is based primarily on economic rationality, but this overlooks the reality of historical context. Our understanding of financial behavior must recognize contextual features from the past that influence contemporary financial behaviors.

Writing in the *American Economic Review*, economists Marianne Bertrand, Sendhil Mullainathan, and Eldar Shafir describe a "culture of poverty," which may appear irrational to those not impoverished, but which may seem perfectly rational given its contextual features.[11] Two factors they cite as the genesis of this culture are *direct experience*, which can provide individuals an understanding of the benefits of financial institutions, and *negative legacies* that cause some to distrust these institutions.[12]

Consider the history of many American Indians who were excluded from citizenship until less than a hundred years ago; experienced a multigenerational pattern of broken agreements, contracts, and treaties; and had limited access to financial institutions. Would it surprise anyone that this group would tend to avoid financial services and products that could help them build wealth?

A quick review of 2010 Census data suggests the lingering impacts of history in the economic challenges faced by many American Indians. First, American Indian homeownership rates were lower than those for the general population, 54 percent versus 65 percent.[13] Second, median household income was $35,062, compared to $50,046 for all Americans.[14] Third, 28.4 percent lived below the poverty level, compared to 15.3 percent nationally.[15] Fourth, about one-third of American Indians lacked health insurance, compared to 15.5 percent for the nation as a whole.[16] Fifth, their labor-force participation rate was 61.6 percent, the lowest among all racial and ethnic groups.[17]

# CHAIRMAN ROCKY BARRETT: NEW LEADERSHIP FOR A NEW TIME

At the dawn of the twenty-first century, the Citizen Potawatomi Nation had approximately thirty thousand members, about ten thousand of whom lived in Oklahoma.[18] Members were plagued by poverty, ill health, bad living conditions, and ineffective self-rule. A long history of broken treaties, land theft, destruction of natural resources, paternalism, and federal policies aimed at eradicating their language and culture had left the CPN with 2.5 acres of trust land, $500 in cash, and a run-down trailer that served as tribal headquarters.[19]

Following a long-established elective process of selecting tribal leaders, in 1985, the CPN voted John "Rocky" Barrett as their chairman.[20] Barrett was instrumental in adopting a new constitution and statutes that emphasized tribal self-determination under federal law and heightened accountability of tribal officials. The new framework reorganized the tribal government into three branches and organizing institutions focused on economic self-sufficiency. His leadership marked the beginning of change for the CPN, and a pattern of economic revival ensued.

Barrett's focus on entrepreneurship and organizational management leveraged tribal sovereignty to provide a competitive edge.[21] To secure loans and attract investors, the tribe adopted uniform accounting standards, eventually winning a national award for transparency in financial reporting.[22] During Barrett's tenure, the CPN experienced more than 15 percent average annual economic growth for twenty consecutive years.[23] By choosing to manage trust fund dollars from the Bureau of Indian Affairs—rather than investing money in failing enterprises—the CPN doubled its returns on investments.[24] Those changes, combined with strong enforcement of the rule of law, led to a period of stability, progress, and prosperity. As important, they led to increasing tribal confidence and pride.

## GAMING: AN ECONOMIC DEVELOPMENT STRATEGY

Gaming became a viable strategy for economic self-sufficiency, in part because of limitations on the range-of-use opportunities on land held by American Indian tribes. Frequently, the land itself was barren and isolated, with limited agricultural or commercial development capacity.

As with other matters involving their legal status, the right to engage in gaming was not without controversy and involved a long list of court actions. In a cornerstone case, *California v. Cabazon Band of Mission Indians* (1987), the Supreme Court ruled that if games of gambling or chance occurred within a state, once or periodically, then American Indians could offer the same games at their discretion. This decision effectively gave tribes the right to operate three types of gaming: Class I (tribal, ceremonial gaming), Class II (bingo, poker nights), and Class III (casinos, pari-mutuel betting, slot machines).

The following year, in 1988, Congress passed the Indian Gaming and Regulatory Act (IGRA), which allowed a tribe to engage in Class II or III gaming only by negotiating with the state and signing an agreement, known as a compact, which then required the approval of the chairman of the National Indian Gaming Commission (NIGC).

In effect, the IGRA's negotiation and approval requirement meant that states could forestall a tribe's efforts simply by not coming to the negotiating table. In one notable case, *Lac Du Flambeau Band of Lake Superior Chippewa v. the State of Wisconsin* (1991, U.S. District Court), two tribes sued the state on the basis that its intent to prevent gaming was evident in its failure to negotiate, and that this nonaction was a violation of the *Cabazon* decision. The court ruled in favor of the Lake Superior Chippewa,[25] a decision that cleared the way for tribes around the nation to begin negotiations to open gaming establishments.

Legal hurdles crossed, there remained operational and executional challenges to gaming as a commercial enterprise. First, there were operational risks, as most tribes did not have significant experience in managing casinos. Second, because of treaties, there were limits on equity participation by outsiders. Third, there were frequently onerous contract limitations. These structural elements made it difficult for some tribes to enter gaming, even when they had legal rights and clear opportunities for a return on investment. In addition, traditional banks would not provide debt capital; as a result, the potential ability of these enterprises to attract outside capital was depressed.

Whether gaming has proved a net positive for American Indians is a topic of considerable public interest and debate, but limited academic analysis. However, at least one pair of economists have attempted to determine the effects by comparing economic outcomes before and after tribes opened casinos to outcomes over the same period for tribes that did not adopt or were prohibited from adopting gaming (known as a matched-pairs analysis).[26]

William Evans and Julie Topoleski found that in tribes with casinos, four years after opening, employment had increased by 26 percent, tribal population increased by nearly 12 percent, and the fraction of adults who worked but were poor declined by 14 percent. In counties where an Indian-owned casino opened, jobs per adult increased by about 5 percent (because of increases in non–American Indian employment).

The research team also found attendant negative impacts: bankruptcy rates, violent crime, auto thefts, and larceny rates all increased by 10 percent in counties in which a casino had opened.

## CPN AND GAMING

In 1982, a bingo hall was opened on CPN tribal land. An outside provider managed the games until 1988, when the tribe took over the facility's management. The bingo hall's successor, the FireLake Grand Casino, was opened in 2005, with poker tables, a keno lounge, and more than two thousand slot machines. The 140,000-square-foot facility was rebranded the Grand Casino Resort and Spa in 2013, when a hotel was added. It stands as one of Oklahoma's largest entertainment complexes, featuring a fourteen-story hotel with two levels of gaming, a spa, high-end restaurants, and a concert venue—the hundred-thousand-square-foot FireLake Grand Coliseum, which draws top-name entertainers. In just over three decades, this once financially moribund tribe had become an economic powerhouse.

*Indian Gaming* magazine provided some estimates of the casino's scope and influence:

> CPN is proud to have generated more than 100 new jobs with the opening of the new hotel tower. The tribe's gaming and economic development operations had a $522 million economic impact in the State of Oklahoma for 2012 . . . include[ing] $68 million in wages and benefits, directly supporting more than 2,000 jobs, and purchases contributing to a $377 million impact on the local economy. CPN is the largest employer in Pottawatomie County by more than three times.[27]

Relationship management with surrounding governments was an ongoing task for the CPN. For example, when the City of Shawnee requested increased tax revenues from tribal operations, the CPN responded with economic impact estimates:

> "Much of the sales taxes Shawnee collects are derived from the turnover of our payroll in the economy of Shawnee," added [Tribal Chairman] Barrett. "We buy in Shawnee. We donate to local charities, local law enforcement, churches, and send every penny of our license tag collections back directly to the schools."
>
> In 2012, CPN donated $203,495 to Oklahoma Schools, made $1.8 million in contributions to local charitable organizations and made $21.3 million in tax payments and payments in lieu of taxes.[28]

## A HAPPENSTANCE MEETING ENABLES COMMUNITY DEVELOPMENT FINANCE

Chairman Barrett and the CPN leadership understood that supporting entrepreneurship was crucial to continued economic revival. They were also painfully aware of the need to increase access to capital for American Indians interested in starting or acquiring firms. One day, while visiting Washington, D.C., Barrett heard about CDFIs and their mission to expand access to credit and financial services in lower-income urban, rural, and Indian communities.

Upon return to Shawnee, Barrett got in touch with Kristi Coker, who worked for the tribal government and had practical experience in community development and economic revitalization. After their conversation, Coker contacted the Opportunity Finance Network (OFN), an industry association for U.S.-based CDFIs.[29] Soon after, representatives of OFN and First Nations Oweesta Corporation came to Shawnee to help establish a CDFI. First Nations Oweesta was a capacity-building institution and the only CDFI intermediary offering financial products and development services exclusively to Indian communities. The two organizations worked collaboratively, and in May 2003 a new CDFI was incorporated—the Citizen Potawatomi Community Development Corporation (CPCDC).

Kristi Coker was appointed the CDFI's first executive director. Recognizing the start-up's need for leadership with banking experience, Coker hired Cindy Logsdon, a fifteen-year veteran of the retail banking industry before serving in the Citizen Potawatomi government's accounting office.

## EARLY FOCUS ON ASSET BUILDING

Even with the CPN's strong levels of commercial growth and asset ownership—casinos, convenience stores, a grocery store, a golf course, a truck stop, and a bank—tribal members were less affluent than their counterparts in the general population.

From the beginning, the management and board understood they were dealing with a specific set of challenges unique to American Indians and at the same time common to rural poverty. Therefore, the CPCDC's mission extended beyond providing loan capital and financial products; the ultimate goal was to guide its members through a transition from being unbanked to traditional banking. As one staff member put it, "I'm trying to spin people into the mainstream financial market."

Initially, the team focused on three programs: a micro business loan program, featuring loans up to $35,000; a commercial loan program, offering loans up to $200,000; and technical assistance, which involved providing nascent firms with consulting and mentoring in the areas of business strategy, marketing research, government contracting, and legal issues. As it built capacity, the organization started to develop financial products to fill an acute demand for unsecured, small-dollar lines of consumer credit.

Central to the CPCDC's approach was its belief that—when working with consumers that often lacked even rudimentary knowledge about personal finance—there was danger in providing programs and services without recognizing the need for complementary education. The inclusion of financial education and credit counseling were foundational.

"Anytime you bring [in] a new product, it has to have an educational component, or it doesn't work," explained Cindy Logsdon, the CPCDC's assistant director.[30]

Because of tarnished credit, many tribe members and employees did not qualify for loans at the tribe-owned First National Bank and Trust, or at any traditional bank. When they needed emergency cash, they turned to payday lenders. The minimally regulated payday-loan industry offered short-term loans—typically between $100 and $1,000—marketed as a quick, easy way to tide borrowers over until their next paycheck. In Oklahoma, payday lenders could charge up to triple-digit interest rates, trapping vulnerable borrowers in a cycle of debt and often costing them considerable multiples of their original loan amounts.

In 2005, as a counter to payday loans, the CPCDC launched the CPN Employee Loan Program. Loans ranging from $500 to $1,500 were meant to compete directly with payday lenders; these were augmented by efforts to provide longer-term solutions to break the revolving cycle of financial hardship.

Through a partnership with the Consumer Credit Counseling Service of Central Oklahoma, the loan program offered CPCDC's borrowers guidance in budgeting, creditworthiness, and managing debt obligations; nonjudgmental financial literacy education; and counsel in establishing productive relationships with banking institutions. Through 2012, more than three hundred loans were made annually. Because these loans were in some ways secured by employment within the tribe and supported by a workplace social network, the loan losses were particularly low at less than 1 percent.

Asset savings were another critical need. In 2006, the CPCDC introduced its Asset Builders Matched Savings program. This initiative also stressed sound budgeting practices and a practical understanding of credit—while featuring a twelve-month matched savings program.

Also known as an Individual Development Account (IDA), the program provided a financial incentive through matching to increase savings accumulation. Adult IDAs were targeted to help participants accumulate assets for a business start-up, homeownership, and credit repair, while the youth IDA—for participants between the ages of fifteen and twenty—was designed to help finance postsecondary education. One of the immediate benefits of the program was a marked increase in creditworthiness, with individual FICO scores rising an average twenty to thirty points.

In 2015, the CPN-owned and -managed First National Bank and Trust was one of only nineteen wholly American Indian-owned banks in the nation.[31] However, the bank was not equipped to provide technical assistance, education, and advisory support services to assist potential customers in asset building. In an arrangement I had observed at other CDFIs, the two financial institutions—the CPN-owned First National Bank and the nonprofit CPCDC—worked together to build financial capacity among the local population. The bank referred customers who were not creditworthy to the CPCDC, and the CPCDC helped them repair their credit until they qualified to become customers of the bank.

By 2009, the six-year-old CPCDC had raised $12 million to address the lack of access to capital and had deployed more than $14 million in loans to Indian entrepreneurs, which in turn had created more than 568 jobs. The organization served about 1,200 people each year with financial education products; of that group, approximately 275 held consumer loans.

The CPCDC became the most active American Indian CDFI in the country. It was also the only one to have transitioned from the Native American CDFI Assistance (NACA) program to the mainstream CDFI funding program as of 2009.[32] In recognition of its achievements, the CPCDC was the recipient of the Community Impact Award at the 2009 Wells Fargo NEXT Awards for Opportunity Finance as well as a High Honors Award from the John F. Kennedy School of Government at Harvard University.

After developing a strong start-up team and solid organizational culture, in September 2011, Kristi Coker stepped down from her role as executive director. Shane D. Jett, a former representative in the Oklahoma Legislature and member of the Cherokee Nation, took the helm.


## RISKY BUSINESS: THE JUMPSTART
## AUTO LOAN PROGRAM

When conducting field research, I have two primary tasks: first, to acquaint myself with "the story"—the narrative history of the financial institution—and second, to examine an exemplar initiative that represents the type of impact the firm intends to make.

We looked at a number of CPN businesses, and after weighing the pros and cons of a range of projects, we decided the JumpStart Auto Loan Program would best illustrate the CDFI's efforts in personal asset building.


## PROVIDING AN ALTERNATIVE TO
## PREDATORY AUTO LENDERS

In 2009, Tina Pollard, the CPCDC's consumer loan coordinator, was exploring ways to address the barriers employees faced in getting to and from work in an area with few mass transit options. She knew that many needed reliable cars as well as affordable financing to pay for them. Oklahomans with low-wage service jobs were especially vulnerable when their cars broke down, and even those with relatively middle-income jobs were not immune to hardship. Many were one breakdown away from a financial shortfall that would send them seeking quick, short-term cash.

Regardless of their income, many CPN employees had FICO credit scores lower than 600 (around this time, the average FICO score nationally was 687).[33] When they needed transportation and a car loan, they had no option but to turn to car dealers offering buy-here, pay-here (BHPH) financing. BHPH dealerships were a lucrative business. First, because the dealers self-financed the cars, they could set prices without regard to the Kelley Blue Book[34] or other prevailing comparable sales prices. Second, because many loans were offered without consulting a credit bureau, the dealers could set very high interest rates. And third, BHPH loan contracts tended toward especially onerous terms. In some cases, if the borrower misses even a single payment, the dealer would have the right to repossess the car and sell it to another borrower, and begin the cycle again.

The CPCDC team knew that many CPN employees who were BHPH customers had payments they could not afford. As a result, some tribe members experienced multiple car repossessions, further damaging already vulnerable credit ratings. This, in turn, prevented them from establishing a track record that would allow them to access less expensive forms of debt. To break the vicious cycle, in 2010, the CPCDC launched its JumpStart Auto Loan Program.

The JumpStart loan was available to active, full-time CPN employees in good standing who had worked for any of the tribe-owned enterprises for at least three years. At the time of its launch, the interest rate was a flat 12 percent, fixed for the term of the loan, with zero down payment. The loan terms ranged from three to five years.

In keeping with the CPCDC's philosophy that financial products go hand in hand with education, loan applicants were required to complete a budgeting and credit counseling session, during which Pollard determined the amount of the loan based on their ability to repay it.

"The budgeting sessions—that's all part of making sure the payments are realistic," Logsdon said. By only approving loans with payments that fit their budgets, the JumpStart program gave borrowers with a tarnished credit history a chance to repair their credit record and, eventually, become eligible for loans with mainstream financial institutions.

"This is also a great lesson that your credit score is your asset," Logsdon added. "You pay less interest when you have a better score."

While determining someone's ability to repay the loan, CPCDC lenders considered more than the FICO credit score and debt-to-income ratio. They focused on each applicant's personal situation, trying to elicit a more nuanced picture of whether he or she was creditworthy.

"We look more favorably at someone who had big medical expenses, and that's why they weren't paying their bills on time, as opposed to [someone] not budgeting their money well," Logsdon explained. At the time of my visit, the average FICO score of a JumpStart loan recipient was 513.

"This isn't a program for someone who can go to the bank and get a 4 percent auto loan," Logsdon noted. When an applicant could qualify elsewhere, Logsdon was pleased to refer them.

## PROTECTING THE LENDER (AND THE CPN)

The CPCDC lending team took steps to protect their loans. As with most auto loans, JumpStart used the car being financed as collateral, and the CPCDC made sure that borrowers purchased cars in the best possible condition. Once they were preapproved for a specific amount up to $15,000, borrowers were eligible to buy a car at one of two approved vendors.

As further insurance, the CPCDC placed a lien on the car. "We make sure that our interest in the car is shown in the state records, so that the loan recipients can't sell it," Logsdon said. "The vendor sends the car title directly to our office, and we hold on to it until the loan is paid off." In addition, the borrowers were required to carry auto insurance. "If the car was totaled, the check would come to us," Logsdon affirmed.

There was yet another element of protection—security. Since all borrowers were employed by the CPN, the car payments were deducted automatically from their paychecks. "When they leave employment, then we could have a problem," Logsdon admitted. If the borrower defaulted on the loan or left employment, the CPCDC would request return of the car.

Despite these precautionary structures, at the time of our visit, there had been some delinquencies. The CPCDC had to repossess ten vehicles over four years. "And we had two loan losses," Logsdon reported.

"[Although] we're addressing the need of making sure that an employee has reliable transportation . . . it's risky for us," Logsdon added.

By January 2014, the JumpStart Auto Loan Program was ready for review. Over the previous four years, the loan portfolio had grown by only ten to thirteen loans a year, with an average loan size of about $10,000. Logsdon had to ask herself a difficult question: Was helping ten to thirteen employees annually worth the trouble? Table 11.1 provides a sense of the loan portfolio's performance by 2014.

Over the four-year period, JumpStart had closed fifty-nine loans and generated $108,303 in income and fees. But there were the costs of funds as well as paying an employee to manage the application process, review loan applications, and conduct budget and credit counseling sessions.

Whether because of low interest among employees, inefficient marketing, or the restrictions on the loans that could be approved, it was clear that the broad impact of an otherwise well-managed program was

TABLE 11.1

The JumpStart Auto Loan Program Portfolio Performance

| | FY2010 | FY2011 | FY2012 | YTD FY2013 | Totals |
|---|---|---|---|---|---|
| Loans closed | 20 | 16 | 10 | 13 | 59 |
| Loan disbursements | $211,330.50 | $172,956.57 | $103,297.82 | $119,923.22 | $607,508.11 |
| Program income (interest and fees) | $ 6,177.72 | $ 28,233.13 | $ 41,263.49 | $ 32,629.38 | $108,303.72 |
| Principal repayment | $ 18,342.32 | $ 61,853.14 | $125,038.62 | $185,499.89 | $ - |
| Principal outstanding | $183,062.00 | $273,007.00 | $269,471.03 | $233,267.83 | $ - |
| Cost of funds | 3.50% | 3.50% | 3.50% | 3.50% | 3.50% |
| Paid in full | 0 | 2 | 1 | 12 | 15 |
| Committed | $ - | $ - | $ - | $ 11,000.00 | $ 11,000.00 |
| Charge-off | $ - | $ - | $ - | $ 14,412.74 | $ 14,412.74 |
| Number of charge-offs | 0 | 0 | 0 | 3 | 3 |

*Source:* Citizen Potawatomi Community Development Corporation, used with permission.

relatively small. The JumpStart team had to ask themselves whether they were sufficiently "leaning into" their base of potential members. Yet they knew that adding marketing expense would make an already costly program even less profitable. Further, relaxing loan conditions would increase risk. And finally, allowing the program to remain small would challenge both its sustainability and their ultimate service mission. They lamented the ease with which loans could be obtained from the competition. Simply put, BHPH dealers asked far less of someone attempting to buy an automobile.

The CPCDC was driven by a mission to offer affordable financial products and services in an underserved market. At the same time, the organization strove to be financially sustainable. The issue faced by Logsdon, Pollard, and the CPCDC was one I had seen before. It was clear that there were many tribal employees for whom the loan was the only alternative to high-cost auto lenders. On the other hand, the program had not received the uptake from potential borrowers they had anticipated.

These "market or mission" dilemmas are common, especially in nonprofit financial institutions. Often, an organization's board requests that more be done to support the target population, while the organization's financial professionals are wary about putting their balance sheets in jeopardy by loading up on risky loans, or in this case, by taking on expensive overhead.

In the end, the JumpStart Auto Loan Program continued.

## ANSWERING THE QUESTION

I was inspired at many points during my time with the CPCDC. I had suspected, but had only casually researched, the challenges faced by American Indians. As a college student, I had read Dee Brown's *Bury My Heart at Wounded Knee*,[35] and the book still sits on my shelf. I was taken then, and since, by these accounts because of an effort to deepen my understanding of people's ability to ignore the dignity and humanity of others.

It was clear to me that the adversity and hardships American Indians faced, historically and currently, were underrepresented in the national discourse on civil rights. As some have described, they are a "forgotten people," and I cannot help but feel that many of the social dislocations stem from pernicious discrimination and a lack of opportunities for self-advocacy. I have even come to believe there is a large-scale, undiagnosed condition akin to group trauma among many groups, and that this trauma manifests in the social problems experienced by American Indians living on and off reservations, including substance abuse, domestic violence, and unemployment.[36] Organizations like the CPN and CPCDC have very real opportunities to improve social conditions through the linkage of asset building, self-governance, employment, and entrepreneurship. They also recognize that healing takes time and care.

I also was powerfully moved because, lurking in the recesses of my mind, was my familial narrative. My ancestors certainly lived and worked in the same communities as American Indians. I wondered if there were more, even a shared heritage.

Using large data sets and statistical techniques, researchers have estimated that as much as 20 percent of American Black ancestry is European. However, much of the prevailing research suggests that the prevalence of Indian ancestry among African Americans is likely overstated, being lower than 2 percent in recent studies.[37]

In my work, I have chosen to study and engage with the groups I do because of my interest in and connection to the economic self-sufficiency of the disenfranchised. Because I do not live in a state with a sizable resident tribe, I am relatively blunted in meeting and engaging with American Indians in daily life. The reality of American Indian history and contemporary challenges seems at once deeply moving and somehow disquietingly distant. Of course, I am intellectually engaged. As an observer, I feel empathy for the struggles faced by American Indians for so long. I also find it telling that it gains so little public attention.

I believe that by writing about my work and sharing stories like this one, I am adding to the recognition of the challenges so many have faced, and still do. I seek out opportunities for fieldwork so that I can gain a closer perspective on what might otherwise be purely theoretical, or captured in spreadsheets. Beyond the benefits to my scholarship, I feel these journeys have led to a far richer life.

## APPENDIX 11.1

### FICO Credit Score

Banks, credit card companies, and other lenders use credit scores to assess the risk of lending money to consumers. A credit score is a number that summarizes a borrower's risk of default, based on a snapshot of that person's credit report at a particular point in time.[38]

Everyone who has a credit history has a score. It is based on the records compiled by credit bureaus, which track everyone's personal accounts, balances, amounts of available credit, and payment histories. The FICO score, created by the Fair Isaac Corporation in 1989, is the most commonly used credit score in the United States. Experian, Equifax, and TransUnion, the three national credit reporting companies, use the FICO model. Because data on individual consumers vary depending on which company collected it, an individual's FICO score calculated by Experian could be different from the score calculated by TransUnion or Equifax. The generic FICO credit scores range from 300 to 850—the higher the score, the lower the risk of default.[39]

## Credit Score Makeup

Although the FICO score is calculated using a proprietary mathematical algorithm, FICO has disclosed five types of information used to calculate the score for the general population:

| Information | Percentage of Overall Score |
| --- | --- |
| Payment history | 35% |
| Amounts owed | 30% |
| Length of credit history | 15% |
| New credit | 10% |
| Types of credit in use | 10% |

Lenders commonly use credit scores because they are affordable and provide a largely accurate picture of a consumer's credit history. They have their drawbacks, however. For example, a considerable part of the FICO score is calculated by looking at the ratio of credit used to credit available to an individual. One could easily improve one's FICO score by increasing the credit limits on his or her credit card accounts.

*Source*: Created by case writer Malgorzata (Gosia) Glinska.

# CHAPTER TWELVE

# Flooding the Food Desert in North Philly

Property entails duties, which establishes its rights. Charity is not a
voluntary concession on the part of the well-situated. It is a right to
which the less fortunate are entitled in justice.

RABBI EMIL HIRSCH[1]

ONE OF the themes of this book is that the environments in which
we live have considerable and long-standing influence on our economic outcomes. Diversity is necessary, yet insufficient to allow for
integration.

One example comes from our popular culture and history. On May
13, 1952, twenty-two-year-old Dick Clark began work as a broadcast
announcer at a local Philadelphia station, WFIL. Only a few years
earlier, WFIL had launched a commercial television station, and it was
now introducing a new programming concept: a pop music dance
television show called *Bandstand*.[2] The new show was led by veteran
WFIL broadcaster, Bob Horn, who chose to program what became
known as the "Philadelphia sound," a type of rock and roll with a
largely Black-derived idiom.[3] The recording artists featured on the
show were integrated, yet the teenage audience that danced on camera
to the music, was not. It became an open secret. It was locally known
that Black teenagers were not desired: "Everybody began to understand, 'Hey, this is a show for white people.'"[4]

Horn's show was popular, but unfortunately for WFIL, in 1956 he was arrested for drunk driving, and as rumors swirled, it soon became clear that his personal reputation could damage both the show and station as a whole.

Because of the show's popularity in the Philadelphia area, WFIL's management offered the hosting gig to Dick Clark. Within less than a year, Clark successfully pitched the show to the American Broadcasting Company (ABC), and on August 5, 1957, *American Bandstand* aired nationally on ABC affiliates. Clark maintained the interracial programming and featured a broad base of performers. For example, in October 1957, the Black singer Johnny Mathis appeared singing *Chances Are*, followed by the white singer Andy Williams singing *Lips of Wine*.[5]

For many viewers across the country, such a diverse staging could not occur without protest in their local, hometown music venues. Despite a diverse musical experience onstage, the show's studio audience remained segregated to the extent that viewers personally unfamiliar with Philadelphia would never have guessed that Philadelphia contained one of the largest Black populations in America.[6] The segregation of music venues was a mirrored reflection of the same demographic patterns in local neighborhoods.

Residential segregation has received considerable attention from civil rights activists, policy makers, and social scientists. In their book *American Apartheid*, sociologists Doug Massey and Nancy Denton note that many Blacks living in metropolitan areas experience "hypersegregation," with rates of Black-white segregation rivaling those of South Africa during the apartheid era.[7]

Two primary indices measure different forms of residential segregation. One, the index of dissimilarity, is a quantitative measure of the percentage of a focal group of residents—for example, the number of Blacks who would need to move to achieve an even distribution across cities. The second, the index of isolation, measures the degree to which a group lives without neighborhood exposure to members of any other racial group. In most major cities, indices of dissimilarity and isolation confirm that Americans live in cities that are diverse, yet not integrated.

Since the publication of *American Apartheid* in the early 1990s, segregation indices have declined, though from embarrassingly durable and sustained levels of separation between the races. In an article with a seemingly upbeat title, "Racial Segregation: Promising News," economists Ed Glaeser and Jacob Vigdor noted that Philadelphia was one of the cities that had shown a decline in segregation in the decade between 1990 and 2000.[8]

By 2010, Philadelphia's index of Black-white dissimilarity had decreased from 0.751 to 0.734. Even at the lower number, this meant that seven out of ten Blacks living in the city would need to move to establish an even distribution across the city's census tracts. In terms of Black isolation, Philadelphia had declined from 0.812 to 0.725, indicating that even by 2010, the average Black Philadelphia resident lived in a census tract in which the Black share of the population exceeded the overall metropolitan average by roughly 69 percent.[9] Each of these declines represented greater than a 5 percent increase in Black-white integration, which is certainly a reason for optimism. Yet, from another vantage point, it also seems to be faint praise. Glaeser and Vigdor note:

> There are still large metropolitan areas with substantial amounts of segregation. Moreover, the past 30 years have brought the least amount of change to many of these areas. This survey is not meant to deny the continuing hypersegregation of a significant number of American cities. This extreme segregation persists and represents a significant challenge for America going forward.[10]

The historical narrative about *American Bandstand*'s laudable effort to program a multiracial slate of performers is at odds with its management's inability to accurately represent the demography of the city in which the show was based. This fact underscores the uncomfortable reality that we are, indeed, both diverse and segregated. Arguably, this is the pattern seen in modern sports entertainment today-integrated field, segregated fans.

A deep review of the literature on segregation and concentrated poverty is beyond the scope of this chapter. Suffice it to say that neighborhood segregation concentrates poverty and social problems. Those of us unfortunate enough to live in segregated minority areas are burdened with substandard government supports, often harsh policing, and fewer goods and services than those of us lucky enough to live, school, and work elsewhere. Segregation becomes the source and reifying force of inequality.

The following section focuses on how a Philadelphia-based community development loan fund (CDLF) developed a program to combat high levels of residential and social segregation and the concomitant lack of housing and services available to residents.

## A HOLE IN NORTH PHILADELPHIA,
## AND HOW TO FILL IT

The Reinvestment Fund (TRF) was a loan fund originally established in 1985 as the Delaware Valley Community Investment Fund (DVCIF). Jeremy Nowak, the CEO when we visited, had been one of the cofounders. For a finance professional, Nowak had the less-than-expected background of a PhD in anthropology. He became energized by community organizing through his interest in increasing access to affordable housing. These early experiences convinced him that capital was a critical component of social change initiatives. "Organizers were quickly becoming community investment experts, whether they wanted to be or not," Nowak recalled.

As we sat in TRF's headquarters near Philadelphia's tony Rittenhouse Square, Nowak described Philadelphia as a "classic industrial city." He noted that as manufacturing had declined nationally, Philadelphia's population and employment base had followed suit.

Nowak's description mirrored the data: The city's population was approximately 1.4 million in 1900, 2.1 million in 1950, and again about 1.4 million by 2009. His diagnosis was that during the 1970s, public policy efforts to desegregate neighborhoods and schools, along with riots, precipitated "white flight." This migration to areas outside Philly-proper increased the population and asset value of the surrounding suburbs, while the city of Philadelphia suffered housing abandonment.

During its period of decline, the city's manufacturing sector—once its economic engine—shrank even more significantly. In 1950, 525,748 Philadelphians—almost one-quarter of the city's population—were employed in manufacturing. By 2000, manufacturing employment had fallen to just 43,600, representing less than 3 percent of city residents. This downturn reflected economic shifts from manufacturing to service industries that resulted in high levels of unemployment and residents who left the workforce altogether. The jobs that many young Philadelphians had prepared to take as adults had vanished. Philly's experience was not unique. Many American cities of the time had similar stories.

Nowak and his peer organizers, committed to improving inner-city Philadelphia, questioned how to collectively stem the losses of jobs and residents and improve the quality of life for those who remained.

Area activists, community organizers, and local leaders decided to formally institutionalize their interests and created the Delaware Valley Community Investment Fund. Nowak agreed to serve as its leader.

Nowak talked to me about the organization's incipient mission to "balance the tension between public purpose and market discipline." When compared with traditional banking, the organization that became TRF would position itself as an intermediary. Reflecting an assumption about how to drive change, its loan fund would be an essential participant in a broader marketplace. TRF sought to demonstrate in the field that some of the perceived differences between a small bank and a loan fund were based less on reality and more on assumption. The name The Reinvestment Fund was chosen later, after agreement that DVCIF was too long. The name change also signaled a change in geographic aspirations. The time would come when there would be a need to support challenges outside the Delaware Valley.

As Nowak saw it, the newly launched investment fund would issue "unbankable" loans (Nowak and I did not agree on what the term meant). It was clear from the outset that the lending would begin and expand without compromising the overall financial stability of the fund itself. At least one reason for an initial focus on self-sufficiency was that there were not especially deep pockets backing TRF. It did not have a substantial base of founding institutional investors, such as banks or insurance companies. Nowak and the group hoped to make use of alternative sources, such as individual investors and religious institutions.

"We started with a very local, very personal, very accountable base of support," Nowak recounted. This meant that careful portfolio management would be critical, including underwriting, managing delinquencies, and working carefully with lendees in distress to avoid losses.

Even with a broad-based, grassroots funding approach, by 1988, TRF had accrued $1 million in assets. Nowak recalled that after its first few years of operation, TRF had garnered recognition from institutional providers, including recognized banks and leading national philanthropies such as the Pew Charitable Trusts, the MacArthur Foundation, and the Prudential Foundation. There was a bit of pride in a locally focused loan fund attracting national support. Also around this time, local community groups had begun to urge banks to invest in neighborhood revitalization projects across Philadelphia.

One of Nowak's strong personal beliefs was that a coordination of sectors played an integral role in community development. Not unlike

Rabbi Emil Hirsch, whose words open this chapter, Nowak believed private-sector organizations had a responsibility to provide for those less fortunate, and assumed culpability in their collective failure to do so. He thought that partnership with organizations like TRF could lead to a greater likelihood of success.

In response to the merger of local Midlantic and Continental banks, community organizers in Camden, New Jersey, suggested that the merged entity invest in TRF. "Banks were starting to now get forced to look at us as a potential intermediary," Nowak explained. "They understood . . . that our mission was permanent."

There was political interest as well. During his campaign for president, Bill Clinton vowed to establish "100 community development banks" following his visits to a number of the nation's prominent community development banking institutions (CDBIs).[11] After Clinton's election, Nowak became a key advisor in the building of what would eventually become the Community Development Financial Institutions (CDFI) Fund. As Nowak saw it, TRF and other loan funds needed equity in order to grow, and the notion of what would become the CDFI Fund could provide some of it. He clarified the point by saying, "We wanted to make sure it wasn't just banks" that were investors.

## A DEVELOPMENTAL SHIFT

By 1991, TRF's sixth year, the firm's asset size had grown to what Nowak recalled as "a couple million dollars." Banks and national philanthropies were no longer novel investors, and more banks were participating in their development deals. Looking back, Nowak saw this period as an inflection point, moving from the "entrepreneurial creative stage" to a "growth stage." He concluded that for TRF to continue to expand, he would need to strengthen the talent pool.

Don Hinkle-Brown first encountered TRF in 1987 when he worked as a loan officer at Midlantic Bank. Midlantic's acquisition of Continental Bank included a Community Reinvestment Act (CRA) requirement, and Midlantic made an equity investment of $62,500 in TRF, along with $62,500 in debt. This was TRF's largest investment at a time when the organization's asset size was slowly climbing to the $1 million mark. Midlantic assigned Hinkle-Brown to TRF's loan committee.

Representing the interests of an investor, Hinkle-Brown's charge was to "watch the money carefully." He became drawn to the organization's mission. He continued to volunteer at TRF while he transitioned to lending roles at several different banks, including Liberty Savings Bank and PNC. During this time, he became increasingly dissatisfied with the traditional banking sector, describing it as "people with wealth getting access to wealth." Hinkle-Brown officially transitioned to the TRF staff in 1991, and by 2009 he had become president of lending and community investments.

As the skills of management improved and the scope of the organization evolved, TRF continued to thrive. In particular, Nowak saw significant gains in the firm's ability to organize bank debt. By the late 2000s, TRF was financing four major areas: affordable housing development, commercial real estate and business, energy efficiency, and community facilities. As investments soared in magnitude, the composition of borrowers began to change. The mature portfolio contained commercial real estate, including supermarkets, charter schools, and housing, with for-profit developers instead of exclusively nonprofit developers. Nowak attributed this transition within the portfolio to becoming "better known with bigger producers."

Making such a transition is not a given in community development. Many organizations are successful at operating within a closely defined local market and set of capabilities. The transition to regional and national sustainability requires the development of capacities for scale.

## FERTILIZING THE GROWTH OF FRESH FOODS

During our meeting with Nowak and his staff, we inquired about projects that were exemplars of the TRF approach. The next sections tell the story of Sullivan Progress Plaza and the effort to bring fresh foods into Philadelphia's inner-city neighborhoods.

In 2010, Treasury Secretary Timothy Geithner, Agriculture Secretary Tom Vilsack, and First Lady Michelle Obama announced the Obama administration's Healthy Food Financing Initiative, a move to bring healthy food retailers into America's "food deserts"—underserved urban and rural communities.

In Pennsylvania, TRF's model of pairing public financing with private investment and mission-driven entrepreneurs had led to the creation of what became known as the Fresh Foods Financing Initiative (FFFI).

It would be easy to assume that TRF's work on FFFI was spurred by the involvement of the First Lady and the support of two Cabinet-level secretaries. Yet actually, TRF's involvement dated to 2004, when TRF initiated an issue identification study and found that the inner-city Philadelphia market had an overwhelming need for grocers;[12] as one staff member explained, "FFFI . . . became a convening and bringing together of supermarket operator-owners." It had the benefit of a diverse coalition of institutions that were committed to solving the grocery problem, and to applying innovative financial tools.

## LACKING SUPERMARKET ACCESS IN NORTH PHILADELPHIA, AND WHAT TO DO ABOUT IT

The Progress Plaza project was unique for a number of reasons: first, the historical and cultural relevance of TRF's partner in the redevelopment of an inner-city supermarket and retail center; second, the challenge of environmental concerns associated with the site; and third, the leverage of a number of funding sources to spread the risks of the deal.

Given their roots in community organizing, it was not surprising that TRF would seek projects to engage partners with long-standing, trusting relationships in the communities where they wished to lend. The wisdom in this approach ensured that TRF would not be seen as another financial provider without knowledge or understanding of the areas in which it operated. TRF recognized that this is a very real challenge for some lenders, and can become stark when there is a demographic mismatch: predominantly white leadership teams and lending staffs working in predominantly minority areas.

Candidly, TRF's approach illustrated recognition of an uncomfortable reality: in a city as racially segregated as Philadelphia, a failure to thoughtfully engage across race and class networks could hamper many well-meaning community development efforts. Hinkle-Brown, who is white, shared his awareness of these issues. He had graduated from Temple University (BA and MBA) and, perhaps of greater relevance, had taught in the school's urban studies program.

Sullivan Progress Plaza, located on Oxford and Broad streets, had a unique link to history, as it was the first urban grocery and retail project led by a notably Black, community-based set of owners. The store came to North Philadelphia through the work of the Reverend Dr. Leon Sullivan, pastor of Zion Baptist Church. Sullivan held a strong belief in self-advocacy and improvement of the social condition of Blacks through economic self-help. One Sunday in 1962, Sullivan directly linked the notion of self-help to investment:

> "One day I preached a sermon at Zion about Jesus feeding the five thousand with a few loaves and a few fish," he recall[ed]. "Everybody put in their bit and you had enough to feed everybody, and a whole lot left over. So I said, 'that is what I am going to do with the church and the community. I am going to ask 50 people to put $10 down for 36 months of loaves and fishes and see if we could accumulate resources enough to build something that we would own ourselves.'"[13]

The response was overwhelming. More than two hundred people signed up for his "10–36 Plan" that Sunday morning. His idea of bringing people together to invest in a community-owned enterprise had caught fire.[14]

Sullivan's initiative was called the 10–36 Plan because of its novel philosophy and structural elements. First, it asked all participants to commit to a long-term investment of $10 per month over a three-year period. Second, it required a commitment from all investors to give to others; in the first twenty months, parishioners would contribute to a fund to create and support the Zion Nonprofit Charitable Trust. Third, the plan stipulated that in the final sixteen months, the fund would establish a for-profit corporation, Progress Investment Associates (PIA). Finally, at the close of the period, each investor would receive one share of voting stock, which would give "voice" to the community.

In essence, this structure created a savings discipline and an equity stake in the economic growth of the community.[15] The plan was part of a suite of initiatives by Sullivan, including the Opportunities Industrialization Centers (OIC), which were employment training facilities, and the International Foundation for Educational and Self-Help, devoted to education in nine African nations.[16] I was familiar with Sullivan's work; however, this particular initiative was something truly illuminating, because of its strategy to fuse local engagement and investment.[17] I had never come across anything like this type of grassroots community development finance activity before.

We toured the site with Hinkle-Brown. While visiting the retail development site, we were introduced to Wendell Whitlock, the lead executive and developer from the partnering for-profit entity PIA. Whitlock talked with visible energy about Sullivan's dream to create the first fully Black-owned, community-owned, locally developed and managed grocery store. The original notion was for the retail center to serve multiple purposes: first, as a center for retail development on a major thoroughfare, Broad Street; second, as a source of goods that were either not available in the community or overpriced at small, neighborhood stores; third, as a job creator, providing employment opportunities before and after the project's completion; and fourth, as an advocate for locally based entrepreneurs by making office space available for them.[18]

Through PIA, the original retail center became a reality in 1968. Ten thousand people came to celebrate the grand opening.[19] Now, forty years later, Progress Plaza was showing wear and tear. When we toured the site, the buildings looked aged and faded, with dated architecture and in dire need of masonry. Progress Plaza looked like an artifact from archaic, run-down Philadelphia.

According to Whitlock, the objective of the PIA-TRF collaboration was to renovate the entire retail block and to attract and support a new, up-to-date, 42,000-square-foot urban grocery offering fresh foods to the community.

Although I was aware that, historically, the area had once been affluent and predominantly white, I also recognized that its relatively low-income, disinvestment impression had resulted from a different wave of flight from the city. Once-thriving North Philadelphia neighborhoods had experienced a steady exit of Black middle-class residents to the suburbs. Ironically, the integration of formerly all-white suburbs by a select set of affluent, advantaged Blacks also lessened the economic and political force that a community like North Philadelphia could marshal. The constraining forces of segregation in some ways supported the shared stake of a broad coalition of Blacks who cut across class groups. As relatively advantaged Blacks left the area, a wealth and leadership vacuum was created, and once flourishing developments like Progress Plaza tended to decline.

I had seen similar exits of the middle class in other urban cities, and even in rural towns. When large-scale development projects like

Progress Plaza step into the breach, they run the risk of being viewed as "interlopers" intent on altering the neighborhood, and perhaps eventually driving out current residents. For a lending organization—especially one with a predominantly affluent, highly educated, and largely white staff—careful navigation of community, political, and business interests would be required to build community trust. This was one reason the partnership with community-based organizations like OIC and PIA were so critical to the project.

## THE "DIRTY" HOLE IN THE PARKING LOT

In some Philadelphia neighborhoods . . . blighted factories and warehouses are the sole remnants of the once vibrant and bustling communities. Many of these sites are brewing with contamination, and their continued neglect poses real environmental and health threats. . . . A disproportionate number of these sites are in African-American and low-income communities. . . . The prototypical brownfield site is an abandoned, idled or underused industrial or commercial facility.[20]

The primary reason that entrepreneurs and developers avoid working in inner-city urban areas is perceived financial risks. One way to lessen these risks is through financial innovations or subsidies that alter the risk/return relationship, such as tax increment financing (TIF) and New Markets Tax Credits (NMTCs).

It is important to note that the perceived risks are an artifact of segregation and attendant white flight. Relatively affluent, often white, investors lack familiarity with neighborhoods like these and have limited knowledge of residents' preferences and tastes. Then there is the potential for negative reactions from incumbent residents. For both investors and entrepreneurs coming from the outside, there is the very real possibility of being perceived as gentrifying "outsiders." Recognizing this risk, TRF's partnerships helped to quell that perception.

A third hurdle in many of these projects is the possibility of environmental issues, which generally cannot be determined before development begins but have the potential for legal and financial liabilities once they are discovered. The possibility of building in a "brownfield" area is a deterrent for many investors who might otherwise consider developing a site for, say, a retail complex or hotel. Brownfield development presents an extra set of legacy concerns that are not a concern in development projects on formerly rural or "greenfield" spaces, where environmental issues are less likely.

North Philadelphia's history as a former industrial manufacturing hub and commercial thoroughfare raised the likelihood of contaminants or pollution that would need remediation. One challenge of brownfield development is determining who is liable for cleanup, especially when firms that once operated in an area are no longer operating or when historical records are unclear about who may have been responsible. There is a very real likelihood of cost increases and construction delays when building on these sites. This alone can deter some investors.

In addition to manufacturing sites, the North Philadelphia area had gas stations, known to store petrol underground in large tanks. As Progress Plaza was redeveloped, the U.S. Environmental Protection Agency (EPA) required that the development site be searched for contaminants, including underground storage tanks (USTs). In any development project, if contaminants are found, the cleanup costs can be considerable, with an average remediation cost of $125,000 per site, according to EPA estimates at the time (2009).

In the Progress Plaza parking lot, workers found an ancient tank with long-abandoned gas inside. In addition to its removal, there was the question of whether the tank had a leak and whether leakage had seeped into the surrounding ground. Gas is considered a volatile organic compound; long-term exposure can cause cancer or damage to vital organs. Depending on age, a UST can also contribute to lead poisoning.[21] A cost-prohibitive environmental cleanup could either scuttle the project altogether or cause a developer to raise rents to offset those costs. This, of course, would counter PIA's desire for a low-cost business development. The project risks were significantly increased by the reality of brownfield remediation, and any financing would require some way to lessen the costs for PIA.

Cities with brownfield spaces would certainly rather know about them and want to mitigate potentially dangerous pollutants. For their part, developers make efforts to help municipalities understand that environmental risks often make outlying, rural spaces more attractive development opportunities. In some cases, subsidies or relief from future liability are negotiated to entice developers into formerly industrial areas; these may come from federal, state, or local sources.[22]

## FINANCING CHANGE ON BROAD STREET

President Clinton yesterday proposed giving more tax credits to businesses that invest in the country's poorest areas, telling audiences in New York City that such spending is . . . a *moral obligation.* . . . Mr. Clinton announced a plan to increase to $5 billion from $2 billion the amount of money available during the next 10 years for his "New Markets" tax credits, a program that gives companies a 25 percent tax credit for each dollar invested in community development projects in poor areas [emphasis added].[23]

In 2004, TRF participated in a public-private partnership—the aforementioned Pennsylvania Fresh Food Financing Initiative—a collaboration of government, nonprofit, and business organizations dedicated to bringing supermarkets and grocery stores to inner cities and simultaneously opening up local job opportunities.

Under the FFFI umbrella, there were four primary players in the Progress Plaza redevelopment project: (1) the Commonwealth of Pennsylvania; (2) The Food Trust, an advocacy group committed to the provision of fresh foods in underserved areas; (3) the Urban Affairs Coalition (UAC), committed to job development for minority workers; and (4) TRF, as capital provider.

The project's financing came from two sources: the portion provided by the state, and the amounts matched by TRF. The Commonwealth's $30 million grant was spread over six years in the following fashion: (1) loan capital and credit loss reserves ($13.1 million); (2) direct grants to supermarket entrepreneurs ($12 million); (3) provision for NMTC ($3.1 million); and (4) overall program management and administration ($1.8 million).

TRF's primary role was to assist in providing financing for potential supermarket or grocery operators; however, its skill in packaging market-rate and subsidized capital would help overcome the real and perceived higher costs of providing fresh foods in these areas. TRF had built a reputation as a financial intermediary through its demonstrated ability to bring other funding sources into economic development projects—a process known as "leveraging."

TRF assembled four primary components into a $117.1 million financing vehicle: (1) a bank-syndicated supermarket loan fund, offering loans of up to seven years to finance a range of project elements, including equipment, acquisition, construction, renovation, and leasehold improvements; (2) funding from the federal government's NMTC program; (3) funds from TRF's internal lending operation (the Core Loan Fund), used for short-term projects that fall outside of traditional loan conditions; and (4) direct grants for predevelopment costs, staff training, security, relocation, demolition, and environmental remediation.[24]

To qualify for any of these funds, a development project had to be located within a low- to moderate-income area that was also underserved by other markets. Progress Plaza qualified on both counts. The nearest supermarket was more than a mile away, quite a distance for someone traveling by mass transit.

Readers will note that New Markets Tax Credits have been mentioned multiple times in this project. The NMTC program was an innovation of the Clinton administration, created under the Community Renewal Tax Relief Act of 2000. NMTC projects offer both tax credit investors and debt investors a way to participate in business development in areas that might otherwise be perceived as too risky by providing a subsidy approximately equal to 20 percent of a project's financing needs. Frequently, the loan portion of the deal is "convertible debt" that becomes equity after the initial period of startup risks has passed, usually seven years. In some cases, this structure provides an entrepreneurial borrower with insufficient capital to meet the loan-to-value (LTV) hurdles that the lender may require.

NMTC financing is limited to projects located in "qualified census tracts" or business entities owned by, or serving, low-income persons. The qualifying location or "footprint" essentially involves two measures: the level of poverty and household income.[25] The Progress Plaza location met three criteria for inclusion: (1) median family income at or below 60 percent of the average median income (AMI); (2) a poverty rate at or above 30 percent; and (3) an unemployment rate at least 1.5 times the national rate.

There are additional criteria for projects that fall outside qualifying areas: the project employs or serves low-income persons (Progress

Plaza had both); the legal entity is owned by low-income persons (a portion of the project would be owned by PIA and a related organization, the Progress Trust); the location is a brownfield site, as determined by the EPA.

CDFIs are the primary recipients of NMTC allocations; however, other entities may also qualify, including minority enterprise small business investment companies (MESBICs). This vehicle was created as a way to attract capital from multiple sources (for-profit, nonprofit, and public) for what are known as qualified active low-income community businesses (QALICBs), mostly real estate and business investments. Many leading CDFIs have used SSBIC funds in a broad range of projects. This approach can also be called an "off balance sheet," meaning that investments are made into a separate legal entity developed with a specific project intent, structure, and delivery of benefits.

An NMTC project must also include a financial intermediary that has received an allocation from the CDFI Fund. By the time of our visit, the CDFI Fund had already awarded nearly $26 billion to five hundred entities, according to each applicant's specific economic development goals.[26] Some applicants, such as TRF, had received allocations since the program's inception.[27]

In these arrangements, the benefits to the tax credit investor must be managed. TRF prepared a review of its Fresh Foods Program for the CDFI Fund and provided advice for others interested in NMTCs:

> In TRF's experience, investors desire an annual yield in the neighborhood of 4.20 percent to 6.40 percent; this yield or discount rate translates into a discounted price paid for each credit of $0.65 to $0.75. The price paid for each credit has a direct link to the size of the NMTC benefit; that is, the lower the price paid per credit, the smaller the NMTC benefit.[28]

The Community Development Entity (CDE) must also receive economic benefit for participation. In this project, TRF was the CDE:

> During TRF's years of experience, we have seen a wide range in the amount of fees and the structure of fees charged by CDEs in NMTC transactions. Typically, [Community Development Organization] fees appear to add up to an aggregate 5 to 8 percent of QEI over

the seven year compliance period, resulting in a direct reduction of NMTC benefit. An example . . . of fees that could be charged in a single transaction include a 2 percent fee charged at the investment fund level, a 2 percent charged at the CDE level and a 0.50 percent asset management fee charged every year of the seven-year credit period. One of the other features of a NMTC transaction . . . is the ability to provide affordable commercial leases by lowering the overall need to service the debt (especially at the beginning of the new development, and before operations or customer patterns have stabilized).[29]

## THE FRESH GROCER

Innovation in financing was one important element of Progress Plaza; the other was locating an experienced urban grocery entrepreneur willing to plant an anchor store in North Philadelphia. (For the purposes of an NMTC deal, this was the QALICB.) The prior supermarket operator had vacated the space in 1999. It had not only languished since then, but the original, decades-old architecture and design would not suit the contemporary aesthetic. As a result, there would need to be a considerable reset of the store, the parking lot, and the storefronts of other tenants. TRF provided the PIA with a grant to help with the demolition cost and associated professional fees.

Don Hinkle-Brown and his team worked with the owners to secure an experienced anchor supermarket tenant. Since grocery stores run on very small margins (often less than 2 percent), it was critical to find a tenant that understood the project's context and yet would still be able to turn a profit. In 2006, The Fresh Grocer (TFG), a company started by two local entrepreneurs, expressed interest. The experienced cofounders, Patrick Burns and Mike Rainier, had been operating ShopRite and Fresh Grocer stores in the area since 1995, with a mix of urban and suburban locations.

There was an additional challenge. Because Progress Plaza was an operating retail center, the project would have to be completed in three phases so as to not disrupt ongoing business. The first phase called for an upgrade of the current facilities, at an estimated cost of $730,000. The second phase would redevelop the existing facilities for the local business tenants and add office space onto a second floor.

The third phase would position the complex's anchor supermarket. In addition to creating three discrete construction risks, this type of plan requires a comprehensive, innovative financing stream throughout. Morgan Stanley agreed to be the New Markets investor that would purchase the resulting tax credits, Progress Trust would be the legal entity that held the land, and PIA would develop and lease the retail facility.

Ultimately, the financing package combined NMTC and other subsidies along with a consortium of banks. The TRF portion of the financing worked as follows:

- A $10 million NMTC investment, a portion of which ($3 million) was later lent directly to The Fresh Grocer team.
- The $10 million loan was organized into two A/B note structures, each with below market interest rates of approximately 3.50 percent.[30]
- An additional $3.7 million in NMTC investment to The Fresh Grocer for the third-stage supermarket construction and installation of a rooftop parking lot. (This investment also had an A/B note structure.)
- TRF also secured nearly $2 million to TFG for equipment financing through its Pennsylvania FFFI, and a $1 million loan using Philadelphia Gap Financing.
- Through a leasehold mortgage, Progress Trust, which held the land, and PIA, the developer, agreed to a lien on the property as a collateral security for TRF. (In 2000, prior to improvements, the land was appraised at $4 million.)

The Fresh Grocer opened on December 11, 2009, meeting the deal's three-part objective: (1) offer fresh, healthy foods within a 46,000-square-foot Fresh Grocer; (2) generate another 38,000 square feet in other retail and office space to encompass both local entrepreneurs and chain stores; and (3) create new jobs for the North Philadelphia community. In February 2010, First Lady Michelle Obama visited Progress Plaza, and subsequent press releases reported the project had created 270 jobs, with a 96 percent minority workforce.[31]

A few months after our field visit to TRF, I came across an article in the *New York Times* about the use of subsidies and incentives to attract healthy grocers to "food deserts." TRF's work in Philadelphia was cited as an exemplar that was influencing legislators and healthy food activists in the New York region:

> Inspired by Pennsylvania's example, New York City officials have developed an initiative of their own to bring new neighborhood markets selling fresh food to areas of the city where they say the need is greatest. . . . The [Pennsylvania FFI] program began with a $10 million allocation, which was renewed twice and matched with $90 million in private funds, for a total investment of $120 million, said Patricia L. Smith, the director of special initiatives for the Reinvestment Fund. In all, the program has resulted in 69 projects in various stages of development, 23 of them in Philadelphia. Five approved projects have gone out of business, a relatively low failure rate, she said. Some 3,700 jobs have been created, said John Weidman, deputy director of the Food Trust.[32]

TRF garnered national attention for its innovations as a financial intermediary and problem-solver. By 2010, the FFFI had "attracted 203 applications from across Pennsylvania, with 88 approved for funding as of December 2009. In total, TRF approved more than $72.9 million in loans and $11.3 million in grants. Projects approved for financing are expected to create over 5,000 jobs and 1.6 million square feet of commercial space."[33]

Yet, Progress Plaza was only one of a number of projects they shared with us. Others involved developing affordable housing units, funding commercial and community facilities, financing charter schools, and helping minority and immigrant entrepreneurs create services and jobs in underserved areas. All employed a combination of novel financing structures, a coalition of participating institutions, and a commitment to the expressed needs of low-income communities. This ability to pull together capital from different sources and funders into a novel combination is an important capability in optimizing the "capital stack" in a project. Organizations that become skilled at this, like TRF, are able to attract novel capital sources and to coordinate the financial structure in a way that adjusts to the unique needs of a project.

As I have cautioned elsewhere, an example is not an endorsement. NMTC financing is a tool in a toolbox. What I hope readers recognize is that this particular solution came from a collaborative arrangement. The Reinvestment Fund brought expertise in the collection and leverage of capital in novel ways; other local philanthropists and entrepreneurs brought funds and their experience; there was a need for an entrepreneur that understood urban markets; and the network, engagement, and support of a local organization ensured endorsement from the community.

Philadelphia is one of the most diverse, multicultural, multiracial cities in the nation. As we have seen in this chapter, integration does not necessarily accompany diversity. Segregation is an antecedent and continuing structure that creates and maintains racial income and wealth inequality. Philadelphia is a complicated place, with a unique history, in which a popular nationally broadcast television show had to deter integration. Decades later, many of the same challenges remain. Context matters. The exemplar in this chapter is valuable, but not in a one-size-fits-all fashion. It needs to be modified in ways that enable it to adapt to other contexts.

The effects of segregation extend to the schools we attend and, yes, where we shop and whether there are fresh foods available. Organizations like TRF convene across business sectors, but also across social boundaries. And importantly, they are intentional about breaking through those divides. They achieve these gains through a cluster of skills that allow them to recognize and effectively confront the environmental, social, and financial barriers. As we have seen in this chapter, their innovation is in their ability to package solutions that address each of these.

# CHAPTER THIRTEEN

# A Bluebird Takes Flight

## A Reinterpretation of Banking at American Express

Anyone who has ever struggled with poverty knows how extremely
expensive it is to be poor.

JAMES BALDWIN, *NOTES OF A NATIVE SON*[1]

IN THE introductory chapter, I shared the personal story of my parents' efforts to socialize me with bank accounts, credit cards, and how best to use them. I understood that this introduction to accounts and debit cards shaped my experience with financial services firms. What I didn't understand was that the behaviors I was socialized to adopt were intentionally designed to benefit financial institutions more than me.

## WHO CAPTURES VALUE: NETWORKS, ISSUERS, OR CONSUMERS?

I was unaware at the time of what has become an important insight: Innovations in financial services are not always developed in conjunction with consumers' evolving needs and understanding of their best uses. While there are increasing arrays of consumer finance products, there is not parallel ready access to strategies on how to use and benefit from them. About the time I received my first debit card, the influential economist, William Silber, argued in the *American Economic Review*:

We often think of technological changes, such as the telegraph or xerography, as *de novo* events . . . but most evidence suggests that innovative activity responds to economic forces. . . . The main hypothesis is quite straightforward: new financial instruments and practices are innovated to *lessen the financial constraints imposed on firms* [emphasis added].[2]

In the late 1970s, around the time I received my card, the Visa brand was something new and debit cards were a recent innovation in retail banking. Like many innovations in financial services, the primary reasons for the launch of debit cards were, first, to benefit payment networks like MasterCard and Visa by increasing transaction velocity, and second, to assist the issuer banks that offered the cards in lowering the costs of providing checking services.

From an issuer's perspective, the prevailing hypothesis was that debit cards would lower costs for banks in two key ways: (1) by removing the paperwork and materials handling expenses of checks and (2) by decreasing transaction errors due to human teller mistakes.

Even executives in the credit card industry acknowledged that the rationale for the cards did not include either consumer demand or their need for usage guidance: "There's no public out there knocking down our doors demanding we give them debit cards," a MasterCard official acknowledged in a *New York Times* article.[3]

The hope of issuer banks and network providers was that the new cards could help to transition consumers from the use of electronic systems for entertainment to their use in everyday life, and would replace a portion of the occasions in which consumers used cash. One of the beliefs that drove the introduction of debit cards was that increasing their share of purchase transactions would make customers more likely to later obtain a credit card, which in turn would lead to a higher likelihood of revolving debt and interest payments.

There was also the notion that debit cards would provide a positive elasticity in spending. That is, if consumers did not physically experience funds leaving their accounts, they might be more likely to spend their money. Increased velocity could mean increased fees.

Electronic banking did offer some benefits to consumers. The ease of withdrawals from a growing base of ATMs and the immediacy of point-of-sale (POS) systems meant avoiding the inconvenience of going into a bank to convert funds from one form to another. However, the ancillary benefits of ATMs to retail bankers would only become clear years later. Over time, ATMs would replace bank tellers. Not only did computerized tellers dispense cash with fewer errors, they worked at unreasonable hours without earning overtime pay and without expensive health or benefit plans. Debit cards provide a case study of the primacy of the interests of financial institutions in innovations, even when they do provide consumer benefit.

## FEES AS INFLUENCE MECHANISM

Whether anticipated or not, free-rider worries rose about payment systerms within banks in November 1978. The Federal Reserve and Federal Deposit Insurance Corporation (FDIC) allowed commercial banks and savings banks to offer automatic transfer of funds from savings to checking accounts. This change provided consumers a means to move money from their interest-bearing savings account into their non-interest-bearing checking account at the last possible moment, avoiding a potential overdraft. Consumers could manage their funds to get maximum yield on their total balances across accounts.[4] The new laws also allowed banks to levy new fees for banking behaviors that were costly: overdrafts, low balances, heavy usage of ATMs and tellers, and even dormant accounts. The expanded base of fees would allow banks to recoup some of the costs of managing expensive systems.

In the electronic banking era of the 1980s, higher-income cardholders essentially paid for technological investments through their higher interest payments.[5] There was also a feeling among many merchants—who also paid a transaction fee for accepting the cards—that the higher-income purchaser was more desirable, so banks decided that one way to segment users by income was to raise minimum balance requirements.[6]

Nearly a decade after their launch, debit cards still had not developed into a market commensurate with the intended benefits to consumers:

> So far, debit cards have not turned a profit for anyone. Usage has not been high enough to pay back the investment in the equipment. "At this point, we need [consumer] education by the financial service institutions," said Mike Strada, president and chief executive of Honor, Florida's statewide debit card network.[7]

The next section of this chapter describes the efforts of a perhaps improbable player, American Express, to attract an entirely new category of consumers into a banking relationship.

## A NEW MISSION IN ENTERPRISE GROWTH

In June 2011, Kenneth Chenault, CEO of American Express (AXP, AmEx), announced the formation of a new group within the company, Enterprise Growth (EG). It was explicitly established to drive expansion into digital and mobile payments.

> "New technologies are redefining the payments business and creating opportunities that go beyond our existing businesses," said Chenault. "The Enterprise Growth group is designed to extend our leadership into the world of alternative payments and *create new fee-based revenue streams for the post-recession environment* [emphasis added]."[8]

To lead the group, AXP hired Dan Schulman from the Sprint Corporation.

During one of his first meetings with EG staff, Schulman asserted, "Technology [is] fundamentally going to change the way you might think about financial services, just as the Internet has redefined one industry after another."[9] He instructed the group "to challenge existing business models" and "to think about the intersection between software, software platforms, mobile apps, mobile technology in general, and financial services."

For EG employees Alpesh Chokshi and Wesley Wright, this was a pivotal moment. Both had worked in AXP's prepaid business since 2005. With Chokshi as president and Wright as the product development lead, they had spearheaded AXP's expansion into gift cards and reloadable cards. When their group was absorbed into EG, they saw an opportunity to move AXP into debit and checking spending. Their initiative was called Bank 2.0 because technology was poised to usher in the "next generation" of banking. This would involve even greater use of digital platforms, data analysis, and product design to reach and serve the unique needs of a new customer franchise.

This was a departure from both AXP's customer base and its business model. The EG unit would need solid answers to questions that extended beyond the projected economic returns the cards could generate: Who would be the new card's customers? Where would consumers use the cards? How would they learn about them? Would the cards carry the AXP brand?

The EG staff had painstakingly researched the opportunities inherent in Bank 2.0, and most prominent was the magnitude of the potential market currently underserved by traditional banking services. Estimates were that more than one in four American households (28.3 percent) were either unbanked or underbanked[10] and were conducting some or all of their financial transactions outside of the mainstream banking system.[11] The box provides relevant background about these consumers.

---

Unbanked and Underbanked Consumers in the United States

In 2011, FDIC surveyed 45,000 U.S. households to determine their degree of participation in the banking system. The results are projectable to the entire U.S. population.

### Definitions and Key Findings

- **Depository Institutions.** Banks and credit unions that provide insured checking and savings accounts up to $250,000. *There are approximately 90,000 depository branches in the United States.*
- **Alternative Financial Services Providers.** Financial institutions that provide any of the following services: nonbank money orders, nonbank check-cashing services, nonbank remittances, payday loans, rent-to-own services, pawn shops, or tax refund anticipation loans (RALs). *Approximately 25 percent of households used some form of AFS in the 12 months prior to the survey. Almost 10 percent used two or more AFS products.*
- **Unbanked Households.** Households in which no individual holds a checking or savings account in an insured depository institution. *8.2 percent of U.S. households are unbanked, up 0.6 percent since 2009. An estimated 9.9M households are unbanked.*
- **Underbanked Households.** Households in which an individual has a checking and/or savings account but used AFS providers in the past 12 months to meet financial needs.

---

*20.1 percent of U.S. households are underbanked, up 1.9 percent since 2009. An estimated 24.2 million U.S. households are underbanked.*

- **Banked Households.** Households in which all individuals are fully engaged in the financial mainstream, and did not use AFS in the past 12 months. *68.8 percent of U.S. households are fully banked, down 2.5 percent since 2009. An estimated 88.2 million U.S. households are fully banked.*

- **Unbanked Cash Households.** Households in which no individual has a depository account, and have not used AFS in the last 12 months. *29.5 percent of unbanked households rely purely on cash.*

- **Employment Status.** Not surprisingly, banking status is positively correlated with employment. *64.1 percent of all underbanked households, however, have members who are employed.*

- **Income.** Having a depository account is positively correlated with income. *40.8 percent of underbanked households make less than $30,000 in annual income. 17.1 percent of all underbanked households, however, make between $30,000 and $50,000, and 18.3 percent of all underbanked households make $75,000 or more.*

- **Home Ownership.** An estimated half of all U.S. homeowners are underbanked (52.1 percent).

*Source*: Susan Burhouse and Yazmin Osaki, *2011 FDIC National Survey of Unbanked and Underbanked Households: Executive Summary* (Washington, DC: Federal Deposit Insurance Corporation Department of Depositor and Consumer Protection, September 2012).

## AMEX'S "CLOSED-LOOP" NETWORK

Even as EG's initial research had produced some promising indicators about the new business model, there was still much that needed to be worked out. AXP cards had a smaller footprint, being accepted at fewer merchants than Visa or MasterCard. This was primarily due to the higher charges merchants incurred for accepting AXP cards—an estimated average premium of 2.4 percent.[12] Nevertheless, AXP's growth had been rapid in recent years. Figures 13.1 and 13.2 illustrate the relative share of payment provider networks by share of merchant transactions.

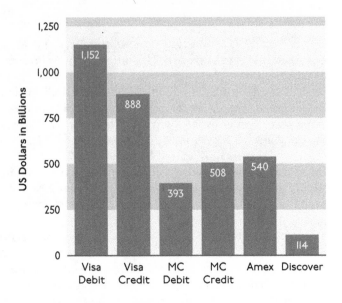

*Figure 13.1* Purchase volume at U.S. merchants in 2011. Data source: Adaptation of data from the Nilson Report, 2012.

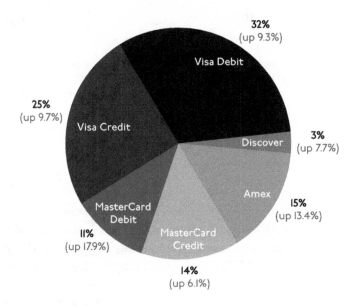

*Figure 13.2* U.S. payment industry market share in 2011. Data source: Adaptation of data from the Nilson Report, 2012.

Behind every AXP transaction were a different business model, set of fees, and pricing structure than those used by competing payments systems such as Visa and MasterCard. In those systems, external banks and financial institutions (called "issuers") owned the relationship with the cardholder. Issuers provided cards that bore a network logo and set the interest rate along with any fees.

The Visa and MasterCard payment networks received their revenues for the ownership and management of the transaction-processing services. Their business models were essentially based on increasing the number of times a consumer used a card. These revenue models are called "transaction-centric" because the larger the number of transactions, the greater the return on the investment in the payments system. In this model, neither Visa nor MasterCard made any loans to the consumer nor received interest on the loans made to consumers for their purchases. Interest or revolving returns, if any, were captured by the issuers of the cards.

AXP's business model was unlike its competitors' in that it served three roles: issuer, lender, and network provider. In this approach, AXP's own banking subsidiaries provided cards to cardholders. AXP received its primary revenues from the discount fees charged to the merchants that accepted its cards. The chief distinction in AXP's "closed-loop" network was that the company was able to leverage customers' spending data to create more tailored rewards and special offer programs.

By comparison, AXP's model was "spend-centric." Critical performance metrics included customers spending higher amounts per purchase, and cumulative purchases over time. The higher spend per transaction made AXP members more attractive to merchants because they were likely to be affluent customers. To help solidify this association among merchants, AXP used internal data to match merchants with wealthy customers who would likely buy their products. In retrospect, it seems AXP had built an early capability in what we would now term "data mining." Because credit risks were borne internally by AXP's banking subsidiaries, any interest on loans to members was another source of revenue for AXP—revenue that Visa and MasterCard did not receive.

## NOT A CREDIT-BEARING RELATIONSHIP

The EG team's working notion was the understanding that the new brand would make an overture to customers who did not qualify for charge or credit cards, and that Bank 2.0 would not require a credit score. Historically, the AXP cardholder was primarily a charge, and not a credit, customer. That is, consumers were not expected to revolve debt and pay interest on their purchases, but to pay in full at the end of the closing period. As a result, credit risks and interest payments were thought of quite differently. AXP tended to focus on the affluent and business consumers who would appreciate the company's rewards and offers. The firm understood that consumers backed by corporate expense accounts and personal wealth would pose less risk of default. Again, there was the promise that digital technology could assist the EG team in attaining a deeper understanding of the habits and needs of their new customers. Innovation would develop along with this deeper understanding.

AXP's business model was supported by an advertising campaign that, from 1987 to 1996, featured the aspirational tagline "Membership has its privileges."[13] Designed to attract affluent customers, ads often featured images of card member celebrities,[14] and the brand became widely associated with exclusivity. In fact, its average annual spend per cardholder tended to be higher than that of AXP's competitors, increasing at a double-digit rate from 2009 to 2011, growing from $11,505 to $14,124.[15]

The distinction between AXP and Visa/MasterCard was also clear to shareholders and industry analysts:

> This contrast is evident in the numbers; Visa has more than 2 billion cards in use worldwide and processes more than 60 billion transactions per year, while AmEx has just 107 million cards in force and processes just 6 billion transactions per year. Despite this disparity, American Express has annual gross revenues of $33 billion while Visa earns just $14 billion per year.[16]

## IT'S EXPENSIVE TO BE POOR

The EG team reasoned that Bank 2.0 was a way to increase AXP's market share by developing an inaugural relationship with a massive untapped group of potential customers. Echoing Silber's notions of the incentives for financial innovation, one EG team member put it this way: "Every company wants to be a growth company. . . . The only way to do that over time is to get new customers."[17]

The group coalesced on the development of an innovative product: a prepaid, reloadable card that could do many of the things one would normally do in a bank. Of course, Bank 2.0 would not actually be a "bank" in the traditional sense, but the working name captured the notion of serving a market segment that historically was unable to access the company's products.

The team recognized that to build a successful product, it needed to better understand how the targeted Bank 2.0 customers transacted in their daily lives. Team members sought to engage directly with the bill-paying experiences of underbanked people who did not have access to credit or checking accounts.

Chokshi, for example, stood in line for at least half an hour before attempting to cash a personal check at a check casher. He found that the standard check casher took between 2 percent and 5 percent of the face transactional value. This process was the first of several in which the underbanked lost both money and time. Once their checks were cashed, they had to stand in another line to get a money order to pay their bills. Given the difficulty of finding time to stand in lines, people often had to contend with late fees. Research from the Federal Reserve Bank of St. Louis confirmed Chokshi's experience:

> Unbanked consumers spend approximately 2.5 to 3 percent of a government benefits check and between 4 percent and 5 percent of a payroll check just to cash them. When you consider the cost for cashing a bi-weekly payroll check and buying about six money orders each month, a household with a net income of $20,000 may pay as much as $1,200 annually for alternative service fees—substantially more than the expense of a monthly checking account.[18]

"Most have enough money to cover expenses," an EG colleague explained. "It's a timing issue. It's cash flow. The populations we're talking about can't take on more debt. They have no savings, they have no flex."

"It's Expensive to be Poor!" was the heading on the EG team's whiteboard. Below it, the stats: "2,300 bank branches closed last year, 95 percent in low-income areas. 70 million people are unbanked or underbanked; they pay 10 percent of their income on fees and interest to complete everyday transactions."

It troubled the group to think that people spent so much money just to change their income from one form to another. Through technology, EG believed it could reimagine what it meant to be part of the financial system. A recent AXP acquisition helped in providing a needed set of capabilities.

In 2010, concurrent with the launch of EG, AXP acquired Revolution Money, a payments company whose technology formed the foundation for a Beta digital payments product—a prepaid card supported by an online platform.[19] This new, reloadable product gave customers a way to conduct peer-to-peer transfers and to make payments online. However, it had not been an outstanding commercial success.

Chokshi wondered if AXP could repurpose the acquired software platform, leverage the EG team's market knowledge, and recast AXP from an iconic brand for the wealthy to an inclusive brand with a much broader reach. He was sensitive to the inherent risks: the all-important consumer adoption factor remained to be seen and required a critical change in financial behavior yet to be proven. Other companies had attempted to rebuild the banking sector and had encountered difficulties. This step required faith.

There were also a host of unanswered questions: How to achieve scale with the underbanked consumer. How to overcome technological hurdles to enable mobile and nonbranch delivery of services. How to adapt to new regulatory requirements. How to get past the scrutiny of consumer interest groups notoriously skeptical of efforts involving middle- and lower-income consumers.

## OPTIONS IN A COMPETITIVE LANDSCAPE

The EG team was not alone in recognizing the opportunities in a changing financial services landscape. The sluggish growth in debit adoption accelerated in the 2000s. Consumers were gradually changing the way they made transactions, as illustrated in Figure 13.3, which shows the relative share of purchases in credit (charge) and debit cards from 2000 to 2014.

As the decade began, credit cards represented the majority of purchase transactions, and by mid-decade debit card transactions exceeded credit.[20] By the end of the period, debit cards accounted for more than two-thirds of transactions. However, in terms of dollars

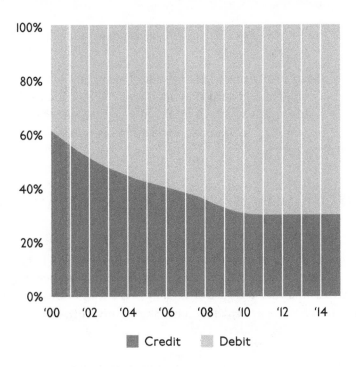

*Figure 13.3a* Credit versus debit, 2000–2014. Transactions; Data source: Adaptation of data from the Nilson Report, 2012.

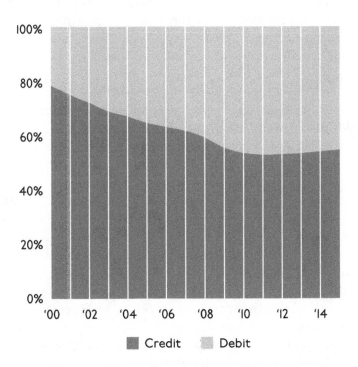

*Figure 13.3b* Credit versus debit, 2000–2014. volume (in dollars). Data source: Adaptation of data from the Nilson Report, 2012

spent, credit cards continued to maintain the predominant share. By 2012, the average credit card transaction was $93, while the average debit card transaction was $34.[21] Taken together, these two charts illustrate a clear size of transaction distinction between credit and debit card usage.

## WHAT DOES IT MEAN TO BE UNDERBANKED?

Although the Bank 2.0 initiative was attempting to serve a new category of consumer, the EG team knew that the term "underbanked" was in some ways deceiving. First, underbanked consumers regularly engaged in financial transactions—they were simply outside of the traditional banking system in their use of cash only, check-cashing centers, or payday lenders. Critics frequently call these alternative financial services (AFS).[22]

In addition to AFS competitors, a cadre of start-ups were leveraging mobile and digital technology and attempting to enter the market with offers of easier and cheaper banking alternatives. For example, Green Dot was testing the marketplace through a partnership with Walmart, Go Bank and NetSpend were forging relationships with check cashers, and Square Cash was providing consumers a send-and-receive money option.[23]

Although the early successes of these players suggested viability, there was a question as to whether any of these new incumbents in the prepaid market would eventually institutionalize and scale. This was two-sided: Their success would help affirm the potential of services for the underbanked, but it would also mean increased competition in a market that presently did not have any large players.

Concurrently, traditional depository institutions were experiencing a change in their financial services footprint. At the time, there were an estimated 96,000 bank branches in the United States, but their numbers had been decreasing significantly, particularly after the financial crisis of 2009. There were economic imperatives pushing this trend. First, the structural costs of branch banking were making it difficult to maintain a brick-and-mortar presence, especially in lower-income and rural communities; and second, real estate, maintenance of physical spaces, and labor costs for tellers, branch managers, and security personnel made paper-thin margins even smaller.

## THE RISE OF ALTERNATIVES

Twenty or thirty years ago, traditional financial institutions fled neighborhoods like Watts, and guys like Tom Nix, co-founder of the biggest chain of check cashers and payday lenders in Southern California, rushed into the vacuum. They built a whole new financial subculture, which now includes . . . more outlets, in total, than all the McDonald's restaurants in the United States plus all the Starbucks coffee shops. [24]

Alternative Financial Services providers generally had radically different business models than depository banks and had developed capabilities that played to the needs of the underbanked—longer operating hours, in-person banking, and convenient locations. Although AFSs were sharply criticized in the public sphere, primarily because of their relatively high interest and transaction rates, they continued to expand their growth and range of services.

Another looming front of competition came from a growing number of traditional merchandise retailers. With extensive footprints and broad customer bases, their efforts were structured around the assumption that offering in-store financial services could also build shoppers' in-store spending.

"You've got to remember, Walmart is intended to be a one-stop shop," said Charles M. Holley Jr., the company's CFO. "The more kinds of services we can offer our core customer . . . the better for them."[25]

Merchandise retailers also sensed a second opportunity: the general distrust of traditional banks. "A lot of [our] members think their bank fees are too high . . . or they're having issues with debit and credit cards," said Jay Smith, Costco's director of business and financial services.[26]

Walmart had sought a banking charter for almost a decade, but after facing considerable opposition from advocacy groups, eventually abandoned the effort in 2007.[27] Home Depot, Costco, Office Depot, and Sears, among others, had also experimented with financial services, but their efforts had shown mixed results.

One challenge that merchandise retailers faced was the skepticism or outright resistance of consumer advocates. On one hand, the consumer advocates appreciated the attempt to serve a broader range of financial services needs. On the other, they were concerned about differences in the level of regulatory scrutiny retailers received relative to traditional depository institutions.

AXP itself had previously entered new markets through cobranded initiatives in their credit card business. In recent years, these partnerships had led to the introduction of the Costco TrueEarnings Card and the Delta Air Lines SkyMiles credit card. The new Bank 2.0 would be an entirely different business model and serve an entirely different customer segment. The question lingered as to whether a partner was necessary.

## ENVISIONING BANK 2.0 IN USE

Consumer adoption and behavior were at the nexus of Bank 2.0's success. To gain a better understanding of the initiative's potential value and returns, AXP modeled and compared the spending behavior of the typical credit card consumer and the new Bank 2.0 consumer (see table 13.1).[28] If the prepaid consumers adopted the cards but failed to use them in ways that sustained the business, the project would be considered a Pyrrhic victory at best. In the hypothetical examples here, the modeled behavior illustrates very different sets of returns and costs.

Another important element of the prepaid strategy would be differences in volume demand. There are substantial numbers of unbanked and underbanked individuals (an estimated 24 million underbanked alone), and the more who became prepaid customers, the greater the opportunity to mine the data for trends and patterns of potentially creditworthy customers. AmEx was betting on the long-term proposition that being underbanked did not indicate "shouldn't" or "couldn't" be banked. They recognized that more than one-sixth of all underbanked households (17.1 percent) earned between $30,000 and $50,000, and nearly one-fifth (18.3 percent) made $75,000 or more.

## AXP'S HISTORY WITH PREPAID PRODUCTS

One of AXP's core, most successful products was traveler's checks, which debuted in 1891, forty-one years after the company's founding.

Prepaid cards and traveler's checks had a number of elements in common, notably that neither involved the extension of credit. However,

TABLE 13.1
Value of Prepaid Versus Credit Card Customers

| Prepaid customers | | | |
|---|---|---|---|
| Sources of revenue | | Sources of costs | |
| Discount revenue | 2.4% | Operating expense | 6.0% |
| Float revenue | 4.8% | Acquisition costs | $7.00 |
| Fee revenue | | Other services | |
| Initial activation/purchase fee | $3.95 | Fraud expense | 1.0% |
| Monthly usage fees | $1.00 | | |
| Direct deposit/cash reload | $0.00 | | |
| ATM fees (in network) | $0.00 | | |
| ATM fees (out of network) | $2.00 | | |
| Foreign transaction fees | 2.7% | | |
| Credit card customers | | | |
| Sources of revenue | | Sources of Costs | |
| Discount revenue | 2.4% | Operating expense | 11.00% |
| Annual fee | $75.00 | Acquisition costs | $80.00 |
| | | Loan loss provision | 2.7% |
| Rate revenue | | Benefits | |
| Regular rate on purchases | 17.6% | Travel insurance | 1.25% |
| Cash advances | 21.0% | Credit insurance | 1.00% |
| Balance transfer rate | 15.6% | Fraud insurance | 0.76% |
| | | Rebates | 1.00% |
| | | Miles | 1.00% |
| | | Cash back | 1.00% |
| Fee revenue | | | |
| Late payment fees | $35 | | |
| Over-limit fees | $25 | | |
| Cash advance fees | $5.00 | | |
| Minimum finance charges | $4.00 | | |
| Foreign transaction fees | 2.7% | | |

These estimated revenues and costs are hypothetical and are not intended to represent actual fees for any credit card or prepaid product, including those of American Express.

Source: Jackie Thomas Kennedy and Greg Fairchild adaptation of company documents.

they differed in distribution models. Traveler's checks were available in financial institutions, prepaid cards in retail stores. The question on the matter of distribution was whether stores would sell the Bank 2.0 product, and how AXP would introduce them.

In 2010, AXP had debuted another prepaid product, the PASS card,[29] designed for parents to give to their young adult children. Effectively, it was an allowance card. Chokshi described it as "driver's ed for the teen's wallet,"[30] and it had clear advantages over cash for parents who could reload the card with their AXP credit card or checking account. One less-preferred element was that the card carried monthly fees.

Around the same time, AXP launched four or five other products, testing to see how each would perform. In retrospect, it could be argued that this was an incubation period in which the company gained valuable experience in the prepaid industry. AXP noted one trend that stood out, however. Prepaid cards across the industry were being offered with the same features usually found in a checking account.

## THE CONVENIENCE OF TECHNOLOGY AND THE *FEEL* OF BANKING

The EG Group considered how the process of opening its new financial services product should "feel," and agreed it was more than simply downloading an app. The Bank 2.0 product launch would have to effectively replicate the service customers appreciated in traditional banks: filling out a brief application, activating a physical card, and moving funds into the card's account would help create a "much deeper banking relationship."

As with many retail products, its success would rely on scale: the margins might be low, but high volume would compensate. The goal would be to provide financial services that came with fewer fees than other prepaid products, and certainly below those charged by AFSs.

Even with a firm grasp of what Bank 2.0 could be, a reloadable prepaid card with direct-deposit capabilities, the EG team considered a number of options—among them, to seek out a partner that could complement capabilities AXP lacked, such as an extensive presence throughout the

United States. The question was how to find a partner that would be familiar with the demographic segment AXP was targeting.

## AN EXPANSION IN BRAND IDENTITY AND BUSINESS MODEL: "FROM EXCLUSIVE TO INCLUSIVE"

A prepaid model, in which AXP accepted a customer's money, was entirely different from postpaid credit, and was more accessible and better suited to APX's new, nontraditional customer. As the group conducted early focus groups, it faced a common challenge experienced by innovators: describing a product and its services to consumers who were learning about it for the first time. Technically, Bank 2.0 was neither a bank account nor a traditional prepaid card. What could AXP call it instead? The company's marketing team concluded that Bank 2.0 was "a debit and checking alternative."

In focus groups, the team described the intended benefits. Bank 2.0 would not charge customers annual or overdraft fees, and a minimum balance was not required. There were multiple ways to load funds for free, including direct deposit and mobile check capture. Peer-to-peer transfers were possible, as was the formation of subaccounts for family members.[31] For some focus group members, it simply seemed too good to be true.

Chokshi described the Bank 2.0 initiative as an "aspirational brand," adding that "safety, security, trust is for everyone, not just the affluent. Millions of people knock on our door and we have to say no to them on the credit card side because they don't have the right . . . credit scores," he acknowledged.[32]

Bank 2.0 was a way of welcoming these same people into the AXP fold.

## WHY THIS COMPANY?

The EG team understood that a key factor in Bank 2.0's success would be concerns among the existing franchise of card members about "diluting the AXP brand." One potential solution would be to distinguish this new customer segment through its distribution channel.

Dan Schulman believed that the biggest impediment to a company's future success was its past success—a tendency "to become wed to what was, and not what could be." He hoped Bank 2.0 could be seen as a complement to AXP's iconic and affluent brand.

The team concluded that effective delivery through novel channels would require investments in systems and expertise that AXP did not currently have, such as those available in retail merchandising and consumer packaged-goods firms. Indeed, Bank 2.0 was a technology product, not just a card—and it had to stand out on the shelf.

As a whole, the prepaid industry presented enormous challenges. Though it was easy for a customer to sign up for a product online, there was no guarantee that he or she would actually use the product. Since part of Bank 2.0's appeal was its minimal fees, AXP wanted its customers to engage fully with the product by signing up for direct deposit. It was felt that enticing, informational material describing the benefits of opening an account was a marketing essential. Bank 2.0 packaging would need to be more than a simple plastic card.

The EG team saw plenty of reasons to move forward: AXP had already spent millions of dollars on the prior digital platform, and the Bank 2.0 initiative was a way to take advantage of that investment. The brand could establish AXP as a player in the expanding world of financial inclusion. And if more consumers wanted to pay with AXP products, it would become harder and harder for merchants to turn them away, especially since AXP had 22,000 ATMs available.

As it happened, the EG group posed a pivotal question: Why develop or purchase infrastructure when you can replicate it? Perhaps potential customers would find a familiar infrastructure both reassuring and easy to use.

## ENTER WALMART

Among the biggest challenges to the goal of "reimagining banking" was reaching consumers where they lived and shopped, and doing so with a brand that was relatable.

A partnership had been one of the team's distribution options, and it came to the fore when Walmart approached American Express about a potential collaboration. For some time, Walmart believed that the company's many locations and service to middle- and low-income consumers lent itself to offering financial services to the underbanked. And, of course, a partnership with a recognized financial services firm could provide value to Walmart's business.

Walmart was far more experienced than American Express in operating within the traditional consumer-products environment, and from AXP's perspective, Walmart possessed attractive criteria to support Bank 2.0. In addition to its 3,295 locations nationwide, the retail giant had an installed base of point-of-sale registers that could serve like ATMs. A relationship with Walmart successfully countered the need to build or open branches.

## FLIGHT OF THE BLUEBIRD

Working collaboratively with Walmart, AXP developed a unique look and feel for its new card. After designing and testing multiple concepts, it finally settled on Bluebird, a card featuring a vibrant blue and teal bird logo. Market testing indicated that the card would be distinguishable from existing American Express cards, and was perceived as customer friendly.

In October 2012, the Bluebird card was launched in royal blue packaging in Walmart stores. The cards were accepted wherever American Express was already accepted, and offered the typical features of direct deposits and withdrawals at ATMs and Walmart stores.

A key element of AXP's strategy was easy account access. Consumers had three options: Opening an account online, through their mobile phones, or in person at a Walmart store, each with only a $5 application fee. There were no credit checks, minimum balances, monthly or annual fees, and—assuming the system worked appropriately—no opportunity for overdrafts. There were some fees, however. A flat fee of $2 was charged for out-of-network ATM withdrawals, and for withdrawals without direct deposit. In contrast, other prepaid card providers typically levied a $5 per month service charge as well as other fees.

"[Bluebird seems] to be competitively priced and is likely to intensify the competitive environment in the prepaid industry," an equity analyst wrote in a note to clients at the time.[33]

Less than a year after launch, the AXP-Walmart partnership added additional features to align the product more closely with traditional banks, including FDIC insurance for accounts under $100,000 and an expanded network of 22,000 ATMs. The relationship between the two companies seemed an important opportunity to learn and innovate together as the product rolled out.

"Bluebird is helping customers streamline everyday money management. . . . [It's] a great option for our active duty military personnel, government employees and other customers, helping them take greater control of their everyday finances," said Daniel Eckert, vice president of financial services for Walmart U.S.[34]

As a sign of Bluebird's growth and diffusion, in 2013, the card was included in a Consumers Union evaluation of more than two dozen prepaid cards, the results of which were published in the organization's magazine, *Consumer Reports*. "Not all prepaid cards are created equal," stated Michelle Jun, senior attorney with Consumers Union. "Consumers can still end up paying more than they bargain for because fees are often poorly disclosed and can pile up quickly."

*Consumer Reports* evaluated twenty-six prepaid cards based on four factors: value, convenience, safety, and fee disclosure. The Bluebird card was top-rated only months after its launch.[35] Three years later, the card still rated a positive mention in the magazine: "American Express Walmart Bluebird was among the top four because it charges no monthly fee and offers some great services, such as bill pay and free access to in-network ATMs."[36]

Though this history is still being written, it provides an important lesson in how effectively large institutions can provide scale to community development financial innovations. More so than smaller organizations, American Express has the potential to reach literally millions of consumers with programs like Bluebird. An important element of this and future innovations will be the leveraging of digital platforms and technology to overcome the structural and cost limitations in banking that may have prevented, or may continue to prevent, some from pursuing opportunities in lower-income communities.

## A FULL CIRCLE POSTSCRIPT

Not long after completing the interviews that formed the core basis of this narrative, I opened my own Bluebird account. I was curious after spending the time learning about the card's development. With three teenagers, my wife and I reasoned that the cards could be educational.

Bluebird accounts allow the holder to create subaccounts for family members, with their own cards, logins, and online services. The interface platform allows the account holder to monitor usage, set spending limits, and receive email alerts when too much is spent within a user-defined period of time.

These were all attractive features in socializing our children on the proper use of financial services, and we presented them with their own Bluebird cards, along with a lecture on how to use them. That was more than two years ago. My wife and I now use the cards to distribute allowance, and our children have begun to use the cards for their online and everyday purchases.

I am not sure how our children will develop their own purchasing habits over time, or when they might graduate to credit products, but I am sure that the Bluebird card is giving them a strong starting point. And as our family navigates relationships with financial services firms, I am certain that payment providers will be learning along with us.

# CHAPTER FOURTEEN

# How I Lost My FOMO

And something which a lot of people don't talk about, but we doubled
the child tax credit, doubled it, and our tax plan also created nearly
9,000 Opportunity Zones . . . providing massive new incentives for
investment and job creation in distressed communities.[1]

"Capital is going to flow to the lowest-risk, highest-return
environment," said Aaron T. Seybert, the social investment officer at the
Kresge Foundation. . . . "Perhaps 95 percent of this is doing no good
for people we care about."[2]

ABOUT FOUR miles from my home in Charlottesville, Virginia, is
the Southwood Mobile Home Park. The neighborhood is substantial, comprising more than three hundred trailers with predominantly
Latino residents. Because of its proximity to the privileged community
and verdant grounds of the University of Virginia, also in Charlottesville, many are surprised to learn there is corresponding inequality and
segregation within our city.

Perhaps change is coming to Southwood. The development is
located on land that has been designated a federal Opportunity Zone
(OZ). This program, a component of the Tax Cuts and Jobs Act of
2017, provides incentives designed to attract investment to projects
in low-income areas. The Southwood project is projected to create a
mixed-income neighborhood: eight hundred new housing units, with
some of the site's 120 acres sold to market-rate commercial and residential developers.

The core innovation of OZ is explicitly financial, targeted toward
beneficial treatment of capital gains taxes. First, the new code would
allow deferral of any capital gains taxes for seven years if invested

in projects like Southwood; second, OZ investors can reduce any taxable gains from these projects by as much as 15 percent; and third, if the investors maintain their position in an OZ fund for a decade or more, they can sell their investment without any taxes owed. The program is applicable to a broad array of capital gains—real estate, equities, mutual funds, even the sale of a business. Combined, these features make OZ investments quite attractive to investors seeking a safe harbor for their prior investment gains as well as provide an opportunity to target those dollars toward underserved areas.

The OZ program is similar in a number of ways to the New Markets Tax Credit, a funding innovation detailed in chapter 12. Managed by the IRS and the U.S. Treasury, OZ sites (approximately 8,800 nationwide) are found in every state, with four in Charlottesville alone. The process to become OZ-eligible is at least partially based on low median household income and other social factors, such as unemployment.

Opportunity Zones were the brainchild of an organization called Economic Innovation Group (EIG), which was supported by a number of prominent businesspersons, including Sean Parker, a founder of Facebook. From the outset, the idea was that financial incentives could bring capital not otherwise available into underserved areas. An early EIG working paper addressed the initiative's intent to assist the unemployed and jobless.

> The proliferation of severely distressed areas around the country has been a drag on the overall health of the U.S. economy. . . . Where GDP growth falters in one area, it has an impact on the U.S. as a whole, not only by acting as a drag on overall production but also because distressed areas are potential markets for consumption of goods produced elsewhere in the U.S. and their weakness has a spillover effect on other communities. . . . A federal subsidy for private activity can knock the community out of the bad equilibrium and help it back on its feet.[3]

Opportunity Zones have certainly gained a great deal of attention. They appear to offer great promise for new investors in economic development; however, questions remain about their realized economic development impact over time. Will OZ investments grow to the levels some proponents claim? Will these subsidies provide the spark that will indeed lead to a leveling across areas? Or will the results be gentrification and high-rise luxury developments?

Candidly, I tend toward a more sanguine assessment. It is difficult for me to avoid seeing OZs as familiar lyrics with a new melody. At one point, I spent time studying NMTCs; and earlier, empowerment zones; and before that, venture philanthropy. I think I will be around to watch the OZ innovation diffuse and disperse into neighborhoods. There will be questions about their efficacy, and I will be interested in answering some of them. This is one of the realities of being a business scholar: there is always something new to investigate, assess, and understand.

## "SO, WHAT ARE YOU UP TO?"

Grad school reunions are opportunities to catch up with former class-mates, and I recently attended my own. Inevitably, the conversations turned to work. More than a few alums shared that they were raising various flavors of venture funds. One was involved in a "Cleantech" fund. Another was a limited-partner investor in a "Regtech" fund. Yet another mentioned an "Insurtech" fund. I nodded, yet wasn't sure I understood what any of these firms might do in the marketplace.

I had some vague awareness of a number of recent "tech" start-ups, generally known by the popularizing term Fintech (a *portman-teau* of "financial technology"). As is often the case with trendy business jargon, what exactly constitutes a Fintech firm is not always clear. I have found that central to most definitions is the application of technology to improve the delivery of financial services across a broad swath of industries—insurance, payments, risk management, electronic trading, and others.

Correspondingly, when asked about my own work, I shared with my classmates the journey that supports this book: "I study financial institutions that operate in underserved markets and address inequal-ity." Admittedly, it is a matter-of-fact, plain-vanilla response. I do not have a cool suffix or a fast-trending brand.

An unexpected, informative benefit of describing your work for others is that they reflect their own worldview when framing their understanding of your work. There are revelations. "Oh, you're study-ing social impact investing." "I see, double-bottom line." "Ethical banking?" "This sounds like Opportunity Zones." Two recent intriguing ones: "economic gardening" and "beehive development."

I suspect each is in some way applicable, yet I am not clear on what exactly constitutes any of these. This ambiguity has caused me to wonder about the benefit of folding my research into a larger, exciting, recognizable business movement that could get quick nods. When pressed for a pithy term, I have generally worried less about having a memorable phrase. Though I have wondered: Should I care?

## RESEARCH AFTER THE REUNION

Not having heard of Regtech before the reunion, I could not find more than a smattering of folks who knew what a Regtech firm was. Eventually, I came across John Humphries's blogpost in *Forbes*:

> Regulatory Technology (Regtech) has emerged as a hot topic in financial services. While some have defined Regtech as a tool to improve efficiency and effectiveness, others describe RegTech as *a phenomenon, a global paradigm shift and a strategic opportunity that will help companies successfully execute their business models in the context of a safe and sound global financial system* [emphasis added].[4]

You have likely heard the popular acronym FOMO (fear of missing out). When reading Humphries's description, I felt uninformed and out of date. As a business school professor, I am expected to stay conversant with important trends. Post-reunion, I was having an insecure, FOMO moment.

To quell my anxiety, I searched our library's databases for definitions, examples, and articles published since 2000 (Dow Jones/Factiva).[5] I looked into a few close cousins, including Cleantech and Greentech. This provided answers—and raised some new questions.

Figure 14.1 shows the number of articles in leading business books, magazines, and academic journals that included the words Cleantech, Fintech, or Regtech between 2000 and 2018. The annual number of articles mentioning each term varies, so I have placed the number of articles mentioning Cleantech on the right axis and represented them as a bar chart. The frequency of the word Regtech is represented by the hashed or dotted line, Greentech by the solid line.[6]

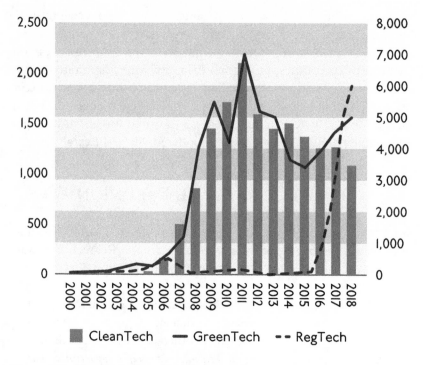

*Figure 14.1* CleanTech, GreenTech, and RegTech.

The visual impression is that all the words experienced steep rises in popularity; two then had noticeable declines. Regtech has drawn marked interest since 2016.

- Cleantech peaked in popularity in 2011 and has since been in a slow decline (down 48 percent by 2018). Greentech mirrored Cleantech, though it was substantially less popular (peaking in 2011 and declining 52 percent by 2015). In 2016 and after, Greentech experienced a resurgent interest, growing an average of 10.3 percent per year.
- The popularity of Regtech is particularly interesting. Humphries's claim of a "phenomenon" is evidenced in articles as early as 2000. For many years, it received relatively scant attention; however, there was a marked rise in interest in 2006 (135 articles). This was followed by a prolonged period of relative decline (by 2014,

it was mentioned in only two articles). For some reason, business writers resumed interest in 2016, and the term rose dramatically (1,526 percent increase in a single year). Only two years later, by 2018, the number of articles mentioning Regtech had more than doubled each year.

From these patterns, one might agree with Humphries's notion that a paradigm shift was underway. But these analyses raised some additional questions: Why the rise, fall, and resurgence? Why did these terms peak in interest never to return? Why did Regtech's escalating, rapid rise happen more than a decade after the word's introduction? How closely related is the popularity of a term to its practice in the field? How often are different terms coined to describe similar approaches? Are Cleantech and Greentech distinct? Is one a subset of the other? Answering these questions might provide an insight into whether being left out of a larger business movement is necessarily a disadvantage.

## A REVIEW OF A FEW RECENT SOCIAL FINANCE MOVEMENTS

In table 14.1, I provide a short (though not exhaustive) list of terms describing various elements of the work I have been engaged in, and definitions of each found in recent articles. Some have been used by practitioners in the field, some by external observers like faculty colleagues. Each became a popular way to describe activity with an objective of integrating societal concerns in business practices.

There was a period when I found myself huddled in meetings with a serious, diligent band of fellow "usual suspects." We would meet in cities across the country to give lectures, share papers, and propose and debate new, inclusive approaches to financial and business activity. We talked about making the business world more inclusive—democratic, equal, just, hopeful.

During this period, one of the first of the movements frequently associated with my work by others was the double bottom line (DBL). This movement was soon followed and exceeded by the triple bottom line (TBL). I devoured everything I could find about each in the hope of providing a language I could use with others when trying to explain what interested me.

TABLE 14.1

Terminology for Integrating Business and Social Concerns

| Phrase | Definition |
|---|---|
| Double bottom line (DBL) | "We think of Double Bottom Line (DBL) businesses as entrepreneurial ventures that strive to achieve measurable social and financial outcomes." |
| Triple bottom line (TBL) | "The triple bottom line (TBL) consists of three P's: profit, people, and planet. It aims to measure the financial, social, and environmental performance of the corporation over a period of time. Only a company that produces a TBL is taking account of the full cost involved in doing business." |
| Ethical investing (EI) | "A set of approaches which include social or ethical goals or constraints as well as more conventional financial criteria in decisions over whether to acquire, hold, or dispose of a particular investment." |
| Impact investing (II) | "Impact investments are made into companies, organizations, and funds with the intention to generate social and environmental impact alongside a financial return." |

As you can see in table 14.1, there are clear distinctions between terms, though they seem fuzzy at the boundaries. From what I can tell, it appears that environmental attention is not included in some definitions of DBL. Triple bottom line appears more rigorous, though perhaps this is because it is perceived as including a larger number of considerations. Triple must be better than double.

Figure 14.2 shows the popularity of each of these terms over time (DBL is shown in the bar chart and is quantified on the right axis). In terms of popularity in business writing, both have an early peak in 2012, followed by a slight decline and then resurgence in 2014. It is also noticeable that both begin declining in mentions of articles dated from 2015 to 2018.

Definitions of the increasingly popular impact investing (II) appear to apply financial services solutions to relatively resilient gaps in social

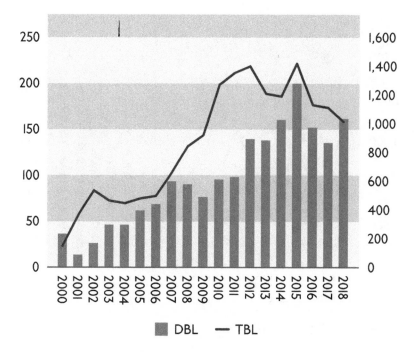

*Figure 14.2* Double and triple bottom line.

outcomes. As with the other terms, I see clear similarities between what I understand to be the II scope and my on-the-ground work in the firms I study. On a number of occasions, II includes the modifier *social* at the front (should there be confusion about where the impact was directed). A leading example of the II ethos is Pacific Community Ventures, one of the financial institutions I have written about in this volume.

As evident in figure 14.3, impact investing was itself predated by ethical investing (EI, shown as a line and quantified on the right axis). When I examined the writing on EI, I found substantial attention in the earliest period (128 articles mentioned the term in 2000). The term had its peak mentions in 2007 (279), then declined through 2015, after which it began rising anew. When I examined II, I found that the term also appears to have had a long history (mentioned in twenty-four articles as early as 2000). It had a very slow rise until 2011, after which it fell for one year and then resumed growing at a slow pace. In 2016, it surged, rising to inclusion in 2,448

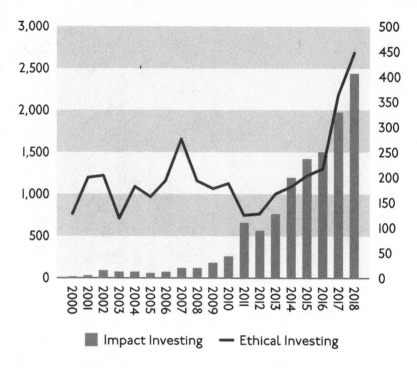

*Figure 14.3* Impact and ethical investing.

articles in 2018. The swings in attention make me wonder whether the frequency of these terms will appear dated five years from now.

## RIDING WAVES

At one point, mission-investing and purpose-driven conferences were "hot"—then, not so much. The conferences gradually fell off in attendance, and then, invites disappeared altogether. It seems all of these descriptive terms are less in vogue, but the evidence on the ground shows there is no less need for an answer to continuing inequality, and for novel prescriptions.

One might ask whether it matters that a phrase rises, crests, and falls out of favor. If the work is ongoing, are we not simply speaking about language? Does the specificity of terms matter? In the next section,

I provide a few examples that can illustrate some of the unintended consequences of jumping on a bandwagon too soon.

## DEFINITIONAL DRIFT

I wrote earlier about fuzzy definitions. This is less critique than observation. When fields are new, confusion about what constitutes a body of work is common. However, there are caveats for new devotees. The following passage is from Gregory Dees, writing in the preface to the *Social Entrepreneurship Teaching Resources Handbook*:

> It is exciting and gratifying to be involved in developing a new field. As an area of academic inquiry, social entrepreneurship is still very young, presenting many opportunities for significant research and teaching contributions. You *can still get in on the ground floor*. However, because it is so new, you are likely to encounter challenges common to any new field.
>
> Another challenge associated with the newness of the field concerns the lack of common understanding of social entrepreneurship. Many people, including many of our academic colleagues, will be unfamiliar with the concept. It has to be explained to curriculum committees, journal editors, *and friends at social gatherings. To complicate matters, there are several definitions circulating* [emphasis added].[7]

Dees's observations were meant for fellow academics and perhaps for investment practitioners. As the shepherd of this movement, Dees appears to be encouraging diffusion and adoption of the social entrepreneurship notion. I can see in his writing that he is creating the "thought umbrella" for others to operate under. This involves writing simultaneously to build engagement and to warn of the risks of a rapidly growing, less understood arena.

One issue in joining a popularizing movement is the likelihood that all engaged are not sure they are interested in the same things. The following quote is from a study of self-identified investors in so-called ethical investing funds:

> [We find] that investors who buy units in ethical mutual funds are often also shareholder activists, protesting at AGMs [annual general

meetings], and they may also invest in socially directed investment vehicles. . . . They have differing ethical beliefs, and are often fairly inarticulate about these beliefs and have a hard time explaining the relation of their beliefs to their investment choices.[8]

Relatedly, I have run across a multitude of investment funds or businesses that are unquestionably working on topics that fit these socially focused descriptions. They are indeed ameliorating social ills or demonstrably improving problems. However, their leaders do not describe themselves in those terms (or are not measuring their social impacts in a rigorous fashion). If a firm does impactful work, yet does not set up a measurement process or call itself a triple-bottom-line firm, is it one?

## THE UPSWING

To gain proponents, movement leaders deliberately select words and phrases to broadcast their missions and differentiate themselves from others. Table 14.2 gives some examples of firms operating in related social business arenas.

These taglines and slogans are certainly motivating and evocative. My worry is that they contribute to a separation that might be less true in practice. I cannot help but ask, would any business or investment firm not make similar claims? Would most business leaders not

TABLE 14.2
A Nonscientific Selection of Exemplar Taglines and Slogans

| Source | Quote |
| --- | --- |
| Prudential | "B Lab helps companies become the best in the world—and best for the world." |
| Global Finance Magazine | "Ommeed Sathe and the business of doing good." |
| Opportunity Finance Network | "Finding and financing opportunities that others miss." |
| Kauffman Fellows | "Patient Capital in an Impatient World." |
| PWP | "Portfolios with Purpose: Investing for Good." |
| Schroder's Asset Management | "Responsible Investing." |

publicize their goal to "seek opportunities others miss"? Would any suggest that they *were not* investing for good?

I suspect at least one reason for the porosity of definitions is that these are framed as unassailable. What is there to challenge or not like in any of the stated business objectives? Another worry about the implications of unassailability is the purported promise of implicit or explicit choices. In a world of finite resources and time, which social change elements are heightened and which are not? What is or is not one fund's operating definition of social impact? Is any impact, without regard to area of focus, applicable? Are all equally valued? Another concern is language that makes promises that a particular framework or approach will miraculously solve long-standing, intractable problems. Consider Humphries's quoted description of Regtech: *a phenomenon, a global paradigm shift and a strategic opportunity*. Is Regtech really all of these? Are writers like Humphries "telling," "selling," or both?

## PROACTIVE OR REACTIVE?

Another challenge in the sphere of "doing good while doing business" is that some brandings seem like reactions to something exogenous. There may be less clarity on what devotees agree with, and greater clarity on what they oppose. For example, I have wondered how much influence the financial crisis, populist movements, and elections have had in encouraging these movements.

In a *New York Times* review titled "Smoothing the Sharp Elbows," Paul Brown begins:

> As you will recall from Ethics and Morality 101—which followed in the wake of the Adelphia, Enron, Tyco and WorldCom scandals, among others—publishers flooded the market with books from academics, consultants and even a few executives, who argued that a relentless focus on the bottom line is not the best way to run a business.
>
> Those authors said that if a company takes into account the interests of all its stakeholders—customers, employees, suppliers and residents of the areas in which the company operates—it will make more money because employees will work harder for an organization they believe in, and customers will be more loyal to companies that share their values.

Having made this argument in the first round of books, publishers are now offering—with decidedly mixed results—new works that focus on how managers can integrate morality and ethics into the everyday tasks of running a business.[9]

## NOT JUST ON THE PAGE

As a business school professor, I frequently attend the keynote speeches of business leaders. A substantial number are CEOs of financial services firms. Whether a finance professional helms a small start-up or a massive, established multinational bank, a recent trend I have noticed is that, at some point, there will be a statement like: "We aren't a financial services firm. We are a tech firm."

I have wondered how this identity applies. Is it an accurate assessment of the strategy or competitive set of the firm? An accounting of the key capabilities brought to bear in delivery systems? Or is it a way to claim adjacency to the slick, flashy world of Silicon Valley instead of what some stereotype as the greedy, stodgy world of banking? I suspect that it varies across firms, and perhaps is a combination of all. Being in finance, but in a deconstructive, disruptive fashion, is more appealing in a human resources context, especially in attracting millennials.

The academic classroom evidences similar tendencies. An article by Abby Ellin on new trends in management education begins:

> In business schools, "green" thinking means more than concern for the environment. Social responsibility (no sweatshops, no Enrons) and economic viability (this is business) are also part of the definition making its way into the mainstream. Many traditional M.B.A. programs have begun to recognize a triple bottom line—of people, planet and profit—and at a few institutions, the marriage of commerce and social responsibility is the guiding principle.[10]

At work, I have observed the launch of courses that became quick favorites, and then just as quickly disappeared. Social Venturing, Social Entrepreneurship, Ethical Business, and Business for Impact are all course titles that have been listed in catalogs. The common theme at the core of each is that, in some fashion, the course attempts to address society's environmental and social concerns through business activity. The issue I have is not their intent. It lies in the front-end framing and patterns of temporality. The courses come and go. The motives behind these courses are unassailable, and there will surely be new ones. The underlying issues persist.

My second concern is the collective swoon for business models at the expense of careful attention to the underlying social phenomena. One example is the recent flurry of interest in Goldman Sachs's decision to pursue a social impact bond (SIB). Heightened expectations were followed by the on-the-ground results:

> The idea of social impact bonds is still very new. The first one was started in England in 2010; Goldman started the first in the United States in 2012.
>
> *The bonds are already being talked about as one of the most promising ideas to come out of finance recently*—providing a new way to fund social programs in an era of government budget cuts. . . .
>
> *But the effectiveness of the bonds has been unclear.* Goldman's first social impact bond to publish outcomes—a program that attempted to reduce recidivism among inmates on Riker's Island in New York—failed this summer [emphasis added].[11]

SIBs offer novel ways to marshal usually disparate groups to solve problems. However, the Goldman experiment is a cautionary tale: excitement about a novel funding mechanism, SIBs, and the involvement of prominent finance professionals create new attention to an old problem.

However, heightened attention can have drawbacks. First, when the experiments fail, what is the lesson learned? An important postscript: In 2018, New York State decided to close Riker's Island after a number of reviews about poor management. This left a question: was the problem with the SIB, or the location chosen? There was a sense of poor management at the site. Unfortunately, what observers may remember is the failure of this program, not the underlying factors that likely contributed. The lesson is that context and details matter. SIBs are exciting, especially when they involve leading firms like Goldman Sachs and the Bloomberg Foundation. But it seems not all was right with the location chosen. Context matters.

## GREAT TASTE, LESS FILLING

I cannot help but compare some business movements to the advertising slogan "Great Taste, Less Filling." The genius of the long-running Miller Lite campaign was the combination of two concepts: While less filling, light beers were generally believed to be watery, and without taste. Full-bodied beers were tasty, but also caloric. If a beer could have both fewer calories and robust taste, then Miller drinkers would tap the optimal beer-drinking experience. I have posited a similar strategy behind some of the terms that rise to popularity in the investment world, and in management generally.

I have come to the conclusion that some, though not all, of these claims are the rhetorical equivalent of the Miller Lite campaign. They offer solutions to seemingly intractable problems modern societies face. They provide the careful, analytical, market-based imprimatur of financial expertise to solve problems like inequality, without the uncomfortable discussions of recalcitrant political, governmental, and social justice issues. In other words, "tasty," finance-based solutions without the uncomfortable discussions we would otherwise have to address. No inequality aftertaste.

The point here is that these are complicated matters that require careful solutions. As scholars, our role is an important one. We should recognize that we can be perceived to be endorsing when we intend to illustrate. We should labor to question, to model, to examine, to report. We should avoid jumping on bandwagons or proffering quick, one-size-fits-all solutions. Context, history, and local knowledge matter. The rush of the latest fad obscures these more sober realities.

## WHAT'S OLD IS NEW AGAIN

Regarding my FOMO, I worry and I do not. Over time, I have become accustomed to the rapid, excited rise of each new business label, followed by a brief period of intense interest and, too often, a corresponding decline. I also worry that overheated excitement early may lead to some unintended consequences later. New movements come and go, rise and fall, because the need is timeless.

One takeaway from "socially motivated" finance is that we are skipping from one iteration to another. Perhaps this is a distraction from more uncomfortable discussions. Perhaps we have tacitly agreed to a separation between the goals of our firms and the resulting impact on the communities in which we live. This is not a new condition. America has both rising inequality and unyielding segregation, and rising nativist tendencies. What to do about these ills is a long-standing concern, with varied prescriptions. Rudyard Kipling wrote of colonialist Britain around the turn of the twentieth century:

> Take up the White Man's Burden. Send forth the best ye breed,
> Go bind your sons to exile to serve the captive's need.
> To wait in heavy harness on fluttered folk and wild.
> Your new-caught, sullen peoples, half-devil and half-child.[12]

Reading this quote from more than a hundred years ago, I see echoes across time, even into contemporary discourse.

John D. Rockefeller, Sr., known as perhaps history's single richest person, was concerned with the great inequality of the late nineteenth century. Perhaps one influence on Rockefeller was his upbringing in a poor, single-parent household. He had a clear sense of his wealth and what to do with it.

> It has seemed as if I was favored and got increase because the Lord knew that I was going to turn around and give it back. . . . I remember clearly when the financial plan—if I may call it so—of my life was formed. It was out in Ohio, under the ministration of a dear old minister, who preached, "Get money: get it honestly and then give it wisely." I wrote that down in a little book.[13]

Rockefeller believed the acquisition of wealth was tied to the philanthropic effort to address societal ills. He was not alone. Another corporate giant, transplanted Andrew Carnegie, published his own treatise on the importance of philanthropy. In "The Gospel of Wealth," he called on those who had excelled in business to take up the cause and direct management of social ills.

> This, then, is held to be the duty of the man of Wealth . . . to consider all surplus revenues which come to him simply as trust funds, which

he is called upon to administer, and strictly bound as a matter of duty to administer in the manner which, in his judgment, is best calculated to produce the most beneficial results for the community—the man of wealth thus becoming the mere agent and trustee for his poorer brethren, bringing to their service his superior wisdom, experience and ability to administer, doing for them better than they would or could do for themselves.[14]

The two business titans had similar concerns, yet divergent views on how to address the problem. Kipling, Rockefeller, Carnegie, and many thinkers of their period and since have arguably been dealing with the concept of *noblesse oblige*—the implied obligation of those with uncommon wealth to care for those without their intellectual, positional, or financial assets. The rub is that *noblesse oblige* has regularly been called out as an argument supporting status and privilege. I am not sure the personal, perhaps idiosyncratic, efforts of powerful, wealthy, well-meaning individuals are sufficient. Our systems are complex; they call for cross-sector, multiple actor, and institutional solutions.

## GETTING BEYOND DISCOURSE: ANOTHER POTENTIAL IMPACT

Business scholars find the motivation to put hand to keyboard for a number of reasons. Often they desire to share findings or theories that will influence fellow scholars to take up their approach or way of looking at the world of markets and exchanges. Some share their work in the hope of influencing those in the finance field by offering up new models to create operational efficiencies, novel investment approaches, and alternative ways to elicit greater profits. Most pursue both of these paths.

Another group of scholars wade into thorny, even controversial topics of public interest—immigration and nativity, racial and gender disparities, residential segregation. They include in their frames the role financial institutions have historically had, and still have, in effecting or exacerbating inequalities between groups. They believe there is even the possibility that research may reveal *inclusive* models that provide prescriptions for financial institutions to operate efficiently and without high levels of risks to produce uncommon returns. I consider myself a member of this second group.

## NOW WHAT?

As I have discussed, this book has shared a professional journey that—as a result of my research and scholarship—only recently prompted me to view my family's personal financial journey through the lens of the overarching financial services system, who it serves and who it does not.

I am still on this journey, and you are as well. Since it does not appear that we have solved the "finance problem" and that the equity markets will not "ensure that discrimination is costly," we will be trekking toward solutions for some time. There are still needed innovations and considerable work to be done—a good deal of it.

What would I recommend to those who have given of their time to read along? In the remainder of this section, I propose some broad thoughts. Complex problems require multiplex prescriptions.

There is substantial benefit in raising awareness. The field of scholarship simply needs more of it. Topics related to how we build a broad-based financial services system demand a broader base of scholars and researchers examining questions and formulating answers. Given the scope and depth of demographic, income, technological, and educational change over the past fifty years, what is needed is a larger group of scholars with a broader base of social disciplinary training and a willingness to ask uncomfortable questions.

Many social science perspectives could help us understand the provision of financial services (or lack thereof). For instance, how, where, and when does bias enter the financial services transaction? What can be done to ameliorate the effects of bias in the transaction? Is it really relevant to match service providers to the populations they serve? What role would bias play, even in quantitative systems, in over- or underemphasizing risks?

We need behavioral measures and data sets. Likewise, data science techniques would help us understand what the relative black box of surveys, bank call reports, or census data cannot. We need new approaches to help us understand behaviors that consumers cannot explain when asked. I should share a note of caution. There is a heated, excited rush to big data and machine learning, and I am not sure the full implications have been considered. For example, there are serious questions about the underlying notions that influence the algorithms created. Computing power without human insight may lead to unintended consequences.

Likewise, we could benefit from more natural experiments, similar to the analysis shared in Chapter 6 about the Latino Community Credit Union. We simply need more scholars with eyes on these questions. And, of course, we need journal editors and scholars to encourage doctoral students to pursue these questions. Subtle "wait until later" messages may be well meaning, but stymie research that is sorely needed.

More scholars need to get into the field, both in research capacities and as advisers to practitioners. I have taken this approach to heart. For some time now, a good portion of my service efforts have been through board work with financial institutions—depository community development financial institutions (CDFIs), Virginia Community Capital, and Virginia's Pension Fund Investment Advisory.

More recently, I accepted an opportunity to join the board of Local Initiatives Support Corporation (LISC). Founded in 1979, it is now the nation's largest CDFI. The organization operates in nearly every state and, in 2018 alone, made more than $1.5 billion in grants, loans, and investments. These funds are deployed across a broad range of programs, including affordable housing, early childhood centers, fresh food initiatives, health care centers, and even after-school athletic facilities. My service on this board has been a veritable "university" of community development knowledge.

In late 2017, I was invited to join the U.S. Treasury's Community Development Advisory Board, which supports the activities of the Treasury Department's CDFI Fund. This has also been a great learning process, especially in understanding how national development policy is constructed. Given my long research on CDFIs, I take this appointment as quite an honor. The worlds of scholarship and practice are not as segregated as we often think. They are mutually reinforcing.

## THOUGHTS FOR PRACTITIONERS

Let us remind ourselves that businesses operate within societies. We have agreed, in most cases implicitly, to support the empowering aspects of the marketplace and ignore the factors in our lives that may contribute to society's challenges. If those of us who are relatively well-resourced intend to ameliorate the issues before us, there are some uncomfortable conversations to be had.

Prevailing data suggest we will continue to go to work, raise our children, and send them to schools in a racially, ethnically, and wealth stratified fashion. As data increasingly indicate, we have only selectively integrated and our separation constrains opportunity. I remain optimistic. However, without intentionality in our policies and, yes, in our investment, we should not expect the problem to "just work itself out" and result in a more accessible set of opportunities. Martin Luther King encouraged us by noting, "The arc of the moral universe is long, but it bends toward justice." I am not always so sure. I believe intentional, purposeful nudges are needed.

Do I think finance professionals, who are frequently advantaged in the educational, social-class, and economic race, should acknowledge these matters? Yes. Do I think they should move their residences and alter where their children go to school? Perhaps.

I advocate that business professionals recognize their advantages, and account for the many that are unearned. Having acknowledged these, they should use their voice and advocacy to reconsider the criteria and structures of their financial services products. They should listen. They could reconsider the processes that lead to important funding decisions in their organizations. They should enter with humility, rather than too easy assurance that their decisions are fully logical and not based on stereotypes. Those who ration capital in our society should take their important role and responsibility seriously.

Do I think that politically based solutions are possible? For sure. However, it may seem dubious given what appears to be a stalled process within the federal government. Here, too, I remain optimistic about the ability to provide outcomes-based assistance, as I have certainly seen novel innovations at the state and local levels.

## GETTING INVOLVED

The finance field is not broken. Of course, there is an easy and clichéd view of the field as populated by actors with questionable morals. As I have stated earlier, this stereotype is a blunt instrument as damaging as any other. What the field needs is engagement with a broader base of actors who bring their unique perspectives to bear.

I have long believed that interrogating and sharing our life experiences provides value, and I encourage others to do the same. This includes testing dominant academic theories against lived experience and inculcating those into data analyses. I suppose I remain an advocate for integration in all things. If there are readers now working in a financial institution, or considering working within one, bring the fullness of your perspective with you. It is needed.

I also recognize that bringing your full self to work is not easy. In this book I have offered a number of examples of firms that have demonstrably benefited when employees carried their networks, perspectives, and demography into their workplaces. Organizations need to be prepared to listen to what their employees offer. Unfortunately, we know from organizational studies that there are pressures to conform to the norm, especially for those in the demographic minority. Far too often, they are not hired. When they are brought into financial firms, they can be discouraged from bringing their "difference" into their work. Knowing that sharing diverse viewpoints is not easy places a special responsibility on organizations to invite and open up the discussion. Our social problems are complicated. When we bring ourselves, we bring our knowledge. It needs to be in the discourse.

## BACK AT THE FAMILY TABLE

On a recent Saturday, I sat down at the kitchen table with my eighteen-year-old son. Over coffee and sandwiches, he told me about a new savings platform he had found. The energy crackled through his voice. He had recently graduated high school, and I was elated he had initiated a conversation about building wealth.

He shared the account's promise: an easy-to-use, intuitive platform that automated savings. After providing access to all of his electronic spending accounts—credit and debit cards, checking accounts—the service would track each transaction. The prime benefit was that the platform would "round up" each transaction to the nearest dollar, and place the remainder into a savings account. For example, if he spent $6.27 on lunch and used a debit card, 73 cents would be removed from his checking account and deposited into one of a preselected set of savings vehicles. For my son, the attraction was its "set-it-and-forget-it" approach. He explained that this was one of the new types of technology that could alter savings accumulation for people like him: busy younger workers who seldom used cash. This was the type of discussion parents can hope for, though cannot compel.

My son and I were pleased with the discussion, but unconvinced about the service. We agreed that while this platform's unique way to save was novel, we both had to do a bit more research. I suggested he look for answers to some questions before deciding whether to open an account: How did the service provider make a profit? And how much, relatively speaking, did they charge for these services?

He asked whether I had any hesitation in our decision not to move forward. Was I creating an obstacle and the possibility my son would miss out? I confessed that I did have a worry, a sense that it would be okay to take our time and see how this latest "next hot thing" progressed. We could wait.

# Notes

## PREFACE

1. Howard Aldrich, *Organizations Evolving* (Thousand Oaks, CA: Sage, 1999).

2. F. Scott Fitzgerald, "The Rich Boy," *Red Book* (January/February 1926).

3. Ernest Hemingway, "Snows of Kilimanjaro," *Esquire* (August 1936).

4. Pamela Newkirk, "Diversity Has Become a Booming Business. So Where Are the Results?," *Time*, October 10, 2019, https://time.com/5696943/diversity-business/.

5. Johan Wiklund, David Audretsch, and Erik Lehmann, "Re-search = Me-search," in *The Routledge Companion to the Makers of Modern Entrepreneurship*, ed. David Audretsch and Erik Lehmann (New York: Routledge, 2016), 233–253.

## 1. THE BEST INVESTMENT I NEVER HAD TO MAKE

1. Antoine van Agtmael, *The Emerging Markets Century: How a New Breed of World-Class Companies Is Overtaking the World* (New York: Free Press, 2007), 3.

2. Agtmael, *The Emerging Markets Century*, 1.

3. Glenn Yago, James R. Barth, and Betsy Zeidman, *Entrepreneurship in Emerging Domestic Markets: Barriers and Innovation Vol. 7* (New York: Springer, 2007); James R. Barth, Glenn Yago, and Betsy Zeidman, *Barriers to Entrepreneurship in Emerging Domestic Markets: Analysis and Recommendations* (New York: Springer, 2006); Glenn Yago, Betsy Zeidman, and Alethea Abuyuan, "A History of Emerging Domestic Markets," *Community Development Investment Review* 3, no. 1 (2007): 1–22.

4. Gregory B. Fairchild, "In Your Own Backyard: Investment Opportunities in Emerging Domestic Markets," (New York: Council of Urban Investors Institute, 2004), https://community-wealth.org/sites/clone.community-wealth.org/files/downloads/report-fairchild.pdf.

5. U.S. Census Bureau: Decennial Census of Population (5-percent sample), "Racial and Ethnic Minorities Refers to Persons That Referred to Themselves as Anything Other than Non-Hispanic White" (1970).

6. U.S. Census Bureau, "Most Children Younger than Age 1 Are Minorities," 2012, https://www.census.gov/newsroom/releases/archives/population/cb12-90.html.

7. In this chapter, and elsewhere in this book, I use terms to describe racial and ethnic groups like white, Black Hispanic, Latino, and others. I recognize that these terms are socially constructed, as are these racial groupings themselves. In most cases, I have defaulted to the official U.S. Census Bureau terms—Hispanic or Latino. In others, I have chosen to use the terms I am most familiar with—Black, white. Some readers may prefer other terms. I recognize that language matters, and have labored to be accessible. In keeping with recent direction from the Associated Press, I have capitalized Black when referring to the racial group or individuals.

8. Erin Duffin, "Educational Attainment in the U.S. from 1960 to 2019," *Statista*, 2020, https://www.statista.com/statistics/184260/educational-attainment-in-the-us/.

9. Susan Aud, Mary Ann Fox, and Angelina KewalRamani, *Status and Trends in the Education of Racial and Ethnic Groups* (Washington, DC: U.S. Department of Education, Institute of Education Sciences, National Center for Education Statistics, July 2010), 123, table 24.1, https://vtechworks.lib.vt.edu/bitstream/handle/10919/83685/StatusEducationRacialEthnicGroups.pdf?sequence=1&isAllowed=y.

10. Aud, Fox, and KewalRamani, *Status and Trends*, 121, table 23.2.

11. Ralph J. Alig, Jeffrey D. Kline, and Mark Lichtenstein, "Urbanization on the US Landscape: Looking Ahead in the 21st Century," *Landscape and Urban Planning* 69 (2004): 219–234, https://www.fs.fed.us/pnw/pubs/journals/pnw_2004_alig005.pdf.

12. John V. Thomas, *Residential Construction Trends in America's Metropolitan Regions* (New York: Diane Publishing, 2009).

13. U.S. Conference of Mayors, "U.S. Metro Economies: GMP and Employment 2018–2020," *Annual Report and Forecast*, September 2019, https://www.usmayors.org/wp-content/uploads/2019/09/mer-2019-09 .pdf.

14. Michael E. Porter, "The Competitive Advantage of the Inner City," *Harvard Business Review* 73, no. 3 (May 1995): 55–71.

15. Porter, "The Competitive Advantage."

16. Jerry Flint, "Credit Cards: Change and Uncertainty," *New York Times*, June 1, 1977.

17. Sharon M. Danes, Catherine Huddleston-Casas, and Laurie Boyce, "Financial Planning Curriculum for Teens: Impact Evaluation," *Journal of Financial Counseling and Planning* 10, no. 1 (January 1999): 25–37.

18. Stuart J. Heckman and John E. Grable, "Testing the Role of Parental Debt Attitudes, Student Income, Dependency Status, and Financial Knowledge Have [*sic*] in Shaping Financial Self-Efficacy Among College Students," *College Student Journal* 45, no. 1 (March 2011): 51–64; Jean M. Lown, "Development and Validation of a Financial Self-Efficacy Scale," *Journal of Financial Counseling and Planning* 22, no. 2 (February 2012): 54.

19. Paul Webley, "The Development of Saving," in *The Interdisciplinary Science of Consumption*, ed. Stephanie D. Preston, Morten L. Kringelbach, and Brian Knutson (Cambridge, MA: MIT Press, 2014), 243.

20. Jeffrey R. Hibbert, Ivan F. Beutler, and Todd M. Martin, "Teacher Versus Parent Influence on Financial Efficacy and Behavior," *Proceedings of the 2004 Annual Conference of the Association of Financial Counseling and Planning*, The Association of Financial Counseling and Planning (2004), 51–59.

21. Douglas B. Holt, "Does Cultural Capital Structure American Consumption?," *Journal of Consumer Research* 25, no. 1 (June 1998): 1–25.

22. Pierre Bourdieu, "The Forms of Capital 1986," in *Cultural Theory: An Anthology*, ed. Imre Szeman and Timothy Kaposy (Chichester, UK: Wiley-Blackwell, 2011), 81–93; Paul DiMaggio, "Cultural Capital and School Success: The Impact of Status Culture Participation on the Grades of US High School Students," *American Sociological Review* 47, no. 2 (April 1982): 189–201.

23. Douglas S. Massey and Nancy A. Denton, *American Apartheid: Segregation and the Making of the Underclass* (Cambridge, MA: Harvard University Press, 1993).

24. David M. Cutler, Edward L. Glaeser, and Jacob L. Vigdor, "The Rise and Decline of the American Ghetto," *Journal of Political Economy* 107, no. 3 (1999): 455–506.

25. Gary Orfield and Chungmei Lee, "*Brown* at 50: King's Dream or *Plessy's* Nightmare?" Civil Rights Project at Harvard University, January 2004.

26. Donald Tomaskovic-Devey, Catherine Zimmer, Kevin Stainback, Corre Robinson, Tiffany Taylor, and Trici McTeague, "Documenting Desegregation: Segregation in American Workplaces by Race, Ethnicity, and Sex, 1966–2003," *American Sociological Review* 71, no. 4 (August 2006): 565–588.

27. Gregory Fairchild, "Racial Segregation in the Public Schools and Adult Labor Market Outcomes: The Case of Black Americans," *Small Business Economics* 33, no. 4 (2009): 467–484; Gregory B. Fairchild, "Residential Segregation Influences on the Likelihood of Black and White Self-Employment," *Journal of Business Venturing* 23, no. 1 (2008): 46–74.

28. I treasure my copy of the deed and bank loan documents (General Warranty Deed, Book 1688, page 278, 28 December, 1945).

29. Hilary Herbold, "Never a Level Playing Field: Blacks and the GI Bill," *Journal of Blacks in Higher Education* 6 (1994): 104–108; David H. Onkst, " 'First a Negro . . . Incidentally a Veteran': Black World War Two Veterans and the GI Bill of Rights in the Deep South, 1944–1948," *Journal of Social History* 31, no. 3 (Spring 1998): 517–543.

30. R. Edward Freeman, "The 'Business Sucks' Story," *Humanistic Management Journal* 3, no. 1 (2018): 9–16; Andrew C. Wicks, "Overcoming the Separation Thesis: The Need for a Reconsideration of Business and Society Research," *Business and Society* 35, no. 1 (1996): 89–118.

31. Nancy J. Adler and Anne-Wil Harzing, "When Knowledge Wins: Transcending the Sense and Nonsense of Academic Rankings," *Academy of Management Learning & Education* 8, no. 1 (2009): 72–95.

32. Richard R. Nelson and Sidney G. Winter, "Evolutionary Theorizing in Economics," *Journal of Economic Perspectives* 16, no. 2 (2002): 23–46; Franco Malerba, Richard Nelson, Sidney Winter, and Luigi Orsenigo, "Product Diversification in a 'History-Friendly' Model of the Evolution of the Computer Industry," in *Dynamics of Organizations: Computational Modeling and Organization Theories*, ed. Alessandro Lomi and Erik R. Larsen (Menlo Park, CA: AAAI Press, 2001): 349–376.

33. Nelson, Winter & Orsenigo, "Product Diversification," 3.

34. Leva M. Augstums, "Thain Says He Will Repay Bank of America for Office Renovation," *USA Today*, January 26, 2009, http://usatoday30.usatoday.com/money/industries/brokerage/2009-01-26-thain-merrill-bank-of-america_N.htm.

35. The "good old boys" network is a slang term for a closed social circle of men that engage in cronyism or favoritism in business dealings. The phrase has other, less pejorative meanings as well. The author Tom Wolfe refers to the network frequently in his novel *A Man in Full* (New York: Bantam, 2001), which focuses on the life of Charles Croker, an Atlanta business leader.

36. Sidney Finkelstein and Donald C. Hambrick, "Chief Executive Compensation: A Synthesis and Reconciliation," *Strategic Management Journal* 9, no. 6 (November/December 1988): 543.

37. Marc Hodak, "Wall Street Deserved Its Bonuses," *Forbes*, February 20, 2009, https://www.forbes.com/2009/02/19/ceo-pay-bonuses-leadership-compensation_hodak.html#254bb8f04749.

38. U.S. Census Bureau, "Median and Average Sales Prices of New Homes Sold in the United States," 2011, https://www.census.gov/const/uspriceann.pdf.

39. Howard Aldrich and Martin Ruef, *Organizations Evolving*, 2nd ed. (Thousand Oaks, CA: Sage, 2006).

40. For more on the eventual program, see U.S. Department of the Treasury, Community Development Financial Institutions Fund, "CDFI Bond Guarantee Program," https://www.cdfifund.gov/programs-training/Programs/cdfi-bond/Pages/default.aspx.

41. Gregory B. Fairchild and Ruo Jia, "Risk and Efficiency Among CDFIs: A Statistical Evaluation Using Multiple Methods," U.S. Department of the Treasury, Office of Financial Strategies and Research, Community Development Financial Institutions Fund, August 2014, https://www.cdfifund.gov/Documents/Risk%20and%20Efficiency%20among%20CDFIs%20Report.pdf.

## 2. A FOOL'S ERRAND? THE RISKINESS OF FINANCIAL SERVICES IN LOW-INCOME AREAS

1. This advertisement underscores Clemens's sense of humor. For perspective, $205 would be $4,427 in 2017 dollars.

2. US Census Bureau tabulations (H001, H018), DEC Summary File 1, Census 2000, https://data.census.gov/cedsci/table?g=8710000US0906105&y=2000&t=Housing%3AHousing%20Units&tid=DECENNIALSF12000.H001&hidePreview=false&vintage=2018&layer=VT_2018_040_00_PY_D1&cid=H001001. Accessing these results requires users to run tabulations.

3. By pluralistic, we mean to indicate that of the residents of the zip code, no single racial or ethnic group composed more than 50% of the population. US Census Bureau tabulations (H006), DEC Summary File 1, Census 2000, https://data.census.gov/cedsci/all?g=8710000US0906105&y=2000&t=Race%20and%20Ethnicity&tid=DECENNIALSF12000.H006&hidePreview=false&vintage=2018&layer=VT_2018_040_00_PY_D1&cid=H006001. Accessing these results requires users to run tabulations.

4. Section 308 of the Financial Institutions Reform, Recovery, and Enforcement Act (FIRREA) of 1989 requires the secretary of the Treasury to consult

with the director of the Office of Thrift Supervision and the chairperson of the FDIC board of directors to determine the best methods for preserving and encouraging minority ownership of depository institutions. Section 308 of FIRREA defines a "minority depository institution" as any depository institution in which 51 percent or more of the stock is owned by one or more "socially and economically disadvantaged individuals." The FDIC's Policy Statement defines "minority depository institution" as any federally insured depository institution in which minority individuals own 51 percent or more of the voting stock. "Minority," as defined by section 308 of FIRREA, means any "Black American, Asian American, Hispanic American, or Native American." The voting stock must be held by U.S. citizens or permanent legal U.S. residents to be counted in determining minority ownership. To understand the definitions, see https://www.fdic.gov/regulations/resources/minority /mdi-definition.html.

5. Office of the Comptroller of the Currency, "Community Development Financial Institution (CDFI) and Community Development (CD) Bank Resource Directory," https://www.occ.gov/topics/consumers-and-communities /community-affairs/resource-directories/cdfi-and-cd-bank/index-cdfi-and -cd-bank-resource-directory.html.

6. H.R. 3474—Riegle Community Development and Regulatory Improvement Act of 1994, 103rd Congress of the United States, https://www.congress .gov/bill/103rd-congress/house-bill/3474.

7. Duane A. Martin, "The President and the Cities: Clinton's Urban Aid Agenda," *Urban Lawyer* 26, no. 1 (Winter 1994): 99–142.

8. The Federal Freedmen's Bank initiative closed in 1874, amid accusations of fraud and mismanagement. Nevertheless, many of the individual banks persisted. For a deeper history of the Freedmen's Banks and their contemporary descendants, see Nicholas A. Lash, "Asymmetries in U.S. Banking: The Role of Black-Owned Banks," in *Global Divergence in Trade, Money and Policy*, ed. Volbert Alexander and Hans-Helmut Kotz (Cheltenham, UK: Edward Elgar, 2006), 91.

9. Saurabh Narain and Christopher Malehorn, "Invest in What Matters: Mission-Oriented Financial Institutions: Perspectives of a Social Investor," National Community Investment Fund, 2018, http://www.ncif.org/sites /default/files/free-publications/NCIF-Invest_in_What_Matters-MOFIs.pdf.

10. David Porteous and Saurabh Narain, "Social Performance Measurement for CDFI Banks," in *Reengineering Community Development for the Twenty-First Century*, ed. Donna Fabiani and Terry F. Buss (New York: Routledge, 2015), 94–109.

11. Russ Kashian and Juan Gómez Casillas, "The X-Efficiency and Profitability of Hispanic Banking in the United States," *Journal of Applied Financial Research* 1 (2011): 38–49; and Russ Kashian, Richard McGregory, and

Derrek Grunfelder McCrank, "Whom Do Black-Owned Banks Serve?," *Communities & Banking*, 2014 Series ß (2014): 29–31.

12. Jake Intrator, Jonathan Tannen, and Douglas S. Massey, "Segregation by Race and Income in the United States 1970–2010," *Social Science Research* 60 (2016): 45–60.

13. "OCC-Supervised Minority Depository Institutions (As of December 31, 2016)," Office of the Comptroller of the Currency, US Treasury, https://www.occ.treas.gov/topics/consumers-and-communities/minority -outreach/minority-depository-institutions-list.pdf.

14. Although low-income areas are perceived to be riskier, some evidence shows that they are not, controlling for other factors. Mills and Lubuele report that low-income communities do not default at higher levels than middle-income neighborhoods. Edwin S. Mills and Luan Sende Lubuele, "Performance of Residential Mortgages in Low- and Moderate-Income Neighborhoods," *Journal of Real Estate Finance and Economics* 9, no. 3 (1994): 245–260. Van Order and Zorn report that low- and moderate-income neighborhoods do not default at much higher rates than higher-income areas. Robert Van Order and Peter Zorn, "Performance of Low-Income and Minority Mortgages," *Low-Income Homeownership: Examining the Unexamined Goal*, ed. Nicolas P. Retsinas and Eric S. Belsky (Washington, DC: Brookings Institution Press, 2002), 322–347.

15. This project—Gregory B. Fairchild and Ruo Jia, *Introduction to Risk and Efficiency Among CDFIs: A Statistical Evaluation Using Multiple Methods*—was released by the Office of Financial Strategies and Research Community Development Financial Institutions Fund, US Department of the Treasury, February 2015, https://www.cdfifund.gov/Lists/CDFI%20 News/DispForm.aspx?ID=101. Portions of this chapter are drawn from that report.

16. Much of this analysis can be found in Fairchild and Jia, "Risk and Efficiency Among CDFIs," 13–71.

17. Gregory B. Fairchild, "Evolution and Development of the Field of Community Development Finance," report to the John D. and Catherine T. MacArthur Foundation, 2011; available upon request.

18. Fairchild and Jia, "Risk and Efficiency Among CDFIs," 4–11.

19. Loans reported through the Home Mortgage Disclosure Act of 1975 (HMDA). HMDA was developed to provide regulators data on whether individual financial institutions are serving the demand for mortgage loans in the communities in which a financial institution is chartered. Our research team did not conduct the analysis presented here. Please see CDFI Fund for more details on methodology and results.

20. The Troubled Asset Relief Program (TARP) was signed into law by President George W. Bush in October 2008.

21. Altman's original study is Edward I. Altman, "Financial Ratios, Discriminant Analysis and the Prediction of Corporate Bankruptcy," *Journal of Finance* 23, no. 4 (1968): 589–609.

22. Daniel Martin, "Early Warning of Bank Failure: A Logit Regression Approach," *Journal of Banking & Finance* 1, no. 3 (1977): 249–276.

23. Sanjiv R. Das, Darrell Duffie, Nikunj Kapadia, and Leandro Saita, "Common Failings: How Corporate Defaults Are Correlated," *Journal of Finance* 62, no. 1 (2007): 93–117.

24. Eigenvector centrality and Bonacich centrality measures are similar calculations, but there are differences between the two that made us consider the utility of both in this analysis. Eigenvector centrality captures how "in the middle" of things any particular point is in a network. This measure is scaled between 0 and 1 and is context specific to the network being studied. Bonacich centrality is similar in that it incorporates how connected various individuals are, but it differs from eigenvector centrality in that it attempts to measure how dominated or dominating a firm is based on where it is connected.

25. For a related approach, interested readers should consult Craig H. Furfine, "Interbank Exposures: Quantifying the Risk of Contagion," *Journal of Money, Credit and Banking* (2003): 111–128.

26. There is no generally accepted measure for Management across regulatory agencies. Regulators and researchers apply the Management measure in a number of ways, including controls, boards of directors and governance practices, record-keeping, and use of information technology. We chose to exclude this measure in our analysis because of the lack of access to such data; our models relied on readily available and objective financial measures.

27. Specifically, we employed Maximum Likelihood Estimation (MLE) logistic regression. Readers interested in the construction and results of the models should consult the appendices.

28. The rural-urban commuting area (RUCA) codes classify U.S. census tracts using measures of population density, urbanization, and daily commuting, https://www.ers.usda.gov/data-products/rural-urban-commuting-area -codes/#:~:text=The%20rural%2Durban%20commuting%20area,The%20 classification%20contains%20two%20levels.

29. Don Graves, "Announcing the CDFI Bond Guarantee Program," U.S. Department of the Treasury, June 12, 2013, https://www.treasury.gov/connect /blog/Pages/Announcing-the-CDFI-Bond-Guarantee-Program.aspx.

30. G. Fairchild and M. Juelfs, "Just How Risky? Comparative Institutional Risks of Minority Depository Institutions (MDIs) and Community Development Financial Institutions (CDFIs)," Community Development Investment Review, Federal Reserve Bank of San Francisco, 2020.

## 3. EFFICIENT? ARE DEVELOPMENT FINANCIAL INSTITUTIONS EXPENSIVE TO OPERATE?

1. Hean Tat Keh and Singfat Chu, "Retail Productivity and Scale Economies at the Firm Level: A DEA Approach," *Omega* 31, no. 2 (2003): 75–82.

2. Rhonda R. Thomas, Richard S. Barr, William L. Cron, and John W. Slocum Jr., "A Process for Evaluating Retail Store Efficiency: A Restricted DEA Approach," *International Journal of Research in Marketing* 15, no. 5 (1998): 487–503.

3. Robert DeYoung, William C. Hunter, and Gregory F. Udell, "Whither the Community Bank?," *Journal of Financial Services Research* 25, no. 2 (2004): 81–84.

4. Ben S. Bernanke, "Community Banking and Community Bank Supervision," speech at the Independent Community Bankers of America National Convention and Techworld, Las Vegas, Nevada, March 8, 2006, Federal Reserve Board of Governors, https://www.federalreserve.gov/newsevents /speech/bernanke20060308a.htm.

5. For examples of analyses using stochastic methods to measure efficiency, see Dmytro Holod and Herbert F. Lewis, "Resolving the Deposit Dilemma: A New DEA Bank Efficiency Model," *Journal of Banking & Finance* 35, no. 11 (2011): 2801–2810; Stephen M. Miller, and Athanasios G. Noulas, "The Technical Efficiency of Large Bank Production," *Journal of Banking & Finance* 20, no. 3 (1996): 495–509.

6. For a list of funds available through the CDFI certification process, visit https://www.cdfifund.gov/programs-training/certification/Pages/default.aspx.

7. James R. Barth, Aron Betru, Christopher Lee, and Matthew Brigida, *Minority-Owned Depository Institutions: A Market Overview* (Washington, DC: Milken Institute, 2019), http://milkeninstitute.org/reports/minority -owned-depository-institutions-market-overview.

8. See Earl L. Brown, "Negro Banks in the United States," PhD diss., Boston University, 1930, https://ia803004.us.archive.org/31/items/negrobanksinunit 00brow/negrobanksinunit00brow.pdf; and Herman Belz, *A New Birth of Freedom: The Republican Party and Freedmen's Rights, 1861 to 1866* (New York: Fordham University Press, 2000).

9. Andrew F. Brimmer, "The Black Banks: An Assessment of Performance and Prospects," *Journal of Finance* 26, no. 2 (1971): 379–405.

10. Brimmer, "The Black Banks," 391.

11. Brimmer, "The Black Banks," 391–394.

12. Brimmer, "The Black Banks," 391–394.

13. Edward D. Irons, "Black Banking—Problems and Prospects," *Journal of Finance* 26, no. 2 (1971): 407–425.

14. Lewis J. Spellman, Alfred E. Osborne, and William D. Bradford, "The Comparative Operating Efficiency of Black Savings and Loan Associations," *Journal of Finance* 32, no. 2 (1977): 565–574.

15. Allen N. Berger and Loretta J. Mester, "Inside the Black Box: What Explains Differences in the Efficiencies of Financial Institutions?," *Journal of Banking & Finance* 21, no. 7 (July 1997): 895–947.

16. Anders Q. Nyrud and Sjur Baardsen, "Production Efficiency and Productivity Growth in Norwegian Sawmilling," *Forest Science* 49, no. 1 (2003): 89–97; Ian Vázquez-Rowe and Peter Tyedmers, "Identifying the Importance of the 'Skipper Effect' Within Sources of Measured Inefficiency in Fisheries Through Data Envelopment Analysis (DEA)," *Marine Policy* 38 (2013): 387–396.

17. Vázquez-Rowe and Tyedmers, "Identifying the Importance of the 'Skipper Effect.'"

18. To test for differences between these groups, we used a method called the Kolmogorov-Smirnov test. This test is a nonparametric model that is used to compare the equality of two sample groups. One of its preferable features is that it is sensitive to differences in both the location and shape of the empirical cumulative distribution functions of the two samples. Interested readers can view a lecture on this topic at http://www.real-statistics.com /non-parametric-tests/two-sample-kolmogorov-smirnov-test/.

19. See Gregory B. Fairchild, Young Kim, Megan E. Juelfs, and Aron Betru, "Good Money After Bad? The Comparative Efficiency of Minority Depository Institutions," *Journal of Developmental Entrepreneurship* 25, no. 1 (2020), https://doi.org/10.1142/S1084946720500028.

20. Douglas D. Evanoff and Philip R. Israilevich, "Productive Efficiency in Banking," *Economic Perspectives* 15, no. 4 (1991): 11–32.

## 4. CHANGING THE WORLD THROUGH THE SOUTH SIDE OF CHICAGO

1. Lorraine Hansberry, *To Be Young, Gifted, and Black: Lorraine Hansberry in Her Own Words*, ed. Robert Nemiroff (New York: Random House, 1995), 20.

2. Steven R. Carter, *Hansberry's Drama: Commitment Amid Complexity* (Urbana University of Illinois Press, 1991); Allen R. Kamp, "The History Behind *Hansberry v. Lee*," *UC Davis Law Review* 20 (1986): 481.

3. Estimate from U.S. Census data, https://www.unitedstateszipcodes .org/60637/#stats.

4. See Otis Dudley Duncan and Beverly Duncan, *The Negro Population of Chicago: A Study of Residential Succession* (Chicago: University of Chicago Press, 1957), for more on ecological and residential succession theories.

5. Ronald Grzywinski, "The New Old-Fashioned Banking," *Harvard Business Review* 69, no. 3 (1991): 87–98.

6. Martin Meyerson and Edward C. Banfield, "Politics, Planning, and the Public Interest: The Case of Public Housing in Chicago," *University of Chicago Law Review* 23, no. 4 (1956): 739–743. The term "tipping point" first appeared in Morton Grodzins, "Metropolitan Segregation," *Scientific American* 197, no. 4 (1957): 33–41. Grodzins credited Meyerson and Banfield with first forwarding the concept based on their observations of housing patterns over time in Chicago.

7. Malcolm Gladwell, *The Tipping Point: How Little Things Can Make a Big Difference* (New York: Little, Brown, 2006).

8. For more economic theories of discrimination, see Joseph E. Stiglitz, "Approaches to the Economics of Discrimination," *American Economic Review* 63, no. 2 (1973): 287–295; Gary S. Becker, *The Economics of Discrimination* (Chicago: University of Chicago Press, 2010); William Darity, *What's Left of the Economic Theory of Discrimination?* (Chapel Hill: University of North Carolina Press, 1988).

9. Grzywinski, "The New Old-Fashioned Banking."

10. Beth Healy, "Problems with Indecorp Sale; Community Protests Shake Bank Funders," *Crain's Chicago Business*, August 5, 1995, http://www.chicago business.com/article/19950805/ISSUE01/10009131/problems-with -indecorp-sale-community-protests-shake-bank-funders.

11. Beryl Satter, *Family Properties: Race, Real Estate, and the Exploitation of Black Urban America* (New York: Metropolitan Books, 2010).

12. Richard P. Taub, *Community Capitalism: Banking Strategies and Economic Development* (Boston: Harvard Business School Press, 1988), 140.

13. In November 2010, my research team and I interviewed Clarence and Lisa Hall in their offices and during travels throughout the south side of Chicago. All quotations in this chapter are drawn from those interviews.

14. The Leadership in Energy and Environmental Design (LEED) green building rating system is "a third-party certification program and the nationally accepted benchmark for the design, construction and operation of high performance green buildings." A LEED rating of Certified, Silver, Gold, or Platinum is based on the number of points a building accumulates in the 136-point system. Silver is the lowest level. http://www.usgbc.org/leed#rating.

15. U.S. Census Bureau, *U.S. Census 2000*, Summary File 1, https://www .census.gov/census2000/sumfile1.html.

16. State of Illinois Department of Professional and Financial Regulation and Federal Deposit Insurance Corporation, ShoreBank Order to Cease and Desist, https://www.fdic.gov/bank/individual/enforcement/2009-07-07.pdf.

17. Kevin Robinson, "Credit Crisis Hits ShoreBank," *Chicagoist*, July 14, 2009, http://chicagoist.com/2009/07/14/credit_crisis_hits_shorebank.php.

18. Steve Daniels, "ShoreBank Shakes Up Exec Suite, Names New CEO," *Crain's Chicago Business*, November 3, 2009, https://www.chicago business.com/article/20091103/NEWS01/200036021/shorebank-shakes -up-exec-suite-names-new-ceo.

19. Daniels, "ShoreBank Shakes Up Exec Suite."

20. Bill Zielinski, "Politically Connected ShoreBank of Chicago Fails and Reincarnated at Taxpayer Expense," *Problem Bank List*, August 21, 2010, http://problembanklist.com/politically-connected-shorebank-of-chicago -fails-and-reincarnated-at-taxpayer-expense-0172/.

21. Micah Maidenberg, "FDIC Sues Former ShoreBank Executives Over Soured Loans," *Crain's Chicago Business*, August 19, 2013, https://www .chicagobusiness.com/article/20130819/CRED03/130819817/fdic-sues -former-shorebank-executives-over-soured-loans.

22. Steve Daniels, "FDIC Settles ShoreBank Lawsuit for $17 Million," *Crain's Chicago Business*, November 20, 2013, https://www.chicagobusiness .com/article/20151120/NEWS01/151119785/fdic-settles-shorebank-lawsuit -for-17-million.

# 5. CORN TOSTADAS AND A CHANGING COMPTON

1. Emory S. Bogardus, "Social Distance in the City," *Proceedings and Publications of the American Sociological Society* 20 (1926): 40–46.

2. Emory Stephen Bogardus, *A Forty Year Racial Distance Study* (Los Angeles: University of Southern California Press, 1967).

3. For more on the measurement of close relationships, see Hugh Louch, "Personal Network Integration: Transitivity and Homophily in Strong-Tie Relations," *Social Networks* 22, no. 1 (2000): 45–64.

4. Miller McPherson, Lynn Smith-Lovin, and James M. Cook, "Birds of a Feather: Homophily in Social Networks," *Annual Review of Sociology* 27, no. 1 (2001): 415–444.

5. For more on Ibarra's work on networks and demography, see Herminia Ibarra, "Personal Networks of Women and Minorities in Management: A Conceptual Framework," *Academy of Management Review* 18, no. 1 (1993): 56–87; Herminia Ibarra, "Race, Opportunity, and Diversity of Social Circles in Managerial Networks," *Academy of Management Journal* 38, no. 3 (1995): 673–703.

6. James R. Elliott and Ryan A. Smith, "Ethnic Matching of Supervisors to Subordinate Work Groups: Findings on 'Bottom-Up' Ascription and Social Closure," *Social Problems* 48, no. 2 (2001): 258–276.

7. At the request of the Wells Fargo team, the names of the firm's owners have been fictionalized out of respect for privacy concerns. All details about

the family, all data about the firm, and the names of all other individuals associated are accurate.

8. City of South Gate, "About South Gate," http://cityofsouthgate.org/257 /About-South-Gate.

9. City of South Gate, "Employment," http://cityofsouthgate.org/303 /Employment.

10. For more on slotting fees, see Guillermo Israilevich, "Assessing Supermarket Product-Line Decisions: The Impact of Slotting Fees," *Quantitative Marketing and Economics* 2, no. 2 (2004): 141–167.

11. Brandon Copple, "Shelf Determination," *Forbes*, April 15, 2002, https://www.forbes.com/forbes/2002/0415/130.html.

12. Charlie Savage, "Wells Fargo Will Settle Mortgage Bias Claims," *New York Times*, July 13, 2012, https://www.nytimes.com/2012/07/13/business /wells-fargo-to-settle-mortgage-discrimination-charges.html.

## 6. A SENSE OF PLACE: INTERPLAY OF GEOGRAPHY AND CAPABILITY

1. The median size of a U.S. home in 2010 was 2,169 square feet. For a listing of median and average home sizes from 1973 to 2010, see https:// www.census.gov/const/C25Ann/sftotalmedavgsqft.pdf.

2. For more on sources of wealth inequality, see Melvin L. Oliver and Thomas M. Shapiro, *Black Wealth, White Wealth: A New Perspective on Racial Inequality* (New York: Taylor & Francis, 2006).

3. Charles Tilly, *Durable Inequality* (Berkeley: University of California Press, 1998).

4. For more on the sense of place in housing, see Bonnie Lindstrom, "A Sense of Place: Housing Selection on Chicago's North Shore," *Sociological Quarterly* 38, no. 1 (1997): 19–39; Joongsub Kim and Rachel Kaplan, "Physical and Psychological Factors in Sense of Community: New Urbanist Kentlands and Nearby Orchard Village," *Environment and Behavior* 36, no. 3 (2004): 313–340.

5. Michael LaCour-Little and Stephen Malpezzi, "Gated Communities and Property Values," Wells Fargo Home Mortgage and Department of Real Estate and Urban Land Economics, University of Wisconsin, Madison, 2001.

6. Oscar Newman, "Defensible Space: A New Physical Planning Tool for Urban Revitalization," *Journal of the American Planning Association* 61, no. 2 (1995): 149–155.

7. Marcelle S. Fischler, "Security Is the Draw at Gated Communities," *New York Times*, August 16, 1998, https://www.nytimes.com/1998/08/16 /nyregion/security-is-the-draw-at-gated-communities.html.

8. Reservation wages, a concept from labor economics, are the lowest wages a given type of worker will accept for a given job. Studies show that different ethnic laborers tend to demand different rates for the same job (i.e., immigrants will frequently work for less).

9. Karen D. Johnson-Webb, "Employer Recruitment and Hispanic Labor Migration: North Carolina Urban Areas at the End of the Millennium," *Professional Geographer* 54, no. 3 (2002): 406–421.

10. Beth Anderson, "Latino Community Credit Union (*Cooperativa Comunitaria Latina de Crédito*): 'Progress with Dignity,'" Duke University Fuqua School of Business, Center for the Advancement of Social Entrepreneurship, February 2004.

11. Noel Poyo and Analisa Nazareno, "Building Economic Power in Immigrant Communities—Lessons from the Field," *NonProfit Quarterly*, August 28, 2009, https://nonprofitquarterly.org/building-economic-power-in-immigrant-communities-lessons-from-the-field/.

12. North Carolina Senate Bill 419 was passed on August 15, 2005, effective January 1, 2006, requiring proof of legal residency in North Carolina before a driver's license would be issued; http://ncga.state.nc.us/Sessions/2005/FiscalNotes/Senate/PDF/SFN0419v1.pdf.

13. "White House Honors John Herrera, Co-founder of Latino Community Credit Union," Z. Smith Reynolds Foundation, July 8, 2013, https://www.zsr.org/articles/white-house-honors-john-herrera-co-founder-latino-community-credit-union.

14. We completed this analysis in 2008. After 2007, a number of other communities also opened LCCU branches, including Winston-Salem, Charlotte, and Garner. This analysis did not include those communities because of the time period of our study.

15. Mike Schenk, "Commercial Banks and Credit Unions: Facts, Fallacies, and Recent Trends, Year-End 2012," Credit Union National Association (CUNA), 11, https://www.cuna.org/uploadedFiles/Advocacy/Actions/Combanks-Cus.pdf.

# 7. WHAT ETHNIC HAIRSTYLING AND CREDIT UNIONS HAVE IN COMMON

1. For more on preferences for Black-serving barbershops, see Quincy T. Mills, "'I've Got Something to Say': The Public Square, Public Discourse, and the Barbershop," *Radical History Review* 2005, no. 93 (2005): 192–199; Quincy T. Mills, *Cutting Along the Color Line: Black Barbers and Barber Shops in America* (Philadelphia: University of Pennsylvania Press, 2013).

2. Virginia had created licensing for all barbers in the state as early as 1962. Any licensee in the state of Virginia must complete at least 1,500 hours of apprenticeship training or schooling before they can apply and take the licensing exam.

3. Mills, *Cutting Along the Color Line*, 235–236; see also Douglas Bristol, "From Outposts to Enclaves: A Social History of Black Barbers from 1750 to 1915," *Enterprise & Society* 5, no. 4 (2004): 594–606.

4. Robert L. Boyd, "Residential Segregation by Race and the Black Merchants of Northern Cities During the Early Twentieth Century," *Sociological Forum* 13, no. 4 (1998): 595–609.

5. Paul Witcover, *Zora Neale Hurston*, Chelsea House Publishing, 1991, 67, also in Mills, *Cutting Along the Color Line*, 60–61.

6. We conducted a number of interviews with Lily Lo and Michael Chan in San Francisco during the week of May 16, 2011. Unless otherwise indicated, all quotations attributed to Lo or Chan derive from these interviews.

7. See Betty Lee Sung, *Mountain of Gold: The Story of the Chinese in America* (New York: Macmillan, 1967); Sucheng Chan, "A People of Exceptional Character: Ethnic Diversity, Nativism, and Racism in the California Gold Rush," *California History* 79, no. 2 (2000): 44–85.

8. Bernard P. Wong, "Chinatown (San Francisco)," in *Asian American History and Culture: An Encyclopedia*, ed. Huping Ling and Allan W. Austin (New York: Routledge, 2015), 147–151.

9. For more about a wave of legislative and social actions to impede Chinese progress and immigration, see Bernard P. Wong, *Ethnicity and Entrepreneurship: The New Chinese Immigrants in the San Francisco Bay Area* (Boston: Allyn and Bacon, 1998).

10. One of the challenges the entrepreneurs had to overcome was technical: Most of the men who would open laundries had no idea how to wash clothes when they first arrived because it was considered women's work back in China. They learned how to wash from the wives in their households who served as domestic servants.

11. Bernard P. Wong, "From Enclave Small Businesses to High-Tech Industries: The Chinese in the San Francisco Bay Area," in *Manifest Destinies: Americanizing Immigrants and Internationalizing Americans*, ed. David W. Haines and Carol A. Mortland (Westport, CT: Praeger, 2001), 111–130.

12. Andrew Gyory, *Closing the Gate: Race, Politics, and the Chinese Exclusion Act* (Chapel Hill: University of North Carolina Press, 1998).

13. The full text of the Geary Act can be found at http://www.sanfranciscochina town.com/history/1892gearyact.html.

14. U.S. Department of State, Office of the Historian, "Repeal of the Chinese Exclusion Act, 1943," https://history.state.gov/milestones/1937-1945/chinese -exclusion-act-repeal.

15. Kenneth T. Walsh, "50 Years Ago, Immigration Changed in America," *U.S. News and World Report*, October 2, 2015, http://www.usnews.com/news/articles/2015/10/02/50-years-ago-immigration-changed-in-america.

16. Chalsa M. Loo, *Chinatown: Most Time, Hard Time* (Westport, CT: Praeger, 1991).

17. The Urban Displacement Project maps four stages of San Francisco's neighborhood change in a comprehensive fashion. See Tanvi Misra, "Mapping Gentrification and Displacement in San Francisco," CityLab, August 31, 2015, http://www.citylab.com/housing/2015/08/mapping-gentrification-and-displacement-in-san-francisco/402559/.

18. "Lee Federal Credit Union Is a True Family Affair," *Credit Union Times*, July 23, 2003, http://www.cutimes.com/2003/07/23/lee-federal-credit-union-is-a-true-family-affair.

19. By the mid-1990s, eleven banks operated in Chinatown, several of which were Asian-serving.

20. The U.S. Internal Revenue Service's VITA Program offers free tax help to low- and moderate-income (generally $49,000 and below) people who cannot prepare their own tax returns.

21. *Kye* clubs are common in Korean communities as a way to support business creation. In these clubs, members pay a monthly fee, and the aggregate amount is given to one member each month to invest as the individual sees fit. Similarly, the *hui* was a lending arrangement among ethnic Chinese business owners who would each put a given amount into a pool and then bid for the aggregate sum. These forms exist in the United States but can run the risk of being considered illegal criminal activity, primarily because they involve transfers of income and interest payments without taxation. There are also some concerns that they involve nonregistered securities.

22. A passbook savings account is one in which the account holder records deposits and withdrawals in a physical passbook. The preference of the Chinese immigrant community for this type of account is an example of the relatively "old-fashioned" banking preferences within this community, and the tacit knowledge of which ethnic Chinese would be aware.

23. Gary Kamiya, "Arise, Tenderloin," *San Francisco*, October 26, 2013, https://digital.modernluxury.com/publication/?i=178974&article_id=1532736&view=articleBrowser.

24. John D. McCarthy and Mayer N. Zald, "Resource Mobilization and Social Movements: A Partial Theory," *American Journal of Sociology* 82, no. 6 (1977): 1212–1241.

25. For a history of the rise of activism in the Tenderloin district, see Christina B. Hanhardt, *Safe space: Gay neighborhood history and the politics of violence* (Durham, NC: Duke University Press, 2013).

26. Kamiya, "Arise, Tenderloin."

27. Patelco was formed in 1936 to serve the employees of Pacific Telephone & Telegraph Company. It had since expanded its field of membership to include employees of more than a thousand businesses and communities.

28. Through shared-branch relationships, members of one credit union could access account services at another participating credit union just as though it were a branch of the credit union of membership. Fees for these transactions were typically around 2 percent.

29. Gary A. Dymski, *The Bank Merger Wave: The Economic Causes and Social Consequences of Financial Consolidation* (Armonk, NY: M. E. Sharpe, 1999).

30. For more on ethnobanks and their performance, see Gary A. Dymski and Lisa Mohanty, "Credit and Banking Structure: Asian and African-American Experience in Los Angeles," *American Economic Review* 89, no. 2 (1999): 362–366.

# 8. CROISSANTS AND CORRIDORS TO WEALTH CREATION

1. Mueller's, "An American Original Since 1867," http://muellerspasta.com /about-us/our-story/.

2. Paul Conley, "The Top 10 U.S. Pasta Brands: Who Owns the Marketplace in 2013?," *Fooddive*, October 24, 2013, http://www.fooddive.com/news /the-top-10-us-pasta-brands-who-owns-the-marketplace-in-2013/185340/.

3. Adrienne Carter, "Marcus Samuelsson, a Chef, a Brand, and Then Some," *New York Times*, August 4, 2012, http://www.nytimes.com/2012/08/05 /business/marcus-samuelsson-both-a-chef-and-a-brand.html.

4. Michael Porter authored one of the more influential articles on clusters. See Michael E. Porter, "Clusters and the New Economics of Competition," *Harvard Business Review* 76, no. 6 (1998): 77–90.

5. See Shun Lu and Gary Alan Fine, "The Presentation of Ethnic Authenticity: Chinese Food as a Social Accomplishment," *Sociological Quarterly* 36, no. 3 (1995): 535–553; Donna R. Gabaccia, *We Are What We Eat: Ethnic Food and the Making of Americans* (Cambridge, MA: Harvard University Press, 2009); Monder Ram, Balihar Sanghera, Tahir Abbas, Gerald Barlow, and Trevor Jones, "Ethnic Minority Business in Comparative Perspective: The Case of the Independent Restaurant Sector," *Journal of Ethnic and Migration Studies* 26, no. 3 (2000): 495–510.

6. All income, housing, and demographic data are from "Quick Facts," U.S. Census Bureau's American Community Survey Office, 1 July 2019,

https://www.census.gov/quickfacts/fact/table/CA,US/PST045219; https://
www.census.gov/quickfacts/fact/table/sanfranciscocitycalifornia,US
/PST045219.

7. Kemp and Roth are US Representative Jack Kemp of New York and
Senator William Roth of Delaware, respectively.

8. Penelope Douglas, Beth Sirull, and Pete November, "Development
Investment Capital: Three Steps to Establishing an Asset Class for Investing
in Underserved Markets," Pacific Community Ventures, May 2006, http://
community-wealth.org/content/development-investment-capital-three-steps
-establishing-asset-class-investing-underserved.

9. The LMI designation indicates persons whose income is less than
80 percent of the area median.

10. See "Investment Criteria," *Pacific Community Ventures* (website),
http://www.pcvfund.com/investment-criteria/.

11. Field interview with Eduardo Rallo, San Francisco. Unless otherwise
noted, all subsequent quotations attributed to Rallo derive from this interview.

12. Field interview with Eduardo Rallo.

13. Pacific Community Ventures, "Social Return on Investment: Executive
Summary 2007," https://www.pacificcommunityventures.org/2015/07/28
/social-return-on-investment-executive-summary-2007/.

14. Penelope Douglas, "The Challenges and Opportunities of Investing in
Low Income Communities: Pacific Community Ventures' First Five Years,"
September 18, 2003, http://www.pacificcommunityventures.org/wp-content
/uploads/sites/6/2015/07/PCV-White-Paper-Challenges.pdf.

15. Douglas, Sirull, and November, "Development Investment Capital."

16. Galaxy Desserts, "About Us," http://galaxydesserts.com/about-us.

17. City of Richmond, California, City Facts, http://www.ci.richmond
.ca.us/DocumentCenter/Home/View/8348.

18. Ryan Lillis, "The Iron Triangle: Richmond's Forgotten Neighborhood," *North Gate News* (Online), December 10, 2004; see also "Richmond,
California," http://www.city-data.com/city/Richmond-California.html.

19. Galaxy Desserts, http://galaxydesserts.com.

20. Field interview with Paul Levitan, San Francisco, November 1, 2010.
Unless otherwise noted, all subsequent quotations attributed to Levitan
derive from this interview.

21. Laurie Gorton, "Oprah Effect Opens Doors for California Bakery, Bak-
ingBusiness.com, July 30, 2014, http://www.bakingbusiness.com/articles
/news_home/Business/2014/07/Oprah_Effect_opens_doors_for_C
.aspx?ID=%7B6478023E-E675-41CF-B5D7-E394CF251D09%7D&cck=1.

22. C.W. Downer & Co., "C.W. Downer & Co. Advises Galaxy Desserts
on Sale to Brioche Pasquier Group," http://www.sbwire.com/press-releases
/release-131344.htm.

## 9. TARGETED PRIVATE EQUITY I: NEIGHBORHOOD INTEGRATION, BLACK CAPITALISM, AND THE INCEPTION OF MINORITY PRIVATE EQUITY

1. Morris J. MacGregor, *Integration of the Armed Forces, 1940–1965*, Vol. 1 (Washington, DC: Center of Military History, United States Army, 1981).

2. MacGregor, *Integration of the Armed Forces.*

3. Nixon had originally presented his ideas in a position paper while campaigning. For more on Nixon and Humphrey's campaigns to promote minority business development, see Roy Seed, "Politics: Humphrey Assails Nixon," *New York Times*, July 21, 1968, 47, http://timesmachine.nytimes.com/timesmachine/1968/07/21/110090190.html?pageNumber=47.

4. John McClaughry, "Black Capitalism," *New York Times*, September 21, 1969, 110, http://timesmachine.nytimes.com/timesmachine/1969/09/21/89375880.html?pageNumber=110.

5. Frederick D. Sturdivant, "Limits of Black Capitalism," *Harvard Business Review* 47, no. 1 (1969): 125.

6. Sturdivant, "Limits of Black Capitalism."

7. See Walter Rugaber, "Stans to Promote a Minority Business Enterprise," *New York Times*, March 6, 1969, 27, http://timesmachine.nytimes.com/timesmachine/1969/03/06/90059574.html?pageNumber=27.

8. For more on the launch of the MESBIC program, see Paul Delaney, "Negro Business Is Assured of Aid," *New York Times*, November 7, 1969, 1, 69, http://timesmachine.nytimes.com/timesmachine/1969/11/07/79434386.html?pageNumber=1.

9. "Arcata Concern Plans to Close," *New York Times*, April 8, 1972, 35, 37, http://timesmachine.nytimes.com/timesmachine/1972/04/08/79466335.html?pageNumber=35.

10. Udayan Gupta, *Done Deals: Venture Capitalists Tell Their Stories* (Boston: Harvard Business Review Press, 2000), 270.

11. This is the popular phrase coined by Marshall McLuhan to indicate the importance of the media vehicle itself, independent of the message that is conveyed. See Marshall McLuhan, *Understanding Media: The Extensions of Man* (Boston: MIT Press, 1964).

12. Officials and managers is a single category. See Gerald Fraser, "EEOC Figures Show Increase in Minority Hiring in Broadcast Industry," *New York Times*, January 3, 1977, 34, http://timesmachine.nytimes.com/timesmachine/1977/01/03/89687569.html?pageNumber=34.

13. Fraser, "EEOC Figures Show."

14. Les Brown, "US Court Voids FCC Equal Employment Rules," *New York Times*, August 9, 1977, 48, http://timesmachine.nytimes.com/timesmachine /1977/08/09/75097548.html?pageNumber=48.

15. Ray Holsendolph, "F.C.C. Acts on Minority Broadcasting," *New York Times*, May 18, 1978, 76, http://timesmachine.nytimes.com/timesmachine /1978/05/18/110955746.html?pageNumber=76.

16. Bari S. Robinson, "Achieving Diversity in Media Ownership: Bakke and the FCC," *California Law Review*, 67 (1979): 231.

17. Gupta, *Done Deals*, 1–27.

18. Clea Simon, "Mining an Untapped Market, Radio One Becomes a Force," *New York Times*, December 25, 2000, https://www.nytimes.com /2000/12/25/business/mining-an-untapped-market-radio-one-becomes -a-force.html?searchResultPosition=1.

19. Steven Overly, "With Purchase of Radio Station WOL in 1980, Cathy Hughes Launched a Media Empire," *Washington Post*, August 11, 2014, https://www.washingtonpost.com/business/capitalbusiness/with-purchase -of-radio-station-wol-in-1980-cathy-hughes-launched-a-media-empire/2014 /08/11/cd0a80fa-20b5-11e4-86ca-6f03cbd15c1a_story.html.

20. Gupta, *Done Deals*, 270.

21. Philip Alphonse, Thomas Hellmann, and Jane Wei, "Minority Private Equity: A Market in Transition," *Journal of Private Equity* 2, no. 4 (Summer 1999): 27–45, https://www.jstor.org/stable/43503224?seq=1.

22. Gupta, *Done Deals*, 272.

23. Kofi Asiedu Ofori, "When Being No. 1 Is Not Enough: The Impact of Advertising Practices on Minority-Owned & Minority-Formatted Broadcast Stations," Civil Rights Forum on Communications Policy, http:// civilrightsdocs.info/pdf/reports/Being-No-1-Is-Not-Enough-Ad-Study -Ofori.pdf.

24. Gupta, *Done Deals*, 128.

25. Noah Samara, Remarks at the National Summit on Africa, February 2000.

26. Multicultural Media Telecom and Internet Council (MMTC), "MMTC Mourns the Loss of Herbert P. Wilkins, Sr., Longtime Board Member and Friend," Multicultural Media, Telecom and Internet Council, December 10, 2013, http://broadbandandsocialjustice.org/2013/12/mmtc-mourns-the -loss-of-herbert-p-wilkins-sr-longtime-board-member-and-friend/.

27. Michael K. Powell, Commissioner, Federal Communications Commission, "Remarks Before the California Broadcasters Association, Monterey, California, July 27, 1998," https://transition.fcc.gov/Speeches/Powell/spmkp814 .html.

# 10. TARGETED PRIVATE EQUITY II: THE ADVAN-
## TAGES OF BEING A MARGINAL MINORITY

1. Erving Goffman, *Asylums: Essays on the Social Situation of Mental Patients and Other Inmates* (New Brunswick, NJ: AldineTransaction, 1968).

2. For more on the potential advantages of socially in-between groups, see Ronald S. Burt, "Structural Holes and Good Ideas," *American Journal of Sociology* 110, no. 2 (2004): 349–399.

3. Paulette Thomas, "A Fund Taps Into a Web of Minority-Owned Firms," *Wall Street Journal*, May 16, 2001, http://www.wsj.com/articles /SB989965870829853798.

4. Years later, StarMedia would have difficulty. The firm was delisted by NASDAQ in 2002 and filed for bankruptcy protection in December 2003. In March 2006, the SEC began a legal action that alleged StarMedia executives improperly inflated revenues in order to meet profit expectations and receive approval for additional financing. Chen settled the suit in March 2011 for $100,000, without admitting or denying the allegations.

5. Venture partners are frequently former entrepreneurs with industry experience but without a great deal of experience in investing. Private equity firms hire them to assist in the pursuit of investments in their areas of expertise. If the relationship between firm and venture partner is positive, they are often invited to become general partners.

6. Rekha Balu, "It's in the Country's Best Interest for Poor Folk to Be Smart," *Fast Company*, FC40, 326 (October 31, 2000).

7. Robert L. Craig, Jerry R. Herman, and Drew E. Crum, "K–12 Education Market," research study conducted by Legg Mason Wood Walker, Spring 2003, 3–7.

8. Craig, Herman, and Crum, "K–12 Education Market," 3–4.

9. U.S. Department of Education, "10 Facts about K-12 Education Funding," 2005, http://www2.ed.gov/about/overview/fed/10facts/index.html?exp. A related chart of ESEA spending can be found at http://www2.ed.gov /about/overview/fed/10facts/edlite-chart.html#5.

10. Patricia L. Donahue, Robert J. Finnegan, Anthony D. Lutkus, Nancy L. Allen, and Jay R. Campbell, *The Nation's Report Card: Fourth-Grade Reading 2000*, National Center for Educational Statistics, April 2001, 43, http:// nces.ed.gov/nationsreportcard/pdf/main2000/2001499.pdf.

11. From case writer interviews and internal document, "Platform Group Project Sunday School Business Plan," January 2003, 3.

12. "Platform Group," 4.

13. "Platform Group," 15.

14. "Platform Group," 15.

15. Craig, Herman, and Crum, "K–12 Education Market," 21.

16. "Platform Group," 16–19.

17. Susan Saulny, "Teachers' Union Is Approved for U.S. Tutoring Program," *New York Times*, March 19, 2005, http://www.nytimes.com/2005/03/19 /nyregion/teachers-union-is-approved-for-us-tutoring-program.html.

18. Susan Saulny, "A Lucrative Brand of Tutoring Grows Unchecked," *New York Times*, April 4, 2005, http://www.nytimes.com/2005/04/04 /education/a-lucrative-brand-of-tutoring-grows-unchecked.html.

19. Saulny, "A Lucrative Brand."

20. Elissa Gootman, "Manhattan: Tutoring Company Files for Chapter 11," *New York Times*, July 7, 2006, http://www.nytimes.com/2006/07/07 /nyregion/07mbrfs-006.html.

21. For more on the likelihood of VC firms' having an exit, see Paul Alan Gompers and Joshua Lerner, *The Venture Capital Cycle* (Boston: MIT Press, 2004), 38, table 9.12.

22. Anya Kamenetz, "For Profit and People: UniversityNow Rides a Low-Cost Wave," *New York Times*, November 1, 2013, https://archive.nytimes .com/www.nytimes.com/2013/11/03/education/universitynow-rides-a -low-cost-wave.html.

23. Kamenetz, "For Profit and People: UniversityNow."

24. Matt Richtel, "In the Venture Capital World, a Helping Hand for Women and Minorities," *New York Times*, June 15, 2007, http://www .nytimes.com/2007/06/15/business/15venture.html.

25. Paul Taylor and the Pew Research Center, *The Next America: Boomers, Millennials, and the Looming Generational Showdown* (New York: PublicAffairs, 2016), Figure 1.1., page 3.

26. Sandra L. Colby and Jennifer M. Ortman, "Current Population Reports, Table 2. Population by Race and Hispanic Origin: 2014 and 2060," March 2015, https://www.census.gov/content/dam/Census/library/publications /2015/demo/p25-1143.pdf, 9.

27. Colby and Ortman, 9.

28. For more on diversity in working teams, see Lisa Hope Pelled, Kathleen M. Eisenhardt, and Katherine R. Xin, "Exploring the Black Box: An Analysis of Work Group Diversity, Conflict and Performance," *Administrative Science Quarterly* 44, no. 1 (1999): 1–28; Pamela J. Hinds, Kathleen M. Carley, David Krackhardt, and Doug Wholey, "Choosing Work Group Members: Balancing Similarity, Competence, and Familiarity," *Organizational Behavior and Human Decision Processes* 81, no. 2 (2000): 226–251.

29. For more on the relationship between unfamiliarity, fear, and danger, see Steven T. Levy and Lawrence B. Inderbitzin, "Safety, Danger, and the

Analyst's Authority," *Journal of the American Psychoanalytic Association* 45 (1997): 377–394; Niklas Luhmann, "Familiarity, Confidence, Trust: Problems and Alternatives," *Trust: Making and Breaking Cooperative Relations* 6, no. 1 (2000): 94–107.

30. For more on similarity in social relationships, see Miller McPherson, Lynn Smith-Lovin, and James M. Cook, "Birds of a Feather: Homophily in Social Networks," *Annual Review of Sociology* 27, no. 1 (2001): 415–444; Evelien Zeggelink, "Evolving Friendship Networks: An Individual-Oriented Approach Implementing Similarity," *Social Networks* 17, no. 2 (1995): 83–110.

31. See Seungwha Chung, Harbir Singh, and Kyungmook Lee, "Complementarity, Status Similarity and Social Capital as Drivers of Alliance Formation," *Strategic Management Journal* 21, no. 1 (2000): 1–22; Alexandra Kalev, Frank Dobbin, and Erin Kelly, "Best Practices or Best Guesses? Assessing the Efficacy of Corporate Affirmative Action and Diversity Policies," *American Sociological Review* 71, no. 4 (2006): 589–617.

# 11. BUILDING WEALTH IN INDIAN COUNTRY

1. Horatio Bardwell Cushman, *History of the Choctaw, Chickasaw and Natchez Indians* (Greenville, TX: Headlight Printing House, 1899).

2. I recognize that terms referring to indigenous North Americans are socially constructed. In this book, I have generally used the term "American Indians" to describe ethnic groups also described as Indians, Native Americans, and by individual tribal designations.

3. Kenneth W. Porter, *The Black Seminoles: History of a Freedom-Seeking People*, ed. Alcione M. Amos and Thomas P. Senter (Gainesville: University Press of Florida, 1996).

4. Daniel F. Littlefield and Lonnie E. Underhill, "Black Dreams and 'Free' Homes: The Oklahoma Territory, 1891–1894," *Phylon (1960–)* 34, no. 4 (1973): 342–357, http://doi.org/10.2307/274249.

5. For more on Black–American Indian relations in Oklahoma, see James N. Leiker, Kim Warren, and Barbara Watkins, eds., *The First and the Forced: Essays on the Native American and African American Experience* (Lawrence: University of Kansas, Hall Center for the Humanities, 2007); William Loren Katz, *Black Indians: A Hidden Heritage* (New York: Simon and Schuster, 2012).

6. First National Bank and Trust Company began when the charter for First Oklahoma Bank, N.A., was approved on June 30, 1983. The Citizen Potawatomi Tribe purchased the bank in February 1989.

7. There are also many unrecognized tribes, which include individuals and groups who claim to be historically, culturally, or genetically related to historic American Indian tribes but are not officially recognized as indigenous nations by the U.S. Bureau of Indian Affairs. As an indicator of the diversity of the American Indian population in the United States, the U.S. Census Bureau's American Community Survey codes 381 distinct non-English languages, and 169 of these are American Indian languages. However, fewer than half a million speak these languages nationwide. See U.S. Census Bureau, "Native North American Languages Spoken at Home in the United States and Puerto Rico: 2006–2010," December 2011, https://www2.census.gov/library/publications/2011/acs/acsbr10-10.pdf.

8. William H. Mullins, "Potowatomie County," Oklahoma Historical Society, https://www.okhistory.org/publications/enc/entry.php?entry=PO026.

9. Vine Deloria and Clifford M. Lytle, *The Nations Within: The Past and Future of American Indian Sovereignty* (Austin: University of Texas Press, 1998).

10. Lawrence C. Kelly, "The Indian Reorganization Act: The Dream and the Reality," *Pacific Historical Review* 44, no. 3 (1975): 291–312.

11. Marianne Bertrand, Sendhil Mullainathan, and Eldar Shafir, "A Behavioral-Economics View of Poverty," *American Economic Review* 94, no. 2 (2004): 419–423.

12. Bertrand, Mullainathan, and Shafir, "A Behavioral-Economics View."

13. U.S. Census Bureau, "American Indian and Alaska Native Heritage Month: November 2012," October 25, 2012, https://www.census.gov/newsroom/releases/pdf/cb12ff-22_aian.pdf.

14. U.S. Census Bureau, "American Indian and Alaska Native Heritage Month."

15. Suzanne E. Macartney, Alemayehu Bishaw, and Kayla Fontenot, "Poverty Rates for Selected Detailed Race and Hispanic Groups by State and Place: 2007–2011," U.S. Census Bureau, February 2013, https://www.census.gov/library/publications/2013/acs/acsbr11-17.html.

16. U.S. Census Bureau, "American Indian and Alaska Native Heritage Month."

17. Kathryn Peralta, "Native Americans Left Behind in the Economic Recovery," *U.S. News & World Report*, November 27, 2014, http://www.usnews.com/news/articles/2014/11/27/native-americans-left-behind-in-the-economic-recovery.

18. Mullins, "Potowatomie County."

19. Blaine Harden, "Walking the Land with Pride Again; A Revolution in Indian Country Spawns Wealth and Optimism," *Washington Post*, September 19, 2004.

20. The Citizen Potawatomi Nation recognizes tribe members based on ancestral records. To be recognized as a member, a person must be the child

of at least one tribe member. According to 2010 U.S. Census data, of the estimated 33,771 Potawatomi nationally, only 20,412 (60.4 percent) report American Indian–only ancestry.

21. The Indian Self-Determination and Education Assistance Act of 1975 helped American Indian tribes break the grip of the Bureau of Indian Affairs and take over operation of everything on the reservations. Tribal governments did not have to pay federal and state taxes on profits, which they were able to reinvest in social services.

22. Harden, "Walking the Land with Pride Again."

23. Citizen Potawatomi Nation, "Citizen Potawatomi Nation Has $506 Million Economic Impact," January 18, 2013, https://www.potawatomi.org /citizen-potawatomi-nation-has-506-million-economic-impact/.

24. Stephanie Innes, " 'Think Like a Sovereign,' Indians Told," *Arizona Daily Star*, November 13, 1999.

25. Rachel Janke, "Tribal Gaming in Wisconsin," Wisconsin Legislative Fiscal Bureau, Informational Paper 87, January 2015, https://docs.legis .wisconsin.gov/misc/lfb/informational_papers/january_2015/0087_tribal _gaming_in_wisconsin_informational_paper_87.pdf.

26. William N. Evans and Julie H. Topoleski, "The Social and Economic Impact of Native American Casinos," National Bureau of Economic Research Working Paper No. 9198, September 2002.

27. Property Review: Citizen Potawatomi Nation, Grand Casino Hotel Resort – Shawnee, OK (2013), *Indian Gaming*, September, 56 http://www .indiangaming.com/istore/Sep13_GrandCasino.pdf.

28. Property Review, 57.

29. Based in Philadelphia, Opportunity Finance Network (OFN) is a national network of community development financial institutions investing to benefit low-income, low-wealth, and other disadvantaged communities. See the website at http://www.ofn.org/.

30. All quotes attributed to Cindy Logsdon derive from a case writer interview with Logsdon, Shawnee, Oklahoma, August 2013. All other information and quotations, unless otherwise noted, derive from case writer interviews with company representatives.

31. Mark Fogarty, "Indian Banks Small in Assets, Small in Number," *Indian Country Today*, September 22, 2015, https://indiancountrytoday .com/archive/indian-banks-small-in-assets-small-in-number-DCxHIW8aQ0 -B9njWCkHm5Q.

32. Donna Gambrell, "Remarks by CDFI Fund Director Donna Gambrell at OFN's Eighth Annual Native Gathering," November 14, 2011, https:// www.mycdfi.cdfifund.gov/speeches/Gambrell-2011-7-Remarks-by-CDFI -Fund-Director-Donna-Gambrell-Eighth-Annual-Native-Gathering-Opportunity -Finance-Network-Conference.asp.

33. Bianca Peter, "What Is the Average Credit Score in America?," *WalletHub*, May 6, 2020, https://wallethub.com/edu/cs/average-credit-scores/25578/.

34. Kelley Blue Book is a service that provides prevailing resale prices of used cars; it is often used to establish used car market prices.

35. Dee Brown, *Bury My Heart at Wounded Knee* (New York: Holt, Rinehart & Winston, 1971); Richard E. Jensen, R. Eli Paul, and John Carter, *Eyewitness at Wounded Knee* (Lincoln: University of Nebraska Press, 1991).

36. Eduardo Duran, *Healing the Soul Wound: Counseling with American Indians and Other Native People* (New York: Teachers College Press, 2006).

37. For studies on the American Indian contribution to Black ancestry, see Rona Yaeger, Alexa Avila-Bront, Kazeem Abdul, Patricia C. Nolan, Victor R. Grann, Mark G. Birchette, Shweta Choudhry, et al., "Comparing Genetic Ancestry and Self-Described Race in African Americans Born in the United States and in Africa," *Cancer Epidemiology and Prevention Biomarkers* 17, no. 6 (2008): 1329–1338; Soheil Baharian, Maxime Barakatt, Christopher R. Gignoux, Suyash Shringarpure, Jacob Errington, William J. Blot, Carlos D. Bustamante, et al., "The Great Migration and African-American Genomic Diversity," *PLoS Genetics* 12, no. 5 (2016).

38. "What Is a Credit Score?," myFICO, http://www.myfico.com/credit education/creditscores.aspx.

39. Gregory B. Fairchild, Christina Black, Liz Jones, and Tierney Fairchild, "Understanding FICO Scores," Darden Case No. UVA-F-1866, University of Virginia, Darden, https://ssrn.com/abstract=3438630.

## 12. FLOODING THE FOOD DESERT IN NORTH PHILLY

1. Peter M. Ascoli, *Julius Rosenwald: The Man Who Built Sears, Roebuck and Advanced the Cause of Black Education in the American South* (Bloomington: Indiana University Press, 2006).

2. John Jackson, *American Bandstand: Dick Clark and the Making of a Rock 'n' Roll Empire* (Oxford: Oxford University Press, 1999).

3. Jackson, *American Bandstand*, 44.

4. Jackson, *American Bandstand*, 44.

5. *American Bandstand*, Season 1, Episode 49, tv.com, http://www.tv.com /shows/american-bandstand/ab-49-johnny-mathis-andy-williams-92402/.

6. Jackson, *American Bandstand*, 74.

7. Douglas S. Massey and Nancy Denton, *American Apartheid: Segregation and the Making of the Underclass* (Cambridge, MA: Harvard University Press, 1993).

8. Edward L. Glaeser and Jacob Vigdor, "Racial Segregation: Promising News," *Redefining Urban & Suburban America: Evidence from Census 2000*, ed. Bruce Katz and Robert E. Lang, vol. 1, 211–234 (Washington, DC: Brookings Institution Press, 2003).

9. "Residential Segregation," Diversity and Disparities (website), Spatial Structures in the Social Sciences, Brown University, https://s4.ad.brown.edu /projects/diversity/segregation2010/city.aspx?cityid=4260000.

10. Glaeser and Vigdor, "Racial Segregation: Promising News," 224.

11. Robert Pear, "A Lending Plan for the Distressed," *New York Times*, January 18, 1993, http://www.nytimes.com/1993/01/18/business/a-lending -plan-for-the-distressed.html.

12. Dwight Evans, "Budget Briefing: Pennsylvania Fresh Foods Financing Initiative," Report on Key Issues from the House Appropriations Committee, March 4, 2010, https://www.ncsl.org/documents/labor/workingfamilies /pa_fffi.pdf.

13. Nathaniel Bracey, "The Progress Movement and Community Development: The Zion Non-Profit Charitable Trust," *Journal of African American History* 96, no. 1 (2011): 90–91.

14. Sullivan's biblical inspiration was the parable of Jesus feeding the multitude found in John 6:1–14. For more on the 10–36 Plan, see Leon H. Sullivan Charitable Trust, "10–36 Plan," http://thesullivantrust.org/about.html.

15. Pratt Center for Community Development, "Zion Non-Profit Charitable Trust (ZNPCT), Philadelphia, PA," http://web.archive.org/web /20070629222112/http://www.prattcenter.net/cdc-znpct.php.

16. Matthew Countryman, *Up South: Civil Rights and Black Power in Philadelphia* (Philadelphia: University of Pennsylvania Press, 2007), 112–114.

17. For more on the Sullivan principles generally, see S. Prakash Sethi and Oliver F. Williams, "Creating and Implementing Global Codes of Conduct: An Assessment of the Sullivan Principles as a Role Model for Developing International Codes of Conduct—Lessons Learned and Unlearned," *Business and Society Review* 105, no. 2 (2002): 169–200. For another approach—an accounting paper that measures the costs to U.S. firms of not participating in the Sullivan codes—see Dennis M. Patten, "The Market Reaction to Social Responsibility Disclosures: The Case of the Sullivan Principles Signings," *Accounting, Organizations and Society* 15, no. 6 (1990): 575–587.

18. Herbert F. Goodrich and Robert J. Sugarman, "Economic Development in the Ghettoes: Some Philadelphia Experiences," *Business Lawyer* 25 (1969): 369–380.

19. Pratt Center for Community Development, "Zion Non-Profit Charitable Trust."

20. Sariyah S. Buchanan, "Why Marginalized Communities Should Use Community Benefit Agreements as a Tool for Environmental Justice: Urban

Renewal and Brownfield Redevelopment in Philadelphia, Pennsylvania," *Temple Journal of Science, Technology & Environmental Law* 29 (2010): 31.

21. Michael C. Murphy and Kenneth R. Crystal, "Redeveloping Former Gas Stations," Retail Law Strategist, Phillips Lytle, LLP, 2009, http://docplayer .net/13077988-Redeveloping-former-gas-stations.html.

22. See Anna Alberini, Alberto Longo, Stefania Tonin, Francesco Trombetta, and Margherita Turvani, "The Role of Liability, Regulation and Economic Incentives in Brownfield Remediation and Redevelopment: Evidence from Surveys of Developers," *Regional Science and Urban Economics* 35, no. 4 (2005): 327–351.

23. David Barstow, "Invest in Poor Areas, Clinton Urges," *New York Times*, January 14, 2000, http://www.nytimes.com/2000/01/14/nyregion /invest-in-poor-areas-clinton-urges.html. President Clinton signed the law creating NMTC on December 21, 2000, just weeks before he left office.

24. Dwight Evans, "Budget Briefing: Pennsylvania Fresh Foods Initiative."

25. For more on the program, see Deborah La Franchi, "New Markets Tax Credits," *Economic Development Journal* 9, no. 4 (2010): 5. An online tool allows a user to search the database to determine whether an address qualifies.

26. La Franchi, "New Markets Tax Credits," 5.

27. The Reinvestment Fund, "New Markets Tax Credits and Urban Supermarkets," Financing Healthy Food Options: Implementation Handbook, September 30, 2011, https://www.cdfifund.gov/Documents/NMTC%20 for%20FUND%20approval%20101911.pdf.

28. The Reinvestment Fund, "New Markets Tax Credits and Urban Supermarkets."

29. The Reinvestment Fund, "New Markets Tax Credits and Urban Supermarkets."

30. An A/B note structure is one in which a loan is split into an "A-structure" and a "B-structure," with the A structure being senior to the other. In effect, this means the A component is paid first. For more on A/B notes, see "The A/B Note Transaction and Documentation," http://files.ali-cle.org /thumbs/datastorage/skoobesruoc/source/CP008_47--McDaniel--A -B%20INTERCREDITOR1_thumb.pdf.

31. Nia Malika Henderson, "Michelle Speaks Frankly About Race," *Politico*, February 19, 2010, http://www.politico.com/story/2010/02/michelle -speaks-frankly-about-race-033162#ixzz4JmvPMGUe.

32. Terry Pristin, "With a Little Help, Greens Come to Low-Income Neighborhood," *New York Times*, June 16, 2009, https://www.nytimes.com /2009/06/17/business/17supermarkets.html?searchResultPosition=2.

33. The Reinvestment Fund, "Success Story: Pennsylvania Fresh Food Financing," https://www.reinvestment.com/success-story/pennsylvania-fresh -food-financing-initiative/.

## 13. A BLUEBIRD TAKES FLIGHT: A REINTERPRETATION OF BANKING AT AMERICAN EXPRESS

1. James Baldwin, *Notes of a Native Son* (Boston: Beacon Press, 1955).

2. William L. Silber, "The Process of Financial Innovation," *American Economic Review* 73, no. 2 (1983): 89.

3. Jerry Flint, "Quick Electronic Banking Slowed by Public's Habits and Fears," *New York Times,* May 30, 1977, D3, https://www.nytimes .com/1977/05/31/archives/quick-electronic-banking-slowed-by-the-publics -habits-and-fears.html.

4. Mario A. Milletti, "Interest-Bearing Checking Accounts—the Ban Is Eroding," *New York Times,* May 8, 1978, D1, https://www.nytimes.com /1978/05/08/archives/interestbearing-checking-accountsthe-ban-is-eroding -regulations.html.

5. William C. Dunkelberg and Robert H. Smiley, "Subsidies in the Use of Revolving Credit," *Journal of Money, Credit and Banking* 7, no. 4 (1975): 469–490.

6. William C. Dunkelberg and Robert Williard Johnson, *EFTs and Consumer Credit* (West Lafayette, IN: Credit Research Center, Krannert Graduate School of Management, Purdue University, 1975).

7. Scott Bronstein, "A Check Writing Nation Ignores the Debit Card," *New York Times,* October 3, 1985, section 3, page 12, https://www.nytimes .com/1985/10/06/business/a-check-writing-nation-ignores-the-debit-card .html.

8. American Express, "Press Release: American Express Announces Executive and Board of Directors Appointments," July 21, 2010, https://about.american express.com/press-release/american-express-announces-executive-and -board-directors-appointments.

9. Jackie Thomas Kennedy and Greg Fairchild interview with Dan Schulman, April 23, 2014; unless otherwise noted, all subsequent quotations by and information about this person derive from this interview.

10. The term "underbanked" refers to households in which at least one person held a savings or checking account, but at least one other had used alternative financial services (AFS) providers such as money orders, payday lenders, and check-cashing services. Those who were "unbanked" did not have any household relationship with a mainstream financial services provider.

11. Susan Burhouse and Yazmin Osaki, *2011 FDIC National Survey of Unbanked and Underbanked Households: Executive Summary* (Washington, DC: Federal Deposit Insurance Corporation Department of Depositor and Consumer Protection, September 2012).

12. Trefis, "How American Express Gains a Competitive Advantage from Its Closed-Loop Network," *Trefis*, March 13, 2014, http://www.trefis.com /stock/axp/articles/230259/maryhow-american-express-gains-a-competitive -advantage-by-using-a-closed-loop-network/2014-03-13.

13. Stuart Elliott, "American Express Gets Specific and Asks, 'Are You a Cardmember?,'" *New York Times*, April 6, 2007, http://www.nytimes.com /2007/04/06/business/media/06adco.html?_r=0.

14. Elliott, "American Express Gets Specific."

15. Trefis, "How American Express Gains a Competitive Advantage."

16. Trefis, "How American Express Gains a Competitive Advantage."

17. Jackie Thomas Kennedy and Greg Fairchild interview with Jon Rosner, April 23, 2014.

18. Martha Perine Beard, "In Depth: Reaching the Unbanked and Underbanked," *Central Banker*, Winter 2010, https://www.stlouisfed.org /Publications/Central-Banker/Winter-2010/Reaching-the-Unbanked-and -Underbanked.

19. Robin Sidel, "Amex to Acquire Revolution Money," *Wall Street Journal*, November 19, 2009, https://www.wsj.com/articles/SB100014240527 48704204304574543462129137096.

20. Federal Reserve System, *The Federal Reserve Payments Study*, July 2014, https://frbservices.org/assets/news/research/2013-fed-res-paymt-study -detailed-rpt.pdf.

21. Federal Reserve System, *The 2013 Federal Reserve Payments Study*, 16, 19.

22. Burhouse and Osaki, *2011 FDIC National Survey of Unbanked and Underbanked Households*.

23. GoBank was a subsidiary of Green Dot Bank.

24. Douglas McGray, "Check Cashers, Redeemed," *New York Times Magazine*, November 7, 2008, http://www.nytimes.com/2008/11/09 /magazine/09nix-t.html.

25. Stephanie Clifford and Jessica Silver-Greenberg, "On the New Shopping List: Milk, Bread, Eggs and a Mortgage," *New York Times*, November 13, 2013, http://www.nytimes.com/2012/11/14/business/major-retailers-start-selling -financial-products-challenging-banks.html?_r=0.

26. Clifford and Silver-Greenberg, "On the New Shopping List."

27. Clifford and Silver-Greenberg, "On the New Shopping List."

28. The main elements of these models are accurate. However, the percentages applied are hypothetical. As a condition of our interviews, American Express requested that we generate percentages for many elements rather than using proprietary firm data.

29. "Amex Launches the PASS," Loyalty Magazine, 13 August 2010, https://www.loyaltymagazine.com/amex-launches-the-pass/.

30. Jackie Thomas Kennedy and Greg Fairchild interview with Alpesh Chokshi, April 23, 2014; unless otherwise noted, all subsequent quotations by and information about this person derive from this interview.

31. Jackie Thomas Kennedy and Greg Fairchild interview with Wesley Wright, April 23, 2014; unless otherwise noted, all subsequent quotations by and information about this person derive from this interview.

32. Jackie Thomas Kennedy and Greg Fairchild interview with Alpesh Chokshi.

33. Robin Sidel and Andrew R. Johnson, "Prepaid Enters Mainstream," *Wall Street Journal*, October 12, 2012, http://www.wsj.com/articles/SB10 000872396390444897304578044313831625492.

34. Walmart, "American Express and Walmart Announce the Addition of FDIC Insurance Worry-Free Check Writing to Bluebird," March 26, 2013, http://corporate.walmart.com/_news_/news-archive/2013/03/26 /american-express-walmart-announce-the-addition-of-fdic-insurance-worry -free-check-writing-to-bluebird.

35. Chris Fichera, "3 Prepaid Cards Worth Considering," *Consumer Reports*, July 2013, http://www.consumerreports.org/cro/news/2013/07/prepaid -cards-worth-considering/index.htm.

36. Jeff Blyksal, "Prepaid Cards Are Getting Better," Consumer Reports, April 13, 2016, https://www.consumerreports.org/prepaid-cards/prepaid-cards-are -getting-better/.

## 14. HOW I LOST MY FOMO

1. "Speech: Donald Trump Holds a Political Rally in Cincinnati, Ohio - August 1, 2019," Factbase, https://factba.se/transcript/donald-trump-speech -maga-rally-cincinnati-oh-august-1-2019.

2. Jesse Drucker and Eric Lipton, "How a Trump Tax Break to Help Poor Communities Became a Windfall for the Rich," *New York Times*, August 31, 2019, https://www.nytimes.com/2019/08/31/business/tax-opportunity-zones .html?action=click&module=inline&pgtype=Homepage&section=Business.

3. Jared Bernstein and Kevin Hassett, "Unlocking Private Capital to Facilitate Economic Growth in Distressed Areas," Economic Innovation Group, April 2015, https://eig.org/wp-content/uploads/2015/04/Unlocking-Private -Capital-to-Facilitate-Growth.pdf.

4. John Humphries, "The Rise of RegTech and What It Means for Your Business," *Forbes* blogpost, December 14, 2016, https://www.forbes .com/sites/forbesfinancecouncil/2016/12/14/the-rise-of-regtech-and -what-it-means-for-your-business/#96fa5305935a.

5. The Dow Jones/Factiva database is an oft-used source for academic researchers and faculty. The database's breadth of thirty-two thousand sources from two hundred countries and in twenty-seven languages allows it to represent a relatively generalizable sample of writing on business issues and topics. The database is searchable by topic and word, such as RegTech, and can be subanalyzed in a number of ways, including by date and source of publication. For more information, see ProQuest, https://www.proquest.com/products -services/factiva.html.

6. There seems some degree of confusion among authors on whether to capitalize the Tech portion of these phrases. In RegTech, it appears the T is almost always capitalized. In the two others, there isn't systematic agreement. I did the word searches with all potential combinations.

7. Debbi D. Brock, *Social Entrepreneurship Teaching Resources Handbook* (Arlington, VA: Ashoka Publications, March 2008), 3.

8. The study of the disparate goals of self-identified ethical investors appears in Richard Hudson, "Ethical Investing: Ethical Investors and Managers," *Business Ethics Quarterly* 15, no. 4 (2015): 641–657; quotation is from 643.

9. Paul B. Brown, "Smoothing the Sharp Elbows," *New York Times*, April 2, 2006, https://www.nytimes.com/2006/04/02/business/yourmoney /smoothing-the-sharp-elbows.html.

10. Abby Ellin, "M.B.A.'s with Three Bottom Lines: People, Planet and Profit," *New York Times*, January 8, 2006, https://www.nytimes.com/2006 /01/08/education/edlife/mbas-with-three-bottom-lines-people-planet-and -profit.html?searchResultPosition=2.

11. Nathan Popper, "For Goldman, Success in Social Impact Bond That Aids Schoolchildren," *New York Times*, October 7, 2015, https://www .nytimes.com/2015/10/08/business/for-goldman-success-in-social-impact -bond-that-aids-schoolchildren.html.

12. Rudyard Kipling, *The White Man's Burden* (London: The Times, 1859).

13. Quoted in Ron Chernow, *Titan: The Life of John D. Rockefeller, Sr.* (New York: Random House, 1998), 55.

14. Andrew Carnegie, *The "Gospel of Wealth" Essays and Other Writings*, ed. David Nasaw (New York: Penguin, 2006), 10.

# Index

Page numbers in *italics* indicate figures or tables.